A Beautiful World

Book I

God Must be Sleeping

Book II

By
Gregg Tyler Milligan

© 2013 2nd Edition
© 2011 Gregg Tyler Milligan
All Rights Reserved.

No part of this publication may be reproduced, stored in a retrieval system, or transmitted, in any form or by any means, electronic, mechanical, photocopying, recording, or otherwise, without the written permission of the author.

First published by Dog Ear Publishing
4010 W. 86th Street, Ste H
Indianapolis, IN 46268
www.dogearpublishing.net

ISBN: 978-145750-650-5

This book is printed on acid-free paper.

Printed in the United States of America

DEDICATION

This book is dedicated to –

April Lynn (Pug) Gallant: By looking up to me when we were only children and still today. From whose love and admiration in me I still find strength. We made it, Pug!

Geno Gallant: I could not have picked a better man to wed my dear Pug. What you have given the both of us is a love worth waiting for. Thank you, brother.

David Carter Milligan II: Within you there have always been shades of glory. Just because you are lost, does not mean you cannot be found. You are not forgotten dear brother.

Tina Marie Milligan: I will always remember you holding on to me during the day-mares, gently whispering over and over, "I got you, Tyler ... I got you." Sweet Sis, you most certainly do.

Sue Marsh: For loving me unconditionally and never letting go ... So, please don't ever!

Debbie Caliguri (your sweet Mother, Father, and Brother): Thank you for taking me in when I was so lost, sick, afraid, and lonely. Debbie, something tells me that Heaven is still trying to figure you out! We miss you so damn much.

Greg Churchill: When I was hungry you gave me food and when I needed a place to rest my weary head you gave me shelter. Because that is what true friends do.

Bruce Cattell: Your memory is a great treasure. Dear friend, it's just not the same here without you.

Pat Palmer: A true Saint in every sense. Because of you, the dream of a beautiful world no longer slumbered inside my heart, but was made real by your faith in me.

Dr. Edward Skinner: For holding me up when it was too difficult to stand.

The Marsh & Lorkowski Families: For accepting me with open arms.

Sambirdio (my brave little kitten): Because of you I found the meaning of love and that there is no difference between Angels and Kittens.

The Mighty Advocates: Who work tirelessly to end abuse, never give-in or give-up, even when the rules, by no means, are in your favor.

Keepers of Law: For protecting the innocent; especially, those who cannot protect themselves.

Peacekeepers: Because you pour compassion all over the world, hope can find its way home.

Warrior Angels: Who fight for justice in a world long without.

To God: Even now, I still hope it was you all those times who saved me when I was broken.

The Abused / Victims / Survivors: To all of you who suffer; for any reason, and for no reason at all. It is for you who suffer, the abused, broken, and forgotten —I promise to do all I can to save you. A promise I will keep —forever.

ACKNOWLEDGMENT (DEAR READER)

I hope where I have put pen to paper enables others to face their own demons and have the courage to do so. To no longer hide from the truth, but face it so they {you} can move beyond despair. And to no longer live within a world of illusion without the strength to fight or weep. In the spirit of *giving back,* if I can give others anything *–let that be hope.* It is for me the only way I am able to heal. It is the precious work behind and ahead of me.

The two books published within this volume under the title *God Must Be Sleeping* were made possible by so many compassionate human beings. I am both amazed and delighted there are so many of you out there in the world, waiting for me and cheering me on still. Because of your love and support, for partaking of my future in its rise to grace, and even when I fell again and again –you were always there to pull me upward.

To all of you, my dear friends, loved ones, and readers, I say: *"Look! This is the house that [we] built. I am the man that lives in the house that [we] built. You are those precious few who live in the heart of this man who lives in the house that [we] built –together."*

Without your help – those of you who love me, read my books, write articles about my literary works, along with supporting my child abuse prevention advocacy – I know with absolute certainty these books could never have been written. This life could never have been lived. My world could never have been so beautiful.

Therefore, my love, my readers, my hope is incarnate within each and every one of you who made these books possible. You who made this life worthy, please take this deep-hearted acknowledgment (it would be fair to also call this my Dear Reader along with My Dedication to You), and allow it to be a kiss upon your soft cheek. The books are complete and although I may write another, the next will never be as these, which are so very special to you and me. So, with the two books under this one volume, I leave with you a parting wish, prayer, and hope. Let me now affirm the reasons behind your pain, agony, and overall suffering – from whatever befell your gentle heart – you are not at fault. You did not dream those most awful things happened to you – no matter what the abusers at great lengths try and claim are false. These atrocities done unto you are not false. They are real. As real as the anxieties and nightmares which now haunt you. I say to you, those who deem them untrue are evil. A blight upon humanity. However, there is hope –I promise it has not flown away. In the darkest of moments, hope lives and remains steadfast; although during these thorny times it is neither spoken, heard, nor felt. I give to you and awaken all these senses and more in night and day. Not just a glimpse or a quick vision, when one does not exist. It does and it has not left you. When you are feeling the crushing weight of despair, I pledge to you that hope is alive, can never die, and is never less there or sometimes gone. I speak from not a vision of hope, but from a real experience. A life I have because of people just as you. It is all that I see and it is not a dream.

Please read these words and let them fall deep inside your heart. They are written for none other than you. [We] stand amid the roar of a thousand abusive voices, decadent actions, ugly struggles, brought upon our heads by many, or by only one. [We] feel the crushing weight of guilt for their actions as well as our own. Our self-tormented culpability worsens what was done unto us by the abusers. However, please remember –*[We] only need to forgive ourselves to heal. [We] need not forgive another's transgressions to move forward. So, please forgive yourself. I need you to do so, so you may then help me.*

I have written within this book the words which spill from my heart like grains of golden sand and there are so many! I used to squeeze my fists tightly and keep all the sand like memories to myself as to not allow them to escape, yet they slip through my fingers and fall to the ground where they are lost among so many other grains of sand, so many terrible memories left by others, and so many dreams waiting to be washed into an ocean of hope. I could not hold on to my pain as it slipped from my clenching fists and wept harder when I saw all the other grains of sand left by you who wept alone and now with me. Tighter I clasped my hand only to one day relax its grip, letting my worries, pain, and misery fall to be with yours. This is where I found salvation and now my life is to save not one who has suffered, but many. Let the waves come crashing and wash our sand of anguish away into that vast ocean of hope. I now see this is not a dream, but a chance. It is hope within hope and why we are here. Why you are here with me now. My dear friend and reader. I will say again and with it I will make this promise to you.

I have come to know why we are here ... we are here to save one another.

And ... I will do just that, because —a promise is a promise.

All my love, hope, and forgiveness —Gregg Tyler Milligan

INTRODUCTION

I HAVE TAKEN THE EVENTS of both sorrow and triumph and provided a safe harbor for them word by word and on to paper in a writing process which has taken over a decade to complete. Contained herein are two auto-biographical books covering the period(s) between 1963 – 1974 & the latter half of 1974 - 1985. Book I, originally published in August 2009 under the title, *A Beautiful World: One Son's Escape from the Snares of Abuse and Devotion,* describes the first eleven years of my life. Book II, titled, *God Must Be Sleeping,* describes the next eleven years of my life. The reason I chose the first 22 years will become self-evident; however, in the most basic of explanations, it is to describe an emergence from the darkness into the light.

Throughout the difficult and arduous task of trying to publish, agents, publishers, and editors alike often said that *A Beautiful World,* was [too dark]. My only response is to say that anyone who suffers, who has been stripped of self-worth and left for dead, who is caught up in a merciless storm of anguish – their story will be [dark] and bleak. However, the reason I describe in graphic and vivid detail throughout Book I/II, the suffering of abuse in every manner, is to show how we can rise above the decadence and into the light; albeit clawing our way. The other reason – these are the awful events that took place and the truth can sometimes be very ugly.

This particular work in which I combine Book I and II is a merciless description of how I found the light in the midst of all that was done unto me by way of physical, sexual, mental, and emotional abuse. Or, in other words, how the light found me.

In order to remain honest, I do not know for sure what [was/is] or from which it came, the fighting spark that caused me to choose a different path and always look for a savior. All I do know is that I was not looking. Most times, as a child or young adult, I had no idea if God existed or cared. What mattered to me was survival; however, not at any cost. Not at the cost of hurting someone else, but a survival that saves [you] and me in the process. As a child and a man, there were and are those people in my life that do not save, but destroy, and like my college track coach Pat Palmer always said about these people, "They have no self love." What a waste my life would be if after surviving the terrible abuse, I would turn out like my abusers. What a terrible waste, indeed.

Therefore, all this life I look for a flutter of hope and chew on the bark of despair from time to time, getting a mouthful of hate, which makes my throat swell until I can barely breathe. My hunger for survival is acute and painful and the process of fighting in a world where only the fittest survive is downright exhausting. The cutting sting of retribution from my own family for writing the first book was awful. I expect the response by these so-called blood relatives regarding this new work to be appalling. But some of them did wrong and it must be called out. For obvious reasons, they are frightened of the truth and refuse to accept responsibility for their actions. They go on about the business of lying, hour after hour, growing weaker and weaker. However, within me, there is still life and I reason that when death does finally come, it will come as I fight. This way, at least gives me a chance to have a better life, and perhaps even a peaceful death.

Not to be fooled, the sharp, stinging pains of abuse, like little pins piercing me, are not gone. I still experience a sensation of intense panic on occasion and have not had peaceful sleep in years –a sleep without nightmares. However, this book, my choice to give back, and my love still strong and given freely, forces me onward and brings with it endless possibilities of a beautiful world. It is what I work for now, telling myself that when it comes to peace, I will at least feel it, and that in order to do so, I must fight until the end.

The strain of surviving abuse holds no more weight upon me because I will not give up fighting. Some have buried themselves in the remnants of their past and died –at times taking with them the innocent along the way. However, the fighting spark that commands me to die upon my feet is enough to give me shelter, make me a better person, and reach out to you in order to do the same. My efforts to break the chains of abuse have flared up, giving me a new vision, helping me realize this was the right thing to do. At first, I thought this was merely survival. Then, my efforts blossomed, drawing nearer and stronger, until I knew that what I move toward is the light.

Dear Reader: I drag myself toward this light and when it gets close I am so excited. I will continue to grope for the latch fastened to the door of opportunity that has been shut in my face, tear it off, and plunge through. In doing so, what is revealed to me are the welcoming signs of many people like you who are reading these words. Who have purchased this book. And knowing this, ignites the spark –the fighting spark in me. I hear your collective voices and read your messages coming from a great distance. And in these moments, I experience a strange thrill that makes me want to spring to my feet and give back even more. It has given me and continues to do so an unquestionable reason to move from the darkness into the light.

PROLOGUE

THE LONG DAYS AND NIGHTS of self-analysis, research, and reflection, which have passed since the abuse ended, along with the love of a few, have given me the opportunity to think of the tragedies Mother and many others forced into my life. With this contemplation there has been a strength that has drawn me out of the pit of hopelessness and despair into which I had once fallen. Mother is dead. Father is dead. But I still live, and in the hope of finding and claiming this life as my own I have built dreams for myself out of the ashes of all that had been taken from me.

I believe in seeking until we find whatever it is we are looking for. So confident in this belief, I never stopped hoping Mother and Father would change. I am blessed to have believed. Without this belief, there would not have been much of a chance of having found my own possibilities of a beautiful world.

I made up my mind as a child that I would not give up. I would make this promise to myself and keep it. I would return to the living even though when first making this promise I did not know I would have something in which to live for; a son, a wife, a sister, a dear friend. With the help of these people, and also [for] them, I have built a wonderful and peaceful home. A home for all seasons, with love and hope, and even a garden that grows nothing but weeds, but they are charming weeds just the same. With a solid education and hard work, I would never know what it felt to be poor again. I would learn to play the piano and there would be no end to music and things to make me sing and act silly. I raised a son to know only love and compassion, and watching him grow up, I prayed deep down in my soul that he would find me to be a good man.

My grief was deep and I know I will never forget the terrible things that happened, and that the old memories of these things and the mother I had loved would force themselves upon me, from time to time, in the form of anxieties and nightmares. However, this new life and plans for it make my grief less poignant.

It was a summer day in 1974 that had been filled with fear and loneliness when I came to leave Mother. I nearly returned to her several times afterwards, begging her to take back a wayward son. However, the path she had prepared for me was obliterated by a tangle of lies, fear, and pain. Everywhere in my life, with Mother, there was desolation and decadence. I had no choice but to make a new path and fearfully I set out to do so. And, like many difficult journeys, there was no evidence of a life worth fighting for, not the love and support of another, of a good-hearted laugh, or a voice of encouragement breaking the dead silence.

Scarcely breathing, I pressed onward, my heart choking more and more by the fear that gripped me. The fear Mother, Father, family, and strangers put inside of me. The door to hope seemed barred, but I forced it open. I crashed through it, inside were endless possibilities, and the realization I was not broken. With little hope, I started over many times, and the gloom fell swiftly about me. There was so many who wanted me to fail, and so few who made sure I did not. It was because of these latter good souls, along with a fighting strength put inside me by something better than all of us, I flung myself forward with a great cry of faith bursting from my heart.

When raising my head at night, I see the stars shimmering in the sky, and can still hear the ripple of a song I once sang to my sleeping infant son. I can see him rising gingerly to his feet while learning to walk for the first time. I can still hear the promise whispered to me when I pray. Admittedly, not until I was far from the scent of death and my own broken hopes, did I actually begin to pray. Before then, I did not feel God was listening. I felt perhaps, He might simply be sleeping. But then, I see Sarah and her eyes light up and she begins to laugh, and she runs to me. And Sue Marsh, who said she will never leave me, and has not, and I will not leave her. These are the prayers answered. When Ashley Marie (Tina) calls for no reason just to say she is thinking of me. There is April Lynn, my Pug, who will defend me to the death. And, Pat Palmer, the father I never had. The keeper of the truth. Of course, I cannot leave out my alma mater, Siena Heights University; My Siena! Where Pat still presides over many fresh faces and his compassion is never-ending. Lastly, there is Gregg II. My son, my Spudie, my light, and my way home.

Somewhere out there is peace and I will find it if it takes me a lifetime. If that means revealing these secrets to you, then so be it, and if I save you, then that would be even better. You would be right in saying the latter is my last hope before this life is gone. Yes, I am still ragged and torn in places. The hardships I have gone through have left their cuts on my soul, and sometimes, usually after a nightmare or when another person is cruel, you will see the deep-seated grief in my eyes. But I draw myself up and the day is glowing with prospect. The abuse did not end me, it came close, but my fighting strength shone through. I fought hard to overcome my weaknesses that seem to have taken so many others from my life, where addictions and hatred plague their every breath. In spite of their greatest efforts, my abusers could not take the last ounce of strength from my body, and they now darken before my eyes until I can no longer see them.

Therefore, I carry a weight but it gets lighter, and the ravages of abuse, of suffering, have not ended me. Look at this wonderful world. Look at its glow. I want to tell you also that I am sorry if you have suffered, but you will come back. Someday. Somehow. I understand it is lonely and terrible. I know you have fallen, but great, ragged arms are open and ready to catch you when you are ready. Until then, I am waiting.

Book I

1963 – 1974

A Beautiful World

One Son's Escape from the Snares of Abuse and Devotion

For [Spudie]. My son. Loving him is the closest I've ever come to believing God lives in all of us. And now, Gregg Tyler II is a man. A kind and gentle soul. My son has become all that is good in the world. He is my better angel. My son is what I always wanted to be and what I will continue to strive for until the end.

PART ONE
Black and Blue Smile

"There are people who have an appetite for grief; pleasure is not strong enough and they crave pain. They have mithridatic stomachs which must be fed on poisoned bread, natures so doomed that no prosperity can soothe their ragged and disheveled desolation."

Ralph Waldo Emerson

CHAPTER ONE

THEN A TEN-YEAR OLD BOY, I stood looking out a grimy window from a tacky house in Minnesota. Father would soon be here. Would he again crash the battered front door inward and rush past me, as if I didn't exist? Or knock gently while seeing me pressed against the dirty glass and smile – happy to be looking upon the face of his youngest son? My heart refused to accept what my mind already knew.

As I stood there, with my far-too-thin body half-hidden in old curtains that smelled of booze and cigarettes, my mother's voice shrieked behind me. "If that queer cocksucker is on his way over here, hell can't be far behind!" I briefly wondered what a cocksucker was.

My name is Gregg. My older brother, who now stands only a few feet away from me, is Carter and he's twelve years old. Somewhere within this small and dilapidated house, is our sister, Lynn. She's eight and most likely hiding in a closet and trying not to make a sound.

My brother, much heavier, almost portly is Father's first son and properly given our father's name. He was much taller than I with greasy black hair that stuck to his chubby face. His eyes were piercing blue, like Father's, and the small of his pupils looked like rounded black onyx. Although he was only twelve, his fingers were thick and man-like. He was solid as a horse and street tough. His wide legs balanced a substantial torso, which was squared off by two broad shoulders. When he bent his head downward, his hair hung catching only a slim blue slice of one eye. With his fists balled, he wasn't just a striking image of Father – he actually became him. It made me quiver in fear and feel a terrible sadness deep inside. When he looked like this, horrible things happened.

In contrast, I was small and frail, hiding behind oversized glasses. My skin would go from alabaster to ashen gray within seconds, depending upon the mode of terror. Both shorter and smaller than Carter, I was meek with thin, dangly arms. I was awkward and broken down. My stomach was sunken to the point that I could suck it in and create a gaping hole flanked by two sets of miniature racks that resembled ribs. When I stood next to my brother, my slender neck appeared better fit for a young girl. Half-moons lay beneath my eyes, but did not quell the deep green color wrapped in circles of gold. I was a squat bony boy, shy and unsure of my surroundings, unlike Carter who was a self-possessed bulk of a sturdy young man ready to do battle. My brownish-black hair mocked my frame, a matted mess of wiry strands that lay flat and lifeless against an undersized skull. Carter was built tough and gave off shiny confidence. I was the picture of weary, soft panic and always plenty nervous. Carter was a death bomb, and I wanted to be like him. Instead, I could only envy his strength and wish for his power, while banging blindly against a world where big brothers like him were better equipped and had the muscle and might to prove it.

My brother and I had our youngest sister to care for as well, whom we called "Pug nose" or "Pug" for short, because her nose resembled a flattened button. Our mother came dangerously close to naming Lynn "Caboose," since she was the last child my mother claimed she would ever have. As it turned out, she would be the last child born to my mother that would survive.

Lynn was a fragile little girl with a penchant for relentless hiding – in closets, under beds, and wherever else she could find room. She was short, as young girls usually are. Black hair rarely cut covered a head much too small and framed her pale doll-like face. Her facial features were diminutive except for large green almond shaped eyes.

There could be little doubt of her mood. When happy, she would form a perfect "O" with her small mouth, pulling her nose downward until it nearly disappeared and took on the shape of a tiny button. Her teeth were a jagged row of miniature Chiclets when she laughed. When sad or frightened, she would press a mangled and worn blanket against the side of her face and suck her thumb. It was a habit she broke years before, but recently had taken up again during times of distress – and therefore, a habit that would take years to break.

Carter and I stood and looked out at the empty driveway. My brother shifted on his feet, still peering out the window in anticipation, and his breath made round steamy circles on the cold windowpane.

After he moved out, Dad would come back from time to time. It was to check up on what Mother was doing, or *whom* she was doing it with, more likely. That is what I thought anyway. It rang true because he never spent much time with us kids, and whenever he was around, he wore an expression of irritation and utter disgust. There was never much talking other than an occasional grunt, which we interpreted to mean, "Hello" or "Get out of the way." Regardless, we never got to say much to him before he and Mother would start fighting, and when they fought, there was always blood.

Once Father arrives, it will break the trance I've yet again allowed to take hold and melt away the disquiet. I have two lives. As I look out the window, standing rigid with my fists clenched under my chin, I think of both of them. One life is made up of heroic fantasies. Often of being a military hero. A high-ranking officer, who performs brave and honorable acts of gallantry. Where I rise above abnormal conditions and always triumph. I was the best in my unit and the one called upon for the difficult missions.

The other life is nothing short of arid torment. A barren and waterless place detached from God. A life where I am not fierce, but clumsy and thin and subjected to coarse decadence. Brutal betrayal rains down on me daily. I am insignificant and have never known true courage outside of my incredible fantasies.

The fantasies are my shield against the savage secrets that sometimes creep into my mind, bringing me dangerously close to insanity. Underneath these childish daydreams is only a thin veil of protection. I have honed the ability to slip into a well-timed fantasy at the speed of light. Moving delicately between fantasy and reality and down a magical well guarding me against evil – this allows me to glide quietly away from the anguish of abuse. Sensing any danger, I am always within reach of this power. It is my only source of life.

In the darkest depths, I need these two lives, even though the one that promises of comfort and security is unreal. Without it, I am left with living the reality of a nightmare.

"Dad's here!" I jumped when my brother yelled, and my mother came running into the living room. Her hair was primped and pulled back with a colorful band, and she wore a deep red lipstick. The desperate effort put into hiding the effects of alcoholism were obvious, and only because Father was coming over. Otherwise, she rarely, if ever, gave much thought to personal hygiene. Mother would seldom brush her teeth, comb her hair, or even bathe. A repugnant habit adopted by her children as well.

Mother was no longer stunning, at least not like she was in her younger days when she had been voted prom queen by the senior class of her high school. I knew very little of Mother, having only gleaned bits and pieces through several thunderous fits of drunken rage and what was told to me by my siblings. Her name was Elizabeth, and she was the last of eleven children. Mother was once something special – referred to by some as a squaw, because of her American-Indian-like beauty. A beauty normally only possessed by Northern women. A dark exquisiteness. She had once been a waitress, kitchen maid, and wife of three former husbands. She grew up in St. Paul, Minnesota, and it was there she met Father at a dance. This was long before the alcohol stole her splendor, or before she simply handed it over without a fight.

Standing now in the living room, the difference was glaring. She had applied rouge to her cheeks, in order to compensate for the natural color now absent, but the fake blush did little to conceal the yellowish-gray of her skin. The flowered smock she wore hung much too loosely, and the low neckline revealed three grotesque bones protruding above the V-cut at the bottom. A pair of brown stirrup pants, meant to hug her thighs, sagged and bunched at the ankles, and I could see where she had cut off the cuff-straps. On her feet were old slip-on loafers without socks, exposing a web pattern of blue and purple varicose veins.

Before me was a woman I rarely saw washed or in clean clothes. Her stunted stick-like figure begged to be young again. By all appearances, her conduct was that of a beauty queen; however, all that was missing was the face and body to go with the confidence. I felt sorry for her and worried Father would find her ugly. The beauty had gone from Mother a long time ago. Left now was something small, wrinkled, and incredibly fierce.

As for Carter, Lynn and me – we knew Mother as a wretched woman who never altered her plans outside the pursuit of her own selfish needs. We could always tell when she was angry. She made our lives unbearable, and her reasons for tormenting us were always kept a secret – but like those of a dictator, they were rigidly enforced. It was more than the alcoholism. Even sober, Mother was spiteful and full of hate. We never understood why she was such a monster.

When I was seven years old, she instructed me to strip down and climb into a tub of cold water. It was afternoon, and she and I were again alone in the house. I was always frightfully afraid of being alone with her, but could never leave. Carter and Lynn were outside and probably close, perhaps in the backyard. Within shouting distance, but it did not matter, because at that age, I would try very hard not to make a sound. I would endure Mother's abuse with obedient silence.

I sat shivering in the tub, with my arms wrapped around my knees tightly pulled against my chest. My testicles ached from the cold water, constricting something in my stomach and making it more painful. Mother took a cup from the corner of the tub, filled it with water, and poured it over my head. Gritting my teeth, I pressed my forehead against the tops of my knees. Still not making a sound, except for the occasional moan I could not help let escape. Even when the little waves of panic played around the edge of my dread, I remained quiet.

It was not until Mother wrapped her skeletal, cigarette-stained fingers around my narrow throat and began to choke me that I broke the silence. Hot urine ran from me and mixed with the cold water. I began kicking frantically, making rattling sounds. Upon letting go, I labored to drag the air down my burning throat. Coughing violently, black spots danced in the air before my eyes. As the air returned to my lungs, the black flecks began to slowly disappear, along with Mother, just as subtle and quiet.

While waiting for our father to arrive, I felt the dread creeping around my belly, and my brother's face was a perfect picture of what I was feeling. We both knew our parents were planning on a night of barhopping. And we both knew how it would end.

Carter had moved from his spot at the window and now stood near the center of the room. It was the vantage point he wanted when Father entered the house. I naturally took my place, off to the side and nearly hidden. Carter deserved the first contact, and if he were lucky, perhaps our father would tussle his hair, or better yet, pick him up and render a giant bear squeeze. Neither would happen.

Carter's excitement would peak while waiting to greet Father, only to be smashed into a million pieces when Father paid him little attention. Like so many times before, I would watch the whole thing play out on Carter's face. There would be this grin sneaking around the corners of his mouth, and his whole face would take on a special light. It was the same light I watched fade, then slowly die when Father left every time.

Father was very handsome – in the old fashion sense. He looked like a comic book super-hero. His hair was black-brown, kept short in a crew cut, and he had deep blue eyes squarely set across his broad face. He had a rugged jaw and protruding cheekbones that made him even more striking. With his smooth shaven face, easygoing grin, neat tie, and blue work shirt, Father looked harmless – even passive. However, we knew differently. We knew he was sudden death. A horrific battle. A calculating man capable of murder.

His children were incredibly afraid of him, and when she was sober, so was Mother. There was good cause to fear our father. He had a short fuse and was violently sadistic. In addition, Father was six feet and thick all over except his gut. His upper and lower torso were substantial and made strong from high school football and years of manual labor while working on the coast survey. He had a wide neck that looked like you could bend pig iron around it. His fists were like bowling balls, and I saw them split the facial skin of both strange men and Mother with one wet popping blow.

Tonight our father entered the house, not with a crash but more of a sheepish lumbering. "Hey, Carter" was all Father said. He then made eye contact with our mother, motioned it was time to go, and left the house.

Mother passed Carter with barely a notice and swung open the battered screen door. Halfway inside and out, she turned and looked at me. "Find your sister. She's run off again and I'll be damned if I'm going to waste my time looking for her." Mother then left the house, and with a bang of the screen door – long missing its hydraulic arm to ease it slowly shut – she was gone.

Once the house was quiet, Carter and I began to cry. My brother looked at the door where our father had stood only seconds earlier. Carter's eyes were pleading with the memory of an image, dreadfully trying his best to make Dad reappear.

"He's not coming back," I said.

"Fuck you, Gregg."

I thought this last remark would be followed by a slug in the arm, but instead Carter only stood there. Dad would come and go, but my brother and I never did ask where he was going when he left, because we were sure it was always some place he would not say. Likely he was heading back to be with one of his new girlfriends, or to the Alibi Tavern, his favorite drinking hole. There was something about his shrewd way of answering our questions, which stopped us from prying. There was also something else; we undoubtedly knew that he just did not want us to know.

I loved Mother, but I worshiped Father. If not for his stiff and impervious exterior which commanded respect, then most assuredly, it was his unyielding quality of something cut ruthlessly from steel. He was vicious to his wife and insensitive to the needs of his children. However, it was difficult not to admire him. He dwarfed everything in his way, and in the afternoon sun, I admired how he cast a long shadow.

It was starting to get dark, and out the window, I saw a neighbor man walking by. He was an alcoholic, like many of the grownups that lived on our street. It was a poor neighborhood and bad part of town. He stopped and stared at me, waved, and then started walking again. "Looks like ole Red is going to the corner store for some Mad Dog," I mumbled.

Carter didn't seem to hear me until he replied: "Fucking drunk . . . They're all fucking drunks." This made me feel a little better. At least he wasn't staring at the damn screen door with that lonely look on his face. It would appear that there was still some fight left in him. We went looking for Lynn.

CHAPTER TWO

OUR NEIGHBORHOOD WAS A CONTORTED dirty forgotten place where the low-income went to retire and die. The last vestige of humanity unwashed. Nothing but old refrigerators tossed out in yards and shacks for houses. Run-down apartment buildings where the hookers stood outside and would show you their titties if you honked at them. Broken glass everywhere, along with needles and liquor bottles. You would be right to call it all these things. My siblings and I just called it home.

At the center of this home was Mother. As long as I can remember, I was her caretaker. I would spend hours in quiet waiting, trying to stay close and unnoticed, at the edge of visibility. If I crowded her, I would pay dearly. I also knew that not being around when Mother needed or wanted me would only postpone the unleashing of hell's fury, which was worse. Therefore, I would lurk around corners and behind doorways, listening to her movements and waiting to lend a hand at a moment's notice. It was a worrisome devotion. A strong and ugly love.

It was not that Carter and Lynn were scrubbed clean of emotion, but the evidence of abuse affected them differently. They found it possible to leave her and I did not. We all discovered the blessed lull between the horrors of Mother's wrath. However, there existed for me some small comfort in knowing she was safe. When Mother was asleep somewhere in the house, I would find sweet relief for a short period, but I constantly checked in on her. My heart would sink upon finding her awake, and I wondered how my siblings could put Mother out of their minds so easily. I hated them for it.

Mother built a relationship with her children based on unadulterated guilt, manipulation, and violence. She used anything that would hold us within her power and replace the wholesome defiance in her children with fear. She told me on more than one occasion that if I told anyone about what went on in the house with her and me, she would say I was lying, and I would be sent away.

At night, Mother would wait until Carter and Lynn had gone to bed before molesting me. In the darkness – always the darkness – with no light or eyes upon her, she would take her liberties while I said nothing and did absolutely nothing to stop her. The blinds were always down, and sometimes there was moonlight that came in thin slits from the bottom of the dark windows. As the tormented moments went by, I would fixate on the horizontal sliver of the only illumination within the room. In that line of brightness, I would find refuge.

It is true I often wished I could leave the house with my brother and sister. And at times I would beg them to stay with me, but they wanted to go and play and be far away from the madness. It was not like that for me. Behind the curtain of my mind, I saw myself finding her dead, and the fear of that was worse than Mother killing me.

The conflict between taking care of Mother and taking care of me was something I did not question. It was more than a part of my sanity. It *was* my sanity. That is all I knew and all that mattered. It even felt like love, and my love for her was every bit as true as her sickness. I would linger and not leave her. I believed that without me she would die. And there were times I did truly save her from real death.

Once I found her gently slipping underneath the water in the bath. She lay motionless and naked. The water a perfectly still shining mirror. There was no vapor rising from the water, now cold, and yet she did not stir. The only remaining dry spot was a circle of flesh surrounding her nose and mouth, and I watched it recede as the water crept inward.

Groping frantically at her arm, I took hold and heaved her upward. She felt as heavy as a bank safe, and I could not lift her out of the tub. Mother was too slippery, and dead unconscious weight threatened to pull her under. She was like a drunken anchor. I knelt pressed against the side of the tub, and held her head, making certain it did not dip under the water.

"Mommy, wake up. Mommy, wake up!" I pleaded and shook her to the bone. I shook her until the water splashed up and over the side of the tub, soaking the floor and me. I shook her until she woke up. When she did, Mother pulled in a tremendous breath, and I could read the angry expression on her face. My heart was pounding so hard I felt it might choke me.

From the tub Mother took hold of both my wrists, and her mouth became a vacant maddening gape. Letting out a deep smoker's laugh that became a growl, she let go a grip of one hand and slapped me hard across the face.

She would have drowned, and I saved her.

I cannot say when the compulsion of living for Mother consumed my every waking moment, but I know that I cannot remember a time when it did not. The feelings of love were real, but Mother had also made an art out of manipulation. It was one of her most prized attributes.

Countless times Mother would hold a knife against her breast while I sobbed uncontrollably, watched, and waited in agony. The tears rolled silently down her cheeks as she stared ruefully at nothing. Not speaking. Just twisting the knife in her hand, carefully and deliberately aiming its point directly at her own heart, but never breaking the skin. I was squatting beside her, occasionally tugging at her free arm. She would apathetically slap me away as you would a fly. Sometimes loudly threatening that she would fall on the knife if I did not move away from her. Then suddenly Mother was finished.

She would drop the knife to the floor and simply sit down on the couch, calling me over to her. When she beckoned, I obediently did as commanded, wanting desperately to believe, but never quite trusting. Within moments, I would be flung back savagely, her hands slapping at my face, her mouth open – and in her eyes, the same quality of hopeless despair she had when feigning suicide.

After each fake suicide attempt, she would beat me for stopping her from going through with it. It was always the same. Imminent death was the plot brought on by an act of simply not having the will to live any longer. And me, running after her, squatting beside her, or pounding my fists against a door or window, pleading with her to stop.

But the choice to protect her was final. The choice not to fight back and resist her was final. It was not just because the beatings would be worse if I did fight back, rendering any resistance futile. It was also because I could not fight the very woman I chose to save. It made no sense to me, and the strength in which to do so did not exist. Even when her long yellow fingernails were around my neck, I would not fight back, nor would I run from her. Not when she opened her mouth and roared, and I was close enough to smell the hatred mixed with booze and cigarettes on her breath. Tearing loose of her violent grip, I would only back away, but never ran. Even when her sickness stole my sleep as the days passed, and I had only the lurid nightmares to keep me company, I would not leave.

Father did leave. He left when I was five or six, I do not remember exactly when or why. There was no fanfare or buildup. I came home from school one day, and Mother said he was gone. This was followed by a tirade of cursing and a beating for good measure. I suppose Father could have left after finding Mother with other men. Who cheated first was a mystery to me. Perhaps he grew tired of coming home to the house in disarray, his children not fed, and the surplus of drunks pouring in and out at all hours. Then there was the constant bickering that would lead to the terrible beatings Mother would endure. The stench of the unwashed marital sheets, which still smelled like other men, would have been difficult to overlook. Father may have justified his own infidelity by telling himself he at least took it elsewhere. He could have left for all of these reasons combined, or just one of them. I do not know.

Father was not a good provider. Beyond the fact he abandoned his wife and children, he did not pay child support. He did not supply his family with any type of food, clothing, or financial means whatsoever, though he made a decent living and could have easily taken care of his family. He squandered most of what he took home on women, booze, and cigarettes. Between one vice and another, he didn't leave much for his children.

When Mother would ask for money, his eyes would grow narrow and dark. He would refuse and say she'd just spend it on booze anyway. Sometimes, he would hold up his calloused hands and show Mother the cracked and worn skin from hard labor to make a point. I knew he could have gone down to the grocery store and filled the cupboards, but I kept this to myself.

Father would go on protesting and telling Mother he did not have any money. "Not after the goddamn government took most of my paycheck," he'd shout. "Why don't you get a fucking job, lazy whore!"

I had overheard enough conversations and arguments over the years to know a bit about Father. He was a man of relatively broad experience in the field of road surveying and postal work. After taking a job as a dockworker for an airline company, Father managed to work his way up to an office position within the freight department. He was even the city dogcatcher at one time and dreamt of running for city council, perhaps even mayor, but like many of his dreams, along with his children, he simply gave them up.

He was the son of a retired cotton mill worker who served proudly in the Marines during WWI. An honor my grandfather often said was lost on Father who had not served. He and his father were never close, but they had quite a bit in common. They both were brutal and sadistic barroom brawlers who, despite their advanced alcoholism, never missed a day of work. They were mean drunks and beat their wives, but never their children. They were gruff and feared men, which they took for respect, and they both felt their lives and children had been an enormous waste of time.

Nothing moved Father to take care of his children. Not even the State could force him to pay child support. He felt such laws were there to screw the working man, and that the stipend the State wanted to charge him for support was plain nonsense. Mother would go to the Social Services Office and complain. However, since she would show up drunk, raging on about how the child welfare system was a total disaster, nothing changed. The people in the Social Services Office sat in tall chairs behind a tall counter and went about the business of doling out misery to miserable people. They moved papers around with slow hands and seemed lost in their own thoughts. Every now and then one of them would let their eyes wander around the room, fix on someone, and then they would shake their head in disgust. It was usually us they were fixing on when they did it.

What little money we had came from the Welfare Department and Mother's more disreputable activities. There were, however, a few occasions when Father would drop a quarter in each in his children's upturned palms. Afterwards, we sprinted to the corner store and quickly exchanged the small token for candy. Any gift from Father was eagerly accepted. Even when Mother threatened to beat us if we did. Of course, she never made her threats in his presence.

I do not know exactly why Father would come back from time to time. Maybe it was easy sex or a sense of familiarity. This had once been his wife and was still the mother of his children.

But it was bizarre to think he would take her barhopping. He must have known she would be parading herself in front of some of the local men she had been with sexually. Father would also have known that both of them became violently jealous when they drank.

Despite Father's shortcomings, Carter gave him infinite love; however, it was not returned. To simply not care, or at least not appear to, was a vicious quality of Father's. This affected Carter greatly, who sometimes looked at Father as though they had met somewhere else, in another time. It was a disconcerting look and I could see that it made Father nervous.

Since Carter was given Father's name, it easily supported Carter's claim that Father loved him the most. However, the urgency to have nothing to do with Carter was evident.

Father's indifference to his eldest son did not deter Carter from pining for his affection. He would sit for hours on the front porch waiting for Father to come back to the house and often Father would not for days. When he did, what excitement Carter had stored for his arrival was immediately dashed when Father paid him no attention. Carter would hide in his room afterwards and cry; sometimes his sobs were so heavy that simple breathing became difficult.

They never played ball together or went fishing. There were never any of the normal father and son activities. Serious anxieties regarding his affection for Father eventually developed into a full-blown reason to hate him. The love Carter felt for Father was abruptly carved from his heart and in time became hazardous.

Although it was the nineteen-seventies: the time of peace signs and "Keep On Truckin,'" Sergeant Pepper's Lonely Hearts Club Band, PONG, Happy Days, and being cool – this was all gone for Carter, and until you are thrust into being a father to your younger siblings, you just don't understand the gone part. He was pushed into the role of protecting his younger brother and sister, and it must have been unbearable for him continually witnessing how badly he had failed.

Early on, Carter was always there, doing what he could to take care of me. He would linger near me as if lying in wait for Mother to attack, and she never disappointed. Before he had the courage to stop her from hurting me, he was forced to watch helpless and frightened. Although Carter did not physically intervene at first, he never left the room. Instead, he stayed and begged with Mother. He sobbed, pleaded, and prayed aloud. It may have been with Mother that I shared the worst and most decadent of experiences, but it was Carter who felt the crushing weight of the world as a helpless spectator. One who bears the burden of a terrible responsibility, but none of the authority or training to carry it through to the end.

My earliest recollection of when he did interfere for the first time was near Thanksgiving. I was nine years old. We were happy to be out of school and even more excited it had snowed considerably. There was a massive weeping willow tree in the field at the end of the street, and it was covered in a cocoon of white frozen powder. Carter, Lynn, and I carefully tunneled our way below the thick low-hanging branches. We were delighted to find ourselves protected from the world in what appeared to be a natural tee-pee of ice and snow.

While the three of us stretched out silently on the winter floor of our willow tree sanctuary, we forgot about Mother. It was actually warm enough to remove our ragged coats, which barely kept the cold out anyway. I do not remember how long we were under the willow, but it was not until the November wind boomed outside and the light began to fade that we decided it was time to go home.

I was the first to walk inside the house. I had no boots, only a pair of old tennis shoes that were once Carter's. I came in the front door with the laces of my snow-wet sneakers flopping and slapping the floor because I still did not know how to tie my own shoes. Mother looked at me, and her face fell to an exaggerated sadness. Her voice took on a droning undertone, almost whiny. I remember it well because it was how she always started out while building toward her violent outbursts. It would reach a climatic point, but by then I was already fighting for my life. My eyes left her face and fell to searching the ground. I thought of running outside and into the night. Into the wet dark snow.

Mother walked over to the couch and sat down, crossing her legs slowly. "I don't appreciate *(coming out appreechhate)* you kids being gone so long," she slurred.

Her movements were deliberate as if she were a guest at a royal dinner party. Carter and Lynn were standing behind me, just inside the door. It was now dark outside, and Mother instructed Carter to turn off all the lights in the house. The only light remaining was a lamp sitting on an end table near Mother's head. It cast a yellow glow against her face, and her cigarette smoke rose up and disappeared under the stained and dented shade. Dust particles floated downward from underneath the lamp. Mother sat smoking and staring right at me. When she took a drag on her cigarette, its ember glowed and cast a blood light over her face.

Carter returned to where he was standing, behind me and in front of Lynn. Mother crushed out her cigarette, stood up, and walked over to where the three of us were. Looking at me, she then put her finger to her lips and said, "Shhh, now be still." The expression on her face never changed as she shoved me backward. It created a domino effect, slamming me against Carter and Carter against Lynn. All three of us fell against the screen door and out onto the porch, where we went skittering down the icy cement steps. Lynn began crying immediately. Both Carter and I helped her up. Having no place else to go, the three of us walked back into the house.

Mother was just inside the door. She told Lynn to go take a bath and Carter to sit down on the couch. I would remain standing near the door. We all did as we were told. When Carter sat down, Mother turned to me, again her expression never changing, and put her hands around my throat. I could hear myself making thick sounds when I began to choke. The inside of my mouth tasted like pennies, and I made quick furious motions while grabbing at her wrists trying to free myself. This time, Carter was no longer simply begging Mother to stop. He was making her.

His hands were now over mine and pulling as well. The three of us were standing together – clenching, with Mother's hands around my throat, my hands around her wrists, and Carter's hands around mine.

Carter screamed, "Mom! No!" – and then to my amazement, released one of his hands long enough to lay a wallop of a backhand across Mother's face. She went reeling backward, breaking her grip. I was immediately filled with sweet air – along with a deep adoration for my brother.

While I was buckled over, fighting desperately to refill my starved flattened lungs, Carter and I watched with curious nonchalance as Mother slid down the wall she hit. She eventually came to rest, splayed out on the dirty living room carpet. She was not unconscious. Instead, only surprised and laid there blinking in the semi-darkness of the room.

Carter pushed open the front door, letting in the cold air and making it easier for me to breathe. Mother continued to lay there and look around the room confused. We saw with a tad of concern that her left ear was bleeding.

I would later suffer the consequences of Carter's heroism. This is why Mother began waiting until he was gone before unleashing on me whatever fancy of madness struck her. However, that night Carter proved to me and himself that he was a true giant, and we both believed in our hearts – to Mother as well.

The endless laborious task of watching out for both Lynn and me gradually took its toll, and Carter was forced to choose whom to protect. He must have been horribly sickened by the difficult decision he had to make. He did the only thing he could, protect our youngest sister by taking her from the house as often as he could – thus, leaving me alone with Mother, as I would not go.

Sometimes, Carter would come home to find the aftermath of his decision. His younger and only brother curled into a ball of agony and lying on the bumpy linoleum kitchen floor. My tattered underwear pulled partway down, exposing the half-moon shapes of Mother's nails that had bit into the soft skin of my buttocks only minutes before. Further reminding Carter he was just barely too late was the thick smell of urine, sweat, and alcohol that still hung in the air.

He would kneel over me weeping, and I could feel the weight of his shaggy hair on my face. I would hear the click in his throat while he sobbed, squeezing my hand tightly. Carter would raise his head to Mother, angry and pleading. At times, he only stared at her and into those dead black eyes. Other times he would shout hoarsely, "Why don't you just leave him alone!"

Lynn would be in the background, screaming as well. A sound too large for her small body. Her tiny mouth gaping, making a lower-case "O." Mother would raise her hand to hit Carter and then lower it. She then would walk away, and we could hear the sound of her collapsing onto the living room couch. As a means of insane justification or to lay blame, we would hear her from the other room, her voice dry and flat, "I told you kids to stay inside."

When Carter's eyes met mine, they would be filled with bitter remorse. There was also something else that passed between us, as it had during the countless other times he found me much too late. When my crotch had been dark with piss, the putrid smell of my own shit filling the room, still spitting out globs of blood – it was as clear as Mother's insanity – what passed between us was life and death.

Lynn, being the youngest, often found herself pitched to the side and forgotten by everyone. Carter was disinterested as older brothers are. It was enough for him to just get her out of the house. I stayed as close as possible, but I had Mother to care for. Mother herself was pitifully indifferent to her youngest daughter's needs.

Lynn had once made a trip round the block on her bike. By the time she came peddling up the sidewalk outside our house, she was in a full panic. She jumped from her bike while it was still rolling and ran inside. A terrible thing had occurred to her halfway around the block. She suddenly did not recognize any of the houses and began to fear that, when she turned the corner again, she would be lost for sure.

Watching Lynn was a heartbreaking experience. You could see qualities of immense joy she consciously kept in check. A picture-perfect young lady without any physical affliction, aside from the inability to say her R's, making her even more lovable. Evident in all her characteristics was a perfectly resolved innocent little girl's way of thinking. However, this was shattered, leaving only the bitter cries of a lonely child.

The abuse Lynn received was not physical torment; instead, it was sexual. It had not been Mother's better nature that kept her from beating Lynn; instead, it had been Mother's worst nature that would rise to the surface, and Lynn as well would not be spared.

Carter and I slept in the same bedroom and in the same bed. Lynn had her own bedroom, and a thin wall separated it from Mother's. Lynn's room was directly across the narrow hallway from the one I shared with my brother, and from where I lay on the bed, I could see both her doorway and Mother's. On some nights, I would see Mother leaving her room and going into Lynn's. Mother would try to remain silent while waking her. It did not matter because I could see perfectly how she would lean over the bed, removing the covers and whispering something into Lynn's ear.

Mother would then take Lynn in hand and lead her out into the hallway, making a sharp turn to the right and into her own bedroom. I watched as Lynn went quietly and saw her facial expression was always tired and sad. The springs of Mother's bed would squeak when they crawled onto it. Sickening anxiety filled me, knowing what I would hear next. The rustling of bed sheets followed by the snap of Mother's elastic band around her underwear as she pulled them down. Not wanting to hear any more, I would bury my head under the pillow and climb frantically toward sleep.

What little protection Lynn had from the beatings was lost in these bitter experiences and the endless neglect. Based on the normal instincts of a young girl, Lynn looked for direction from her only parent. What she received was the uninterested reflections of a woman who had no desire to be a mother.

Often, if I did not remind her to use the restroom, Lynn would soil herself. Without the proper attention, she would occasionally end up with a terrible rash on her genitals. Having no one else to care for her, and being too young to care for herself, I would have to administer first aid. Finding old creams under the bathroom sink, I would give instruction on how I thought they should be applied. It was embarrassing guesswork and a parent's responsibility.

I fed Lynn when I could. When I would often steal food for myself, I always made sure to take something for her. Although the apple tree in the backyard or the field at the end of the block was my private refuge, I shared them both with Lynn. She would sit next to me, usually a leg touching a leg or her arm resting against my side. Lynn understood the quiet and enjoyed it as much as I did. What protection and shelter I could give her, I did. However, it was limited by the constraints of my own frailties. Like Carter, I sometimes had only enough strength in order to survive and care for myself.

Lynn had a reflective temperament, but it was frequently overshadowed by anxious concerns that we were always about to be harmed. As a result, she would cling to me or my brother and warn us against an impending doom. She did not cling to Mother or trail behind her like most little girls. Perhaps she knew even then, the impending doom was Mother herself.

Carter and I had to become her guardian and neither of us were prepared for fatherhood. We were children, and the only examples we had were the unsettling observations of two parents possessing abusive characteristics. We were poor excuses for caretakers, and Lynn was abandoned, suffering the ravages of carelessness and no one to help her.

Carter, Lynn and I had four older sisters. By the time I was ten, they had all systematically moved out – escaped. The two oldest half-sisters, Jessica and Lauren, had married the first man that came along and asked. Ashley was living with the boyfriend who impregnated her, and Madison, for the time being, lived with Jessica. It was a temporary arrangement and the best she could do on short notice. When the older siblings took themselves out of the picture, with them went the protection we once had.

Lauren, the oldest, was in her early twenties and on the very few occasions when I saw her, she already looked much older. She was slim, tall, and always brooding about something. She did not look like any of us and had none of the physical characteristics passed down from a mother we all shared. Her hair was platinum blond and kept short. Her appearance matched her clothes, which were always screamingly clean. Her eyes were unfriendly and when she looked at me, I was frozen on the spot.

Two years younger than Lauren and hard as nails, that was Jessica. She drank, smoked, cursed, and could whip a whole lot of ass whether it was a man or woman. Jessica could "knuckle up," as the saying goes, and she relished in it. If she were drinking in a bar, which she often was, and a fight broke out, it was Jessica who probably started it. When she was in her early teens, she was short, squatty, and pleasingly round. At eighteen, she looked to be assembled together with just the right amount of smooth, compact curves. With one exception, she had a big behind that earned her the nickname *bubble-butt*. Jessica also did not look, or act, anything like Lauren. Especially when comparing Lauren's eerily controlled temper, long slender frame, and flat almost non-existent buttocks.

Jessica took to alcohol early on and drank so much that slurring her words became a natural part of her vocabulary. She often had blood seeds in the corner of her eyes from either leaving a hangover or working like hell to prepare for the next one. Like Lauren, she kept her hair short. It was a reddish auburn and brought the brown out of her beautiful, almost perfectly round eyes. However, when she drank her eyes were pretty no more and looked exactly like Mother's. And when she wore her hair a certain way, she even looked a little like Mother too, and often she had the same nasty disposition.

Still, there was also this other sweet side of her that came out sometimes. You had to catch her in those sweet moods, which usually occurred right after she had a couple sips of wine. However, a few more sips and she was yelling at you about being too loud.

I loved Jessica even if she did scare me sometimes. There was this time I had started choking on a jawbreaker while playing down the street, only a couple houses down from where we lived. I started to gag and immediately ran home. By the time I reached our yard, the world was going black. Jessica was there and just about ready to pull her car out of the driveway. The next thing I remember, she was holding me over the sink with her finger down my throat. I coughed up the jawbreaker and took in huge gulps of air. When the danger subsided, I started to cry. Jessica held me as my head rested on her shoulder. Rocking me back and forth, she just kept saying, "It's okay, baby – it's okay." It was easy to love someone like that.

Ashley was six years older than me, and when she lived at home, she did her best to protect me from Mother. Her defiance was a harsh tax on Mother's convictions. One evening in an outrage, Mother went after Ashley in a drunken frenzy. Ashley drew a knife she had pulled from the kitchen drawer and held it to Mother's throat. That was the end of Mother's attacks against her. Ashley left for good the next day.

Rebelliousness was inherent in Ashley's nature. It was as if she came into this world to discourage all fools. She seemed to possess endless courage, and it filled me with both dread and amazement. I admired her strength and loved her so much that I would think breathtaking thoughts about her, turning them repeatedly in my mind.

She was a natural beauty. Her thick auburn hair was combed straight down past her shoulders, and she often wore it pulled back with a headband. The first thing you would notice were her eyes. They were sharp and glinted when the light touched them. Adding to their unique beauty was the fact one was green and the other blue. Her nose was thin and perfectly narrow at the point. She had a doll's mouth, full and soft. Although Ashley was barely sixteen, her body was that of a grown woman.

Ashley would become pregnant soon after she moved away to live with a boyfriend. She would carry the child full-term, and regardless of Mother's protestations, she would keep the baby. At first, she wearily considered an abortion. Alone, she pondered this choice endlessly. There was no parental guidance. Mother had mocked her, ironically calling her a whore. According to Mother, it was yet another act of defiance brought against her personally, as if Ashley got pregnant out of spite.

And finally there was Madison. Madison had left in a hurry, as they all did and for the same reason – Mother. In one of the last terrible arguments she would have with Mother, she packed what she could and ran. I watched Madison go, and I wept, but did not ask her to stay. Even then, I knew it would have been unfair to do so.

Madison was two years younger than Ashley and four years older than me. Her mouth at one time had been almost voluptuous, but habitual muscular tension had drawn it close and made a deep line on each lip. She was still very pretty with long brown hair often tied in a ponytail and short with mild curves. Her eyes were dark, almost black, and they shimmered when she laughed. Her face was eager and mature for such a young girl and bore the high cheekbones of a native Indian. Her ears were much too large for her head and at times would poke through her hair. Their pale color would contrast sharply against her dark hair, making you notice them even more. She had small hands, almost too small for her body, and they moved graciously like those of the blind. I remember her hands while holding me on her lap. I remember that the most about Madison.

With our sisters gone, and Mother to deal with, our lives were not like most kids', but there were a few children in the neighborhood with whom we made friends. The Jacobsons, who lived directly across the street, had three children our age and gender. Kyle was my good friend, Louis and Carter buddied up, and Lynn befriended Alexis. Although Mother, her madness and my need to stay near her prevented frequent interactions with the Jacobsons, they gave us all brief, desperately needed moments of childhood play.

School however was a different story. In the fall, when most children were going about getting ready for the academic year, purchasing new clothes and supplies, I along with my brother and sister were mentally preparing ourselves for another year of humiliation. Somewhere hidden inside each of us, secretly waiting to explode, was the fear we all felt – remembering how we would be tormented by the other children. Our clothes were hand-me-downs from Goodwill or the Salvation Army and were never a good fit, either too big or too small. The trousers were littered with patches sewn on by their former owners. Every stitch was worn thin and stretched to the breaking point. The fabric was shiny with wear in places, and the shirts, dresses, and pants stank of stale cigarettes and mothballs. We looked and smelled poor.

Our hair was shaggy and unwashed. Our faces were often dirty, and mine was sometimes bruised, albeit lightly, which generally looked to be the result of innocent play with other boys. During the school year, Mother was always careful to hit below the neck, and she intentionally avoided the legs and arms. Occasionally, there would be the remaining bluish hue of her fingertips as a result of her choking me. Mother would use flesh-tone makeup to conceal the marks, and I was desperately afraid it would rub off and someone would notice. We drew no attention nor did we seek it. Confessing to a teacher was out of the question. If not for the fear of retribution, it was inconceivable to imagine divulging what dirty little secrets were kept hidden in the darkness of Mother's room.

Because of constantly wetting the bed, I often smelled as if I had bathed in urine. The odor emitting from damp yellow underwear hung to the crotch of my pants. The schoolchildren would point their fingers, laughing and holding their noses when I walked by. My siblings and I were relentlessly targeted when it came to the other children. They would tease us incessantly. We were easy prey. The poor always are.

I would sit facing away from the other children in the cafeteria, in order to hide as best I could the State–provided free lunch. Both hungry and humiliated, I would quickly gobble down the food. When the other children traded snacks, I could only watch with envy. Making it worse, from time to time a well-meaning lunch lady would take up a collection of treats for me. Reluctant children would hand over their pudding cups and sweet pies. Once laid out before me, I would greedily eat the vast array of colorful delicious snacks. They were scrumptious, but did not douse the bitter taste of shame in my mouth.

Academics were an afterthought compared to the basic needs of survival. We missed a significant amount of school. Mother would sometimes forget and think it was summer. My siblings and I never brought this to her attention. Instead, we would stay home, choosing rather to take our chances with Mother than face the humiliation of other children and the stresses of schoolwork far beyond our comprehension. We all fell behind and were below the recommended reading, writing, and arithmetic levels. At ten, I still did not know how to tell time or tie a shoelace. I would steal the homework from book bags and lockers of other children and copy the assignments. I cheated on tests – if I did not cheat, I flunked.

Each school year, the lessons became more difficult and the children more sadistic. Barely passing each grade level, we were more broken and no smarter. At the end of each year my brother, sister, and I sighed with relief. We would find some comfort in not having to contend with yet another meaningless prospect of disgrace – one less reason to feel *dunce* was stamped upon our foreheads, no need to worry about readying ourselves for school after long sleepless nights. When summer finally arrived, it brought with it the chance to let the shame of the school year die away.

Summer also meant not having to desperately conceal my "tics" from the eyes of the cruel schoolchildren. My obsessions ran the gamut from constantly needing to get the saliva out of my mouth to touching and re-touching objects. I was also absolutely certain for about six months that I would die of a heart attack. I remember when it all started.

It had been with a film we watched in school about a boy my age. The similarities between the boy and me filled me with terror. His parents fought, children shunned him, and he was lonely. The film cut to a time earlier that morning and showed the boy's parents fighting. Later, the boy asks his father to play catch and his father refuses. The boy was already wearing his baseball glove, and I felt sorry for him even more.

At the end of the film, the boy boards a school bus. Minutes later, he walks to the front of the bus and asks the driver to stop. He speaks in a low, almost inaudible voice that seemed to come from a deep and empty place. I sat watching the movie knowing exactly from where that voice came. The driver stops the bus, and the boy descends the steps. You saw his Converse high-tops, and then his ankles turn, legs buckle, and then he falls without a sound.

I watched, fighting back tears, while my anxiety blossomed. The film skips to a doctor telling the boy's parents that he died of a broken heart. The mother and father did not sit together. I noticed they were not holding hands. It bothered me a lot that they seemed not to care about what the doctor was saying.

That afternoon it began to build up inside me. The boy in the film kept weaving in and out of my head. It worked on me until I was convinced it could happen. The fear dragged at me, and I waited for the moment when I would die of a broken heart.

I needed constant affirmation my heart was beating. So, I ran from morning 'til night in order to feel the hard rhythm of my heart slam in my chest. As soon as the pounding subsided, I was off and running again. The worst of it was when I could not leave Mother in order to run outside. Disappearing into the bathroom or out of Mother's sight, I would press my hand against my chest and concentrate until I thought I could feel a beat. It was pure agony, but I still chose to stay with her. A choice I made easily when it came between Mother and me. Mother always came first.

Life was a long period of agony and waiting. We were hungry all the time. The food was scarce, and the kitchen was off limits according to Mother – who usually announced this with her belabored decree – "The kitchen is now closed." What little food we might have found in there would have been beyond consumption anyway due to aging, mold, or roach shit.

With this lack of food, we had to resort to stealing from the corner store. The store was at the end of the block, luckily within walking distance from the house. The storekeeper was a bitter, rotund Hungarian. His eyes glittered blue sparks, piercing out of dark caves. The skin beneath his eyes went blackish brown when he became angry. His nose canted to the left and was badly pocked. It looked broken and I wondered how he could breathe through it.

When I first started stealing, I would panic and stand there like I was frozen in mud, letting the storekeeper scream and cuss and get close enough almost to catch me. Later I learned the trick was to wear an old hat to hide stuff under, or pants with deep pockets, and just waltz right out of the store. In the winter, I would wear a big floppy coat, but that would not work in the summer.

Mother also frequented the corner store to get her booze and cigarettes. The storekeeper had everything crammed inside that small and crowded corner grocery. He sold what you needed or wanted, and that was what mattered. He even cashed paychecks and food stamps. You couldn't use the stamps to buy booze or cigarettes, so the keeper would let you purchase the legal items, *what you needed*, and you worked it out so you had cash money coming back. With that, you purchased *what you wanted*.

I went on stealing when I could, and the storekeeper never bothered to throw me out when I returned. He probably figured the money Mother spent was worth the occasional snack he lost. Things went on as they always did. The only time I was ever chased beyond the parking lot of the corner store was not by the old Hungarian, but by a bread delivery driver.

I had snagged not a loaf, but a whole rack of bread from the back of the truck. I remember the small parking lot had just been freshly tarred and lined, which had a sweet industrial smell to it. As soon as I took off running, I could hear the driver shouting after me. I was hungry –no, starved – and by the time I crossed the street, he was already gaining. The rack was awkward and difficult to run with, so I dropped it. Regardless, he continued after me. I tore down the sidewalk, my hair plastered to my skull in sweat strings with my arms pumping like mad. I could hear his harsh breathing and knew he was closing in. He wasn't yelling any longer, and I felt his fingers brush the back of my shirt lightly, making me scream. With a newfound burst of energy, I pulled ahead and left him far behind. I did not dare look back until I was nearly to the field.

The chaos of our home life suffocated the normal activities of childhood. Seasons and holidays came and went. Christmas was something trivial, unimportant and without meaning. I certainly did not have gifts to brag over the next day with my only friend Kyle. When I got back to school after Christmas break, I would always lie and say I got a truck or a BB gun.

If Mother felt the urge, she would allow us to put out the old fake tree Father had brought home before I can remember, or the Christmas Wheel. The Christmas Wheel was fashioned like an old desk fan with the same shape and size, but instead of a series of blades and protective meshing, there was a large round plastic disk made up of various pie-shaped colors that would be projected on the wall. The tree was store-bought and looked it. It was made up of several wire attachments supposed to be the limbs, and glued to those were artificial bristling quills painted white. Most of the quills were gone, leaving bare spots when the tree was assembled. The wire limb attachments would stick into three green wooden rods filled with holes. One of the rods was lost, so it was now a much shorter fake tree with a bad case of the mange.

We would turn off all the lights and aim the Christmas Wheel at the tree. It would go round and round, making this low throbbing noise. With the lights off it was much better, because you could not see how ugly the tree was or that it didn't have any decorations. When all the lights were off, including the Christmas Wheel, you could not see there weren't any presents under the tree either. That was Christmas.

There may have been Thanksgiving too, but I do not remember it. Therefore, I do not have any grief for what was gone because it does not stick in my mind as a memory.

There were a few winter experiences though that I can warmly recall. I would sometimes go skating with my brother. When we were skating, Carter and I were happy. We would go down to the fire station, pulling one another on a sled, and then strap on our skates and chase each other around the rink. The skates were hand-me-downs from older siblings. Often, I would be wearing girl skates, which were still too large; however, newspaper made them fit.

The fire station sat on top of a large hill, which was great for sledding. Its steepest slope was just below three enormous doors, and behind the doors were the huge fire trucks. Below the hill was a sunken expanse of land that always flooded when it rained and made a perfect ice rink in the winter.

The fire station would use the thick hoses from one of the engines to fill the recessed area. Sometimes, Carter and I would watch the firemen prepare the rink. The best part was watching the hose stiffen right before the water came gushing from the end. The station maintained the rink, and the locals looked forward to its opening every winter, but not as much as I did. It was a safe place full of fun, and best of all, within walking distance from home.

We would sit atop the big hill that overlooked the ice rink and watch the other skaters go whizzing by, shouting at the neighborhood kids we recognized. Sometimes when the fire station served hot chocolate, we'd drink so much that our small bladders felt ready to burst, and we'd be forced to sneak a piss in back of the fire-red brick building. We would skate and sled for hours until our fingers and toes, wrapped in plastic bread bags, were frozen. But we would not go home. Sometimes we waited until the fire siren blew, signaling the rink was closing. The time spent away from Mother did us good. It made us strong.

The birthdays also came and went without parties or friends. There was a moratorium on sleepovers, what few we had from time to time, which was a blessing in disguise. During these painful few, Mother would always be involved somehow. She would force us along with our friends, which were usually Kyle, Louis, or Alexis to sleep all together on the living room floor. She would explain loudly to them that this was so she could keep an eye on me. Because she believed, I would do the most atrocious things with Kyle if left alone with him.

Mother would then flop down in between us and promptly pass out. The last sleepover ended with Mother urinating and defecating herself while she slept. Kyle, who was asleep to one side of her, ended up getting some of it on him. He woke up feeling the wetness. When he realized he got a good dose of Mother's excrement on him, he started to gag and then he puked all over the blanket on the floor. Mother kicked him out of the house and told him to go home. She cussed him out pretty bad, calling his mother a whore and said he could go fuck himself and the horse he rode in on – one of her favorite lines. Louis was there as well, and he left with his brother. Carter and I cleaned everything up including Mother, gagging ourselves, but we did not puke. Maybe it was because of all the practice; somehow we had gotten used to Mother crapping and pissing herself. Regardless, that ended the sleepovers once and for all.

Desperate, I thought once about trying to tell these things to the store-keeper at the corner store, although he hated me for stealing from him, so much he would throw lit matches at me and chase me away. I also thought about telling a kind-faced neighbor. I would tell them the whole story – even the embarrassing parts about the bad stuff in the bedroom. Nevertheless, I knew that if I went and told anyone, Mother would come and drag me back home, and the man at the store or the neighbors would let her do it. They were afraid of her. More than they cared about me.

I could not tell a social worker either. They only came to the house by appointment, and Mother would get prepared. Mother would mark the day and time on a piece of paper, and stick it to the front door as a reminder. She would make us clean the house, and then she would hide all the booze. Mother would open some windows to air out the smell of stale wine and whiskey, even if it were winter. If the social worker asked why it was so cold, Mother would probably tell her the furnace was old, and we could not afford to get it fixed. That would get her sympathy.

I had seen how Mother was good at playing people when she wanted something and how she could easily get people to feel sorry for her. She was also very good at telling people what they wanted to hear. Mother would be sick from not drinking, and I bet she played that up for the social worker too.

I had watched many times, when, shortly after these visits, she'd be at the corner store buying alcohol and doubled over in pain because it had been awhile since her last drink. Sometimes people in the store would ask her if she were all right. Mother would tell them she had cancer and they would get this sad look on their face. Then, she would be really pissed off because she had to wait and buy booze until the people she lied to left the store.

After me and my siblings were finished cleaning the house, we would be sent away before the social worker was supposed to arrive. Mother told us that if we came back before the social worker left we would, in her words, "Pay the price." That meant we would get a serious beating.

Therefore, we never came back until the blue car with the yellow city emblem on the door was gone. When the social worker finally left, we would come home. Before long, the house looked like it had never been cleaned, and Mother looked like she had never been sober.

I thought about telling someone all the time. Perhaps Kyle or Mr. and Mrs. Jacobson. I would tell them the whole story, but never did. What stopped me was not just shame, but fear as well. Fear of Mother.

Mother had made sure to provide me with detailed insight of the consequences. Not only would I be taken away, but I would be sent to a boys' home where the older boys would cut off my winkie. She also told me that they would make me put their cock in my mouth, and I would have to suck on it until the white stuff came out, and then I would turn into a queer for sure.

I did not know if any of this were true, but I knew Mother was not lying when she said I would "*pay the price*" if I ever told anyone. I knew that was real. As real as the tears rolling down my face. It did not make any difference, because before Mother's warnings, I knew in my heart that I would never tell anyone. I would continue to keep my grief and the truth silent.

CHAPTER THREE

As the sun started to set, Carter and I were underneath the apple tree in the back yard, enclosed by its thick foliage. It was a place we could go when scared or lonely. It was also close to home if Mother needed me. Carter sat down on an old crate smuggled from the corner store's dumpster. On the side of the crate, down one of the slats, was written in big orange letters: SUNKIST. On the ground, directly behind where Carter sat on the crate and near the edge of where the low-hanging branches met the earth, there was a mound of dirt. Stuck in the center was a cross made from two Popsicle sticks tied together with kite string. From the stains, one appeared to be grape and the other strawberry.

This was where the bird Carter shot was buried. The bird he hit with only one try from his *Super-Sonic-Slingshot,* earning him a "double high five" from his younger brother. Both nervous and curious, I remember running over to it, excited at the prospects of returning the fresh kill to my big brother – the hunter. Only when I got up close, I saw it was still twitching. As it suffered and lay dying, its yellow beak opened and shut in a slow-motion fashion that made it look like it was trying to speak. Together, my brother and I picked it up and wept as the blue-black feathered bird bled all over our hands, shuddered once more, and then died.

I stared at the dirt pile, and the thought of the bird never feathering another nest seemed peculiar to me. It'd be quite dead and stiff by now, and part of me, curious about death, wanted to dig it up and take a look. I thought better and gave up the idea. Carter and I sat saying nothing. We took in the quiet and sweet smell of apples mixed with lilac. He rocked back and forth on the four corners of the crate, and I sat down with my back against the trunk. He was staring out through a small clearing between the branches and leaves at the stutters of fading light. I was staring at him. The quiet was good. This too would be behind us soon.

There was a terrible feeling messing around in my gut. It wasn't anything unusual because I always felt this way. Well, at least since I realized what kind of family I came from. Poor white trash. Drunken parents. Abused. Neglected. Molested. Hungry; always hungry. The feeling kept tapping something in the back of my mind. I looked at Carter. Could he be feeling this as well? Something told me that he was.

Carter got up from his box and crouched down in front of the crawl space used to enter and exit the apple tree. He was busily picking at a callous on his middle finger; what Carter called "The Fuck You Finger."

"Are you going in the house?" I asked.

Carter replied, "Yep, and so are you."

Trying to sound as sarcastic as possible, I replied, "Just great." I was eyeing Carter suspiciously. After all, he couldn't catch me if I took off running. Although I was two years younger, I was thinner and faster. I liked to run. *If it wasn't for the malnourishment, I bet I'd be the fastest kid on the block*, I thought. I was still fast even up against the older kids, like sixteen years old, who were almost adults; hell, some of them were driving. It was a pretty big deal that I could outrun someone as old as that in years, who had a driver's license. And on more than one occasion, I had to.

"Do we have to go inside right this minute?" I asked. I wanted to stay longer under the sanctuary of the apple tree. Moreover, I didn't want to be in that house.

Carter looked at me curiously. "Hey," he said, "are you a pussy?"

"No," I said. "But you're a faggot."

Carter was already pushing past the branch when he called back to me, "Come on, pussy; we gotta go find Lynn."

I was at a loss. It wasn't that I had forgotten Mother's instructions to us as she left for the bar that we had better find our little sister. It was that I was in disbelief. Here it was, the first time we get some peace and quiet with Mother out of the house, and Carter wants to go looking for Lynn, who's probably hiding under a bed and playing with her dolls. None of her dolls had any clothes anyway because they were lost after Carter and I stripped them all down and made 'em screw like real people. I never told Carter this, but I'd get a pretty mean boner when rubbing the smooth crotches of the boy and girl dolls together. What really gave me a weird feeling in my groin was when the girl doll had nothing on but a little skirt and I'd lift it real slow, like 'round the backside.

I was still too young to know how to masturbate or what in the world it was in the first place, but I liked the feeling the whole ordeal gave me. It wasn't like being with Mother when she'd make me hard by flicking it with her thumb and forefinger. Then she'd get angry that I was and hit me in the stiffness with the back of her hand. She would grab my hand and shove it between her legs, telling me that she's keeping an eye on my winkie and if he got hard again, I knew what was coming. I'd push up and pull back when she told me. Sometimes my hand would start to get sore. Sometimes after she was done, I would have to lie next to her and get poison whiffs of Mad Dog and cigarettes. I would fight the urge not to puke, feeling her pressed up against me. Sometimes against my groin – and I'd want to wash my hand real bad. I'd keep it down by my side so I wouldn't smell her juices, but I could feel them drying and getting sticky. After Mother finally passed out, I'd go and scrub my hands. It didn't matter. That smell would last for days.

When I got up to follow Carter, I saw something sticking out of the back of his pants. "Hey, Carter. What's hanging from your back pocket?"

He sort of reached around and felt his butt until he happened on the string hanging down.

"Oh, nothing," he said and then shoved the string back into his pocket.

I remember seeing something like that at Kyle's. The Jacobsons went to church every Sunday, and Kyle told me they were Catholic. They had religious stuff all over their house. There was a picture of Jesus on the wall in the living room, and another where he was eating dinner with his friends hanging in their kitchen. Carter and I sometimes went to church with the Jacobsons. This was one of the few times I felt all right about being away from Mother, but only for a short time. I thought the night service was the best. It was quiet, and there were less people. During mass, I would close my eyes and try not to think of the bad things. I always felt better in church. I felt safe.

I figured Carter had stolen the religious thing when he was over playing with Louis. I did not think there was anything wrong with stealing it. I sometimes thought of pretending to put money in the basket they passed around at church and then taking some out instead. Kyle said Jesus understood when people stole things because they were hungry or poor. I figured Carter took it because he thought it would help him.

"That's okay, ya know," I said. "I pray a lot."

We were now standing just outside the apple tree. I could see Carter was embarrassed. "That's cuz you're gay," he replied and started walking toward the back door.

It didn't mean much to me, what he said. I knew it was because he was ashamed. We were beaten for showing any sort of emotion. Once, Mother caught me and Carter holding each other, laughing and jumping up and down. We had gone on a coin hunt where we would find the loose change that fell from the pockets of the men Mother had over to the house. Carter and I would go on a coin hunt every now and then, and if we were lucky we found enough coins to buy a few treats. We would pool our money together and spend it all at the corner store. When Mother caught us dancing around, she slapped both our faces, telling us we were queer for each other. That was when she said we could not sleep in the same bed any longer because we would do nasty things. If we cried that made it worse.

"Let's go inside," Carter said again.

We passed under the aluminum awning that extended beyond the rear of the house. When it rained, it sounded like bullets and the spindly metal braces holding up the awning vibrated. I would put my forehead against them, and it would make my whole head buzz.

Carter said that lightning was going to strike the metal one day and kill me instantly. "It'll blow your stupid fucking head off," he'd say and then laugh really hard.

I told him: "You wouldn't be laughing if that happened – nope. You'd be screaming your stupid fucking head off."

It was no good protesting any further once we reached the back door. For a moment, there was hope when Carter hesitated. But then he grabbed my arm and said we'd go in the front door. I knew why he changed his mind, but didn't want to say out loud. Like me, he didn't want to be near the basement.

A bright lance of fear shot through me remembering when Mother fell down the basement stairs. In a rush, I suddenly remembered Mother near the top step, flailing with her arms trying to keep her balance and then falling. She actually reached out for me, groping wildly. Falling, bouncing, striking each step, and finally emptying on the cracked asbestos tile of the basement floor with a sickening thud.

It wasn't the fall that made me shriek in terror. That had happened too quickly to react. It was how her body laid twisted while still just inches from the last step. She lay ridiculously over to one side and near her head were pieces of bloody dentures. I don't remember running down the stairs, but I remember kneeling next to my mother, waiting for some sign of life. I remember thinking that the pungent odor of feces must have been the result of her extreme tumbling. Later, a brief inspection would reveal the odor had been coming from me.

"Don't leave me," I said abruptly.

"I'm not," Carter said, "but I should make you look for Lynn yourself while I go over to Louis's." The single moment of fear that Carter was half-serious passed when he smiled a bit at the end of his last statement. It was still no use trying to talk him out of going back into the house. I never really had a chance anyway; any opportunity that I may have had was now gone. It had dissipated along with the serenity felt only minutes before sitting underneath the apple tree.

"You coming?" Carter said.

"Yeah," I replied. We turned and walked toward the backyard gate in silence. The house gave off a deserted feeling, although I knew Lynn was somewhere inside. Luckily, we had time to find her before our parents returned.

We were through the wooden gate and passing the kitchen window. I looked at Carter, but his face did not change. In the reflection of the kitchen window, I saw mine had not either. Both of us looked afraid.

CHAPTER FOUR

A COUPLE HOURS LATER, AFTER SEARCHING the house, checking to make sure Lynn wasn't hiding in her usual places, we went back outside and searched in the darkness. We looked in the backyard, behind the lilac bush and underneath the apple tree. We frantically walked up and down the sidewalk, past the neighboring houses. The cement was cold and hard beneath our bare feet. My brother tried running ahead of me, but was afraid to leave me too far behind so he doubled back, grabbed my arm, and we both ran back toward the house. It seemed like a long time had gone by. I wanted to scream out Lynn's name, but didn't want to draw attention to us.

We came back to the front porch, but instead of going inside, we cut away and ran to the side of the house nearest the driveway. This part of the house was dark except for a small illumination that spilled out from a low-watt light bulb burning in the foyer, atop the stairs leading to the basement.

The moonlight was enough to see the cheap aluminum siding that ran the length of the house, and I trailed my hand along its side for balance. "Watch out for broken glass," Carter hissed. "You don't have no shoes on."

Upon a closer inspection and more light, I would have seen the pitted remnants and small pockmarks left by empty whiskey and wine bottles that our mother had thrown and shattered against the house. There was so much glass strewn along the base of the foundation that, when the afternoon sunlight glanced off the jagged edges, it sparkled like pretty diamonds.

Carter looked in the backyard one more time while I waited by an old latch fence that had not swung evenly since the day Father attempted to install it. Father wasn't a handyman, and coupled with his drinking, even minor home projects never seemed to get done properly – when they got done at all.

Soon, our mother and father would be returning from another night of drunkenness spent at the Alibi Tavern or Mickey's, and it would be as bad as usual, but worse for me and my brother if we did not find Lynn by the time they arrived. They would be drunk and already fighting. And there would be blood and lots of it.

I needed to look through the kitchen window, so I climbed the squat wooden gate and stood on the quarter-inch slat below the ledge. It was just the right height. Even under my light weight, it creaked and groaned. The lip of the board dug into the bottom of my bare feet, and I immediately began to feel a dull ache work its way up my ankles.

We had checked the kitchen before leaving the house, but I wanted to check again. Regardless, looking through the kitchen window was an old habit. It was from there I could sneak a peek inside when checking in on Mother. It proved to be the best place to look for her. I was too short to reach the other windows with nothing to stand on. The living room window was low enough to the ground, but the curtains were usually pulled shut. And if she wasn't in the living room, she'd be sitting at the makeshift kitchen table. The kitchen was where she hid her booze most of the time, and you could set your watch to her needing a refill.

As long as I can remember, there were never any screens on the windows, and I never gave it much thought as to why. Lucky for me, because I would have had to deal with removing it, and that would give Mother another reason to beat me. She found enough reason already.

Pressing my palms just under the top of the window frame, I pushed up. At first, it did not budge. I pushed again, this time using my legs to push, which sent a shooting pain from the bottom of my feet all the way to my butt. There was a popping noise followed by a low hush, and the window slid upward. Just a crack, but that was enough to smell the familiar stench of lingering booze and rotting garbage.

In the backyard, I could hear Carter still looking for Lynn, who he thought might have slipped outside after we had left the house. I turned my face away from the kitchen window and caught a cool breeze. A bitter wind, my mother called it. But it wasn't bitter at all. It was very fresh and sweet. My empty stomach clenched violently. I had not eaten since the day before, and then it had been only a half-folded piece of bread with the moldy parts pulled off, smeared with what was left of the syrup. The cool wind blew again and brushed the long and unkempt hair from my face, causing me to close my eyes.

I heard Carter coming and climbed down from the gate, meeting him at the opening. His face was now very close to mine, and I noticed he was crying.

"I can't find her, Gregg. Mom's going to beat us."

Our father was an iron-jawed, powerful man, but he never physically harmed us. However, all bets were off when it came to our mother. When Father beat her, she would return the favor to her children. And she dealt me the most vicious beatings of all. Perhaps that's why Carter was weeping. He was thinking of what would come of me.

While we embraced, I felt the cool wind on my face again. Then I pushed away from Carter and forced a smile. "We'll find her. She can't be too far."

Carter shook his head remorsefully. "Well, we looked everywhere," he said.

Silently, we walked to the front of the house toward the porch. The outer search was over, and we needed to look inside one more time. We mumbled a little to ourselves and each other, but mostly shuffled along in silence. Carter muttered something about hiding as well and then said nothing. And then for a moment, we thought we heard Lynn crying in the house.

Carter cautiously ascended the cracked porch and I followed close behind him. He stopped and stood directly in front of the door, looking at the lighted windows of the living room. It was a small house and Mother always said: "This ain't a home . . . it's a house! It's love that makes it a home!" She was right about that. This was a house.

We opened the door of the house and went in. Something was squirming around in my head, going round and round, and I tried to get it out, but just couldn't. It made me dizzy and sick in my belly. I had a sense of being in a waking dream and a terrible thought rolled toward me: *Lynn is dead and that is why she does not answer.* That is why she cannot hear us. I quickly pushed the thought away, but it was too late. The thought stiffened the hair on the nape of my neck and a sense of lightness washed over me. The harder I tried to push the thought away, the stronger it came back. *Lynn is dead.* Just then, a bolt of lightning exploded in my head. All of a sudden, there was a sound I remembered, a smell I remembered. *Shit*, I thought. *Here comes the tick again.*

"The Tick" would show up whenever I was nervous; I'd start to repeat my words and actions until they ran their course or something else grabbed my attention and shook me loose. Most times, whatever snapped me out of it was worse than the rambling or constant touching and re-touching of an object. The first time this happened to me was right after one of my "day-mares."

That did it. Thinking of having what Ashley called an "episode" knocked the thought Lynn was dead out of my head and settled me down a lit-tle. Enough to pull it together and not slip into one of my walking night-mares. Good thing too. If I had gone on, Carter would have had to slap me across the face to get me back on track.

Just inside our front door, Carter took a few steps toward the kitchen. "Lynn," he called. "Come on! Answer me!"

We promised we would never tease her again, if she would just come out from wherever she was. No more making her drink out of the toilet or stick-ing gum in her hair. *Just please be okay*, I thought. *Please. Please. Just be okay.* Maybe Lynn just needed a little coaxing. Maybe, after all, she needed a whole lot more attention. Last in line and stuck behind six other kids had to be a tough spot. I suppose we just never thought much about how we were treat-ing her when we all were stuck in the same miserable place. Maybe, after all, this house finally got the best of her, and she let it swallow her whole.

Then suddenly it occurred to me. "The attic!" I said aloud. Carter jerked back, as if I just smacked him in the nose. "Oh man! I ain't going up in that attic looking for her," I said with a noticeable quiver in my voice.

Carter looked toward the bedroom with the attic, where a dark square that hovered above the closet framed the opening to what we both swore was the gateway to hell. "Not yet anyways, but we might have to," he said.

Hearing these words made me squirt a dribble of hot piss into a pair of underwear much too large for my body and long past needing a good washing. Didn't matter. The piss would just be joining the many stains in the front and running a close race with those in the back rendered for much of the same reason.

There was nothing to protect us in this goddamn house. There were places around the windows and doors you could look through to the outside. Mother told us that the house had been condemned, which she said meant we were not supposed to live there according to the law. It was like bragging when she said it, but made me feel tired.

The house was an ugly ranch, a squat tacky square with a broken roof that sagged in spots and leaked. In the daylight you could see it lean somewhat, depicting a shimmering dilapidation. The cement steps leading to the front porch were broken, revealing tiny pebbles hidden under the concrete. In the sunlight, the house looked as if it was dying, and from inside, nothing was keeping out the wind or the fear.

Carter took in a breath, which startled me for a second, and I jumped to the other side of him.

"Cool it, Gregg! You almost made me piss my pants!"

I thought to myself, *Beat ya to it*, and turned away so he didn't see my cheeks flush.

"Lynn!" Carter yelled, and I jumped again.

"Let me know when you're going to yell," I said. He just gave me one of his disapproving looks, and I couldn't help but think of how much he looked like Dad when he made those faces. I bet if I told him, he'd find that a pretty neat compliment. Perhaps he'd work it around his head most of the day and turn it into something useful when the pain was real sharp and his heart was breaking all over the place.

"Lynn!" he called again, and there was a note of dumb terror in his voice. "Lynn! Lynn!" There was no answer. The house was empty.

Then, through the dank air stale from too many cigarettes, we heard the horrible sound of a child crying.

CHAPTER FIVE

I SWORE TO MYSELF I WAS LEAVING THIS place. The longer I stayed, I knew Mother'd kill me for sure. She'd hit too hard or strangle me for a bit too long during one of her drunken rages; my lights would go out, and I'd have only myself to blame. It would be my fault entirely. After all, I was the one that stayed behind.

The abuse was leaving dirty little secrets buried deep down inside me. I knew I wanted to learn things. I wanted to know what it felt like to look at the hands on a clock and tell what time it was or to tie my own shoelaces. I was tired of getting beaten for not finding her cigarettes, or worse, her making me do those other things. I worked so hard. I made every effort to say and do the right thing, which meant not pissing her off. And then there was how good I got at forcing a smile and the words, "I love you Mommy," right after she slapped me in the face or popped me in the scrotum. The breath gone from my lungs, but I got the words out nonetheless. The worst was pretending it didn't tear me apart to lie next to her after sex. The worst by far, but I managed to be convincing. So convincing, I started to believe it was my choice, and this was when I first started thinking about suicide.

I'd make a plan to get away. Not just me though, I'd work out a way to get Carter and Lynn out of here as well. It'd be a simple plan that would start out by getting a hold of Lauren. I'd heard she had a nice house somewhere in Minnesota and that perhaps she, along with her husband, might be willing to give us a place to live. Bring us in as sort of a charity thing, but at least we would get out of this place.

I wasn't real sure if Lauren would really take us in because that information was passed on to me by Jessica. She was one to drink a bit too much and had a nasty habit of squeaking a lie right out of a truth. Even if it was a lie, I didn't care. The comfort it gave me was more than anything I had to the contrary and if a lie got me from one day to the next, then I'd take it.

Jessica's drinking made her an unlikely candidate for taking in me and my siblings. Jessica did not want us living with her anyway. According to her, with two kids already and a husband stepping out with another woman, she had enough problems of her own.

Getting out was the only way to save my life. I'd make sure I was a part of all those learning things I'd missed out on. I would study hard, fix on the tough subjects in school, and hang on until the knowledge was cemented in my head. At only ten years old, I knew things. Things that were going to help me survive.

Carter's head snapped back, as if he ran full speed into a low hanging branch. "Did you hear that?" he said, and then before I could answer: "That goddamn crying! It sounds like Lynn!"

I heard it all right. In no time flat, it knocked the recurring fantasy of getting out of this shit-hole of a life clean from my brain. We began to creep toward the direction of the sound, taking a few steps, stopping to listen for another shriek, and then bracing ourselves for when it happened. We were now where the edge of the short hallway cut into the living room.

A cool breeze was blowing, and it was too cold to have come from inside the house. In one of the three bedrooms lining the hallway, I figured there was a window either left open or broken – just about every mirror and window in the house was cracked with chunks of glass missing, which we were always cutting our feet on because we were usually barefoot.

I whispered, "Carter, I think a window's open."

My already small, prepubescent testicles, shrunken from fear, squeezed to the size of raisins when he replied: "It ain't a window. It's coming from the attic."

My mind rattled and I swore, for a split second, there was an old witch hovering just above the floor, only a few feet from me and my brother.

A few more steps down the hallway and we were just outside the first of the three bedrooms, the one with ceiling access to the attic. Carter picked up a dead cockroach that had squished itself between the base molding and the dirty shag carpet.

He examined it as if stalling for time and then flicked the infestation away. It hit the cheap paneling making a 'tick' sound.

Grateful we weren't going inside the bedroom just yet, I took the opportunity to catch my breath. It felt like a thousand needles in my lungs, pecking at my chest. I glanced over at Carter, who was hunched over, leaning against the wall. I asked, "Do you wish Dad was here?"

Tears came to his eyes. "Eat shit, Gregg," Carter said and once again looked toward the open doorway of the bedroom.

Still, no sound. Not even a peep. As a matter of fact, we began wondering if we had heard Lynn at all. We did notice that this was certainly the bedroom from which the wind was blowing. A quick peek into the bedroom revealed that the only window was shut, which further solidified our gnawing suspicion that the square piece of plywood covering the attic opening wasn't secure. We poked our heads in sync through the doorway leading into the bedroom, leaving our feet firmly planted in the hallway. When we crossed over the threshold separating the doorway from the hallway, the sounds started again, this time louder as if amplified by our acute fear. Carter gave a quick jerk of his head to the left, and I followed suit.

"Shit! The goddamn attic panel is slid over," Carter nervously whispered. "Oh man . . . she can't be up there," he said, as if to wish this whole scene away. The wind was blowing straight down from the attic. The panel door was slightly askew, creating a small pie-shaped opening that forced the wind to whistle. It was more like eerie singing.

Carter was now standing directly in front of the closet. The slatted folding door was butted up against the wall and pushed to one side. It had been broken off its sliding hinge the day Mother yanked it open – when she had found Carter and Lynn hiding in the closet and naked. Mother was furious and beat them both mercilessly, calling them perverts and incest demons. It had been all my fault.

Through the years, with each and every beating, between the incessant abuse and neglect, I would grow wiser. I would learn it was unsafe to trust Mother. That day would come soon, but it had not yet come the day I betrayed my brother and sister.

The closet had a step-up with a three-foot platform below a wooden rod for hanging clothes. We would pretend it was a spaceship. With the closet door closed, the sunlight would shine through the individual wooden slats, creating a multi-striped pattern against the interior walls and across the base in which we sat. It added to the fantasy that we were landing on the moon.

That day, Carter and Lynn were playing spaceship, and I stood outside the closet and convinced them they needed to remove all their clothes and give them to me. They did. I quickly hid their clothes under the bed and ran to get Mother. I had honestly thought she would find my silly joke amusing and we would all laugh. When she came bounding into the bedroom with me in tow, I began to realize my joke was going to have terrible consequences, but it was too late.

I stood with my back pressed against the far bedroom wall while Mother pulled my brother and sister from the closet. Their giggles turned to screams when the door crashed open. Our eyes met, and I saw the confusion and pleading glances from Carter and Lynn. Mother thrashed their naked bodies with a belt she had picked up off the floor.

My unsuspecting siblings tried desperately to protect their exposed genitals while the leather hammered away at their pink flesh. When Mother had finished, she turned to me. With only a slap across my face, she was gone. It was the one time in my life I had hoped she beat me. Beat me until unconscious, so I could pay for my sin and afterward know the familiar grace of nothingness.

From our vantage point, Carter and I could see into the closet and up into the attic opening. Through the sliver of darkness, I saw a small yellow eye coming toward us. It grew larger as it came closer to the triangle-shaped opening, and we took about four steps backward. I sidestepped to the right, and the eye appeared to follow me while floating just above the attic door panel. Its movement was purposeful, and every now and then, it would stutter crazily, slanting and tilting, and then right itself again.

"Shut up," Carter hissed. I did not realize that I had been moaning out loud. It pissed me off, but I didn't say anything. He too was making noises, muttering under his breath, and there was this low grunting noise coming from his throat.

Carter and I watched the yellow pupil move lazily from side-to-side – and at one point, it seemed to dip past the opening of the attic, breaking the plane between one dimension and the next. I thought to myself that this most certainly was an optical illusion and a very good one indeed.

Something moved just behind the eye in the attic darkness. It passed by slowly, moving to the left. I knelt on the bedroom floor, bending in order to get a better look at what it was. With my neck craned upward, I peered into the space above the closet. Neither Carter nor I was willing to get closer to the closet at this point.

"What in the fuck is it?" Carter said out loud.

I pushed my glasses up the bridge of my nose and strained to focus. "I don't know, but it looks like it's attached to the eye," I said.

My glasses were too large for my face, but they were the best we could do with the public assistance we had from the State. Being on welfare was our main source of income after Father left. Mother would get a monthly check along with food stamps. In addition, the State paid our utility bills along with the mortgage and we still had no money.

I remember Mother telling me that she spent over a hundred dollars to get my glasses for me. I knew it was a lie, but I would never correct her. That day, she went on about all the sacrifices made over the years for her children and the burden we placed upon her. It got her worked up into another frenzy, causing her to slap me across the face so hard it sent the glasses flying, leaving a deep cut over the bridge of my nose. She cracked the frames, but Carter glued them together with Super Glue. I remember him telling me that you want to be careful not to get the glue on your fingers. To add emphasis, he told me about this kid he knew that accidentally glued his penis to his hand. They had to cut some of his penis away to get it loose. That was a lie as well, but it was a funny story, and I liked it.

Now, in the bedroom, the light of the moon coming through the window lit up Carter's face. He looked worried.

I suddenly realized that Carter's hand was in mine. I must have grabbed it without noticing. Normally, Carter would not have allowed the affection and quickly flung my hand aside. He would then say, "You a fucking queer or somethin'?" It was more of an indictment than a question. Mother had often said I was queer. She frequently told Carter that he needed to keep a close watch on me because I was prone to engage in some sort of deviant sex act with Kyle. I wasn't queer and never knew where she'd gotten that idea.

The yellowish light in the attic flickered, or 'blinked,' and then went out completely. We could see it was real dark up there. Dark like the black monument with a black angel above it in the local cemetery. You couldn't see it at night, and when I ran through the graveyard one evening on a dare, I ran right into it. I busted my lip on one of the angel's outspread wings, and the impact cracked a chunk of it right off. It must have been old and crumbly like many of the statues. The end of the angel wings were thin as well and worn from years of weather. It could have already been cracked from me and Kyle taking turns shooting it with his Red Rider BB Gun. We must have peppered those wings pretty good – especially because we were only about four feet away. So close that one time a BB ricocheted and hit Kyle in the leg, which he said stung like a bitch.

Maybe it was just morbid curiosity or just plain stupidity, but I reached down, picked up the broken piece, and shoved it in my pocket before taking off again. I remember thinking the next day that when I died, there'd be an angel wanting his wing back. It spooked me so badly that I went back and laid it at the base of the headstone. I backed up a little to take another look, and that angel perched atop the headstone now appeared to be staring down at the busted wing.

Just then, we heard a loud thump. Whatever it was, it was moving and had managed to walk or crawl over the ceiling right above us. This got us going again, and we ran from the bedroom. About the time we hit the hallway and were soon to be out of the house for good, we heard another scream. This time, there was no doubt about it. Lynn was in the goddamn attic.

Standing perfectly still next to Carter, I waited for another sound. We had stopped in the hallway, both looking fearfully back at the bedroom. Long black segments of terrible thoughts clicked past just behind my eyes, and I thought of my recurring day-mares. The same feeling that crept into my gut right before I sunk into them was gradually gaining speed.

Fear always set off the memories, and they would trigger the goddamn day-mares. The day-mares, or episodes, began soon after the molestations by Mother. During the day-mares, my thoughts would roar by too fast to grasp, but time would slow considerably. I would run in all directions, screaming obscenities, climbing deeper into a delusional state of panic. There was a feeling of dull rage directed at no one in particular, but if my mother tried to grab hold of me, I would beat her with my little arms. Most of the time, I ran too fast for anyone to catch me. I would run as fast as my legs would carry me through the small house, and if I managed to make it through the front door, I would go sprinting away.

The episodes came not only during the day, but in the night as well. Occasionally, breaking free of my siblings who tried desperately to hold on to me, I would exit the house. Running past all the homes in the neighborhood, with the coolness of the summer evening on my face giving me more speed, I'd distance myself even further from those in pursuit. The anger and panic would dissipate, replaced by an overwhelming sensation of freedom.

Unaware that I was slipping further into the trance-like state of another episode, Carter was trying to tell me something. His voice drifted in and out, becoming nothing more than an echo losing its power after each consecutive repetition. The long black tunnel I was now tumbling downward was a sweet release, and I simply let it take over.

When the episodes first started, I used to fight them because I was afraid. However, as the pain piled up, I stopped fighting them altogether. Within the dazes, I had strength and courage. They were my blanket against a worn-out world.

I was now completely under the hypnotic stupor, and I no longer felt the pangs of hunger or bewilderment of what lie ahead. I was a super-hero. It caused me to make right what so many had wronged for far too long. My fury was so powerful, I could even taste blood. A thought came to mind that not only could I taste blood, but my mouth seemed to be filled with it. It was so vivid that I could even smell the iron and feel the congealed consistence running over my tongue and down my throat.

From what seemed a great distance away, I could hear high-pitched shrieks. Closer now.

"Let me go! Let me go!" The voice sobbed and whimpered, and with each cry for mercy, I grew stronger.

No, I thought. Louder yet, I could hear their shouts of pain and agony. It was a remarkable sound, and I relished in it.

"Let me go! Gregg!" With this last, something popped inside my head. The words were right, but the voice was all wrong. This was not Mother's demanding and impatient voice. The voice seemed to be terrified, pleading, and Mother never begged. "Let me go, Gregg! Goddamn it, wake up!" It was Carter's voice I heard, and with this realization, the episode ended abruptly.

I was suddenly thrown against the wall of the hallway, smacking my head hard enough to cause a great light to explode in front of me. As I continued to ascend the ladder leading from my fantasy nightmare, I realized that Carter was kneeling a few feet from me. He was holding his right hand over his left shoulder.

Carter then moved his hand from what appeared to be a wound and turned in my direction, looking only at my feet. "You fucking maniac!"

He barely got the words out, choking on each one as he did so. "You fucking cocksucker!" He wiped away at his shoulder and I had a clear view of why he was bleeding. The last thing I saw before puking all over the front of my shirt was what appeared to be a clear impression left by a small bite. I had really clamped down on his shoulder. Mixed with his sweat and a small splotch of blood was an ellipse of tooth-shaped tiny red cuts.

When the sickness passed, I walked over and knelt down beside Carter on the hallway floor. He was still pretty pissed off, and right about then, all I wanted to do was disappear into the blackness of the night. My heart was still fluttering inside my chest, and I waited for Carter to really cut loose and leave me to deal with this situation all by myself. He'd done it before, many times, when things got real bad with Mother. He'd take off for the field down the street to hide out and smoke cigarettes with Louis until things blew over. I would tell him not to go – beg him not to – and he would just walk past me and out the door as if he didn't care about what was going to happen to me. I hated him for that and envied him at the same time. But right now, I did neither.

It was a hopeless ordeal for both of us. Any choice we made would end in defeat. It was a question of the lesser of two evils. When Carter would leave me, he did sometimes ask me to go along. I wanted to go with him more than anything, and I'm sure he saw that in my eyes. Maybe that is why he did not linger when waiting for my decision. Most times, he was already walking past me and through the door before my answer was even out.

I wanted to go with my brother. Even if it meant being teased by him and Louis or choking on a cigarette just to be accepted. I would have gladly been the brunt of their jokes, but we both knew that it was impossible. Just as Carter had no choice when it came to caring for Lynn and taking her from the house, I had no choice but to stay with Mother. Torn between staying and leaving, I chose to stay. Leaving with Carter, I believed, would have led to Mother's imminent death. A fate worse than freedom.

It was unfair of me to beg Carter to stay – to expect him to join forces and align ourselves against the common enemy of our mother. Of course, it was unfair, but it was an act of desperation. Descending upon us like an enormous hand and flattening our bond were the choices we both continuously had to make. To stay or leave was only one of them – and like so many other terrible choices we faced, it was slowly ripping apart our brotherhood.

"Carter," I said, "we have to get Lynn." There was no reply. Carter continued to sit motionless and stare at the growing drops of blood. We had to get going. It had been far too long since we first heard Lynn scream. Mom and Dad would be home before morning. The bars closed around 3:00 a.m., and it was nearing that time.

At the thought of our parents returning, my heart fluttered again. I put my hand on my chest to quiet the fluttering and waited for Carter to gather himself up. My head was filled with a hollow drumming sound, and I was scared to death not knowing in what shape we would find Lynn.

Carter stood up, and without further mention of the biting incident, he said, "Let's go." We walked back into the bedroom. The same bedroom Mother used to have sex with other men, when she wasn't using the bed Carter and I slept in. The same bedroom where I had laid down with her — afterwards just wanting to scrub myself clean, but not being able to do so – fearing the bath would have wakened Mother who was already stirring. Instead, I lay awake next to her trying not to think about what just happened. Trying also not to think about all the men who paid to lay with her in the same bed.

There were other places we would have rather been. There was the physical and sexual abuse, which was bad enough. However, Mother and Father were in the business of "Do as I say and not as I do." Mother made me out to be a sexual deviant, but then prostituted herself out to the neighborhood men and sometimes took care of business in the very bed I was to sleep afterwards. Father beat Mother for having affairs with other men, but slept around himself, which was what prompted most of their brawls. Mother would surge into every one of their vicious fights screaming about all the women Father had had sex with, and Father would never deny it. In fact, he would brag about his affairs and sometimes even go into detail. He once told Mother that he liked to have sex with women that were, "heavy in the front and big at the bottom," – unlike Mother, he'd say, "who was nothing but ugly bone and had no more good fucking left."

The standards to which we were held as children were beyond attainment. Yet, our parents achieved nothing.

I remember an evening when my mother was entertaining a man she had picked up in a local bar. I always knew when she was going to be bringing a man home. Mother would put on one of the few dresses that had not been shredded by Father's rage. She wore a lot of mascara, bright green or blue, and her lipstick was put on so thick it would flake in spots. Mother would somehow make her hair big and puffy like cotton and then coat it with so much hairspray that when she patted it you could hear crackling noises.

Her dress was way too short, showing off the top of her nylons where they hooked to a garter belt. Completing the outfit would be a pair of either red or black high-heeled shoes, and when she bent over to buckle the straps, I saw she was not wearing panties.

She had instructed me to sneak into the bedroom and steal money from the man's wallet while they had audible cruel sex. Their grunts and groans were enough to turn my stomach, and the pressure from crawling along on my belly nearly caused me to vomit. I did as I was told and slid backward out of the bedroom. After finishing with my mother, the man dressed and discovered the money missing. My mother stood aside while he beat me, calling me a "nigger thief." She said and did nothing.

As we went back into the bedroom, Carter called out toward the closet. "Lynn! Lynn!" But there was no answer. I jumped every time he shouted. "We've got to go up there," he said.

It was more of a crawl space than a closet. The platform base was a couple of feet above the floor. Once inside the closet, Lynn could easily stand. Her head came within only four inches of the attic opening. Carter and I had to squat bent over upon entering the closet, but we could sit cross-legged comfortably inside the closet walls. Standing upright, we could also pop back the panel door and pull ourselves up and into the attic without any difficulty. With the use of a small three-rung stepladder, Lynn could easily do the same. When the stepladder was placed atop the platform of the crawlspace and she stood on its top step, she would be waist-high inside the attic. Then, all she would have to do is lift one knee up, place it on the attic floor, and crawl inside.

"Go up in the attic and look around," Carter said.

An image of my head being lopped off the moment it stuck through opening of the attic flashed across my brain and caused me to immediately reply, "No fucking way."

"You're a pussy!" Carter said. It was a lame attempt to force me into going, and he knew it.

The attic is going to kill me after all, I thought.

On the nights when Mother was using the bedroom I shared with Carter to *entertain*, I sometimes slept in this bedroom – Mother's room. It was also called the sewing room, because that is where she kept the old Singer sewing machine. The kind that had a metal push plate for your foot. I would watch Mother operate it sometimes, but that was when I was much younger and when she still sewed like normal mothers.

As I would lay there sucking in the dust from the dirty sheets, I would try not to hear the rattling and bumping of whatever lived in the attic. I believed the noises came from all the monsters who had found this house, with all its evil, a comfortable place to reside.

I would lie awake with all the memories of the things Mother did to me in the same bed. The same things she did with strangers.

I would lie awake and the dark would play tricks on me – like when I thought the old sewing dummy had been Mother hiding in the shadows. I could not breathe until I realized it was not her.

This room was filled with awful memories and a dark scary attic.

The thought of having to ascend into the attic, without even a flashlight, was too stressful to bear, and I began spiraling toward another episode. Carter must have noticed; therefore, he rendered me a swift but solid slap across the face. The room, although dark aside from the moonlight, flashed in many different colors. First a pure, dazzling white. This was most beautiful. Then it flashed a lovely green. Then it flashed red, and I, again, was completely aware of my surroundings.

"Don't trip out on me, Gregg. We have to go . . . We have to get up there now!" Carter was right, of course. It had been several minutes since we last heard anything, and for all we knew, Lynn was suffocating right above us.

I could hear my mother sanctimoniously bleating out the words, "Why didn't you boys help her?" The little voice in my head returned, *Why didn't you*? Ah, yes, there was wisdom in that voice, but I would have never allowed it to speak aloud – I mean, if you knew what was good for you, and I knew quite well. I learned all the wrinkles of the games the liars played. And knowing this did not make me happy. Wisdom, I had found out, never did.

We moved closer to the closet, and therefore toward the attic. Carter was standing close enough to rest one hand on the platform and the other on the cheap molding that framed the outside of the closet. I imagined something big and hairy reaching out of the darkness and grabbing his hand, pulling him inside the closet and up into the attic.

Then I saw something in the corner, and my heart sank. Just inside the closet, sitting directly beneath the attic, was the stepladder – the same one Lynn sometimes used when she wanted to reach something high above the kitchen counter. Now that we were right up on the closet, I could make out the three worn steps fastened with rusting metal tubes.

"She used the ladder to get up there. Oh, shit. She's up there," I muttered to myself, but Carter, standing so close, heard every word.

"No shit, Sherlock," he replied, another one of his famous truisms. He pulled the stepladder out of the closet, and set it inside the bedroom. We both climbed inside the closet at the same time, and in the narrow opening, our shoulders bumped. "Watch the bite, you freak!" Carter hissed. I could see the scarlet blood creeping through his shirt.

The attic was directly above us, and I could smell the aging wood and blown insulation. *That must be what hell smells like*, I thought.

Once inside the closet and crouching on the platform, I stood up too far and banged part of the attic panel with my head. I ducked so quickly it banged back down against its frame, but did not fall back into place.

"Go ahead and open it, Gregg! Hurry!" Carter said.

"Fuck no!" I said, and my voice was shaking badly.

The attic panel was now more askew, turning the former pie shape of an opening into a wedge. A puff of wind blew down on top of my head that felt like cold breath.

Carter whispered, "On three. I'll hit the attic panel and you stand up and look inside…Ready? One…two…"

"Wait!" I shrieked.

But it was too late. There was a loud bang as Carter punched the thin plywood panel of the attic door, and it flew off haphazardly. First hitting the rafters and then coming down hard and bouncing against the ceiling. It made a rattling sound and came to rest somewhere just above our heads. The damn thing sounded like it was going to come crashing right through the drywall of the ceiling.

The wind blew down from the attic and carried along with it a rancid smell. The air came in both warm and cold pockets. Unexpectedly, there came another bump, and it sounded close, followed by a very loud and familiar scream. I felt woozy, like I was going to pass out. As I began to slip further away, mercifully down to a soundless depth, I heard the scream again, and this time, I was positive it had come from Lynn.

CHAPTER SIX

CARTER STOOD WAVERINGLY, TRYING TO hold me steady. Inside the attic, the screams grew louder. At first, they sounded far away, but were not far away at all. They were right above me. The unconsciousness I was fighting made them appear that way.

"Wake up, Gregg!" Carter shouted, and an eerie feeling slid around my brain.

"Poke your goddamn head up there!" he said.

This time, I did what Carter told me to do. I was too tired and weak to fight him any longer. I slowly stood up, and standing completely upright, my head cleared the opening to the attic, leveling off at the top of my shoulders. My head was now completely exposed, and I braced myself for the decapitation that most assuredly would come from behind.

"What do you see?" Carter asked, and I could hear the anxiety in his voice. I could feel his chest heaving in and out against my side.

"Nothing," I replied and secretly thanked God. Inside the attic, there were long wooden joists, which stank of rot.

There were other objects strewn about, but I couldn't make them out. To be honest, I didn't want to know. My eyes adjusted, and I saw one of the objects against the far wall directly in front of me. It was an old highchair, and it looked as if whoever placed it up there had simply tossed it against the wall. One of its legs were busted and left dangling by a piece of thin wood. A vent was cut out to allow the attic to cool, and I noticed this was how the air was blowing in from outside. I was admiring the round hole, which looked like a ship's portal, when a gust of wind that felt like more cold breath blew against my face, making me scream.

"What the fuck?" Carter yelled.

"Nothing! The wind scared me."

"Well, is Lynn up there or not? Christ! We heard her scream!"

Before I could answer, the broken leg of the highchair caught a bit of wind and banged against the attic wall. I screamed again, and when I did, I dropped so fast it felt like the earth dropped out from underneath me. One of my legs kicked Carter, knocking him off balance. He fell, his body pushing mine forward, causing me to smack my face on the side of the closet wall. Had he not reached out and braced himself, I would have absorbed the full impact of both our bodies.

There was the familiar taste of blood almost instantly. I figured I had swallowed enough of it over the years to equal what my heart pumped throughout my entire body. We both continued to fall, crashing downward, and ended up splayed like pixie-sticks atop the platform of the closet. Legs and arms were so tangled it was difficult to tell where Carter's appendages ended and mine began.

"For fuck's sake, Gregg!" Carter shouted.

I wanted to leave and give up entirely. I looked toward the bedroom and thought that if I were to push hard enough off the wall behind me, I could clear Carter and leap from the closet. It was an inviting prospect. I would run away and this time for good.

We were both gasping and covered in sweat. My upper lip stung and had a sandpaper texture to it. It felt swollen already and threatening to burst. Somewhere nearby, a motorcycle blatted. "Hogs," we called them and they were everywhere.

"Mom!" I blurted. "Mom will be home soon!"

Carter saw the fear in my eyes and scrambled away, untangling us both, stood up and pulled me to my feet. We were moving again, and soon I was standing upright inside the attic opening. The thought of my head being lopped off was now a dull fret.

"Lynn! Lynn!" I cried. Nothing. Not a sound.

I turned around, doing a full 360. My eyes adjusted, and something in the corner of the attic moved. It moved and wept. "Lynn?" I said cautiously. It was Lynn all right, and she was huddled into a ball and squished into a corner.

With as much urgency as I could muster, but still sound calm, I called to her. "Lynn, come over here!"

She did not reply and only sat motionless.

Carter yelled, "Lynn! Get down! Mom and Dad will be here soon!"

Upon hearing Carter's last words, Lynn began to cry out loud. "Dad's going to kill me! Mom said Dad's going to rape me and kill me!"

She kept repeating these words, and it made me cold inside. Our father would have never hurt Lynn, and perhaps this is what made Mother angry. Before my parents left, Mother must have made sure to leave Lynn absolutely convinced Dad would hurt her in every way possible.

Mother never beat Lynn; instead, she used a form of mental torture that left Lynn frozen and shattered – an emotional anguish that would draw from her a profound and soundless weeping.

Mother often warned Lynn that she was going to be raped by one of the neighborhood boys while she slept in her bed. She would describe in great detail how the twin boys down the block would take turns. It was easy to believe Mother, because the identical brothers that we liked to call *the twins,* had already been arrested. It could have been for burglary for all we knew, but it was enough to make Mother's stories believable. They were so believable that Lynn lived in constant fear and stopped leaving her bedroom window open at night during the summer, regardless of how hot it was – even when the heat became so stifling it seemed to suck all the air out of her room.

If it was not the horrific stories of rape and molestation Mother was force-feeding Lynn, it was the brutal destruction of her dolls that Lynn was subjected to. Mother would take what few dolls Lynn had and tear them apart, leaving pieces of them all over her bedroom. There would be a mass of arms and legs scattered all over Lynn's room, miniature pink limbs snapped off, broken and twisted torsos strewn in many directions. Her playthings ruined.

Lynn would kick the portions of worthless plastic into her closet and shut the door. She then lay atop her bed, crying so hard that she would eventually fall over on her side with her hands between her thin little girl's legs and fall fast asleep.

"Lynn, what did Mom tell you?" I asked, each word coming out more gently than the last.

In long harsh shaking breaths, she said, "Dad was going to pull my underwear down and put his thing in me until it bled, and cover my mouth so I couldn't breathe."

I could both hear and see Mother telling Lynn this. Her words would have a tone like honey, but would hang in the air, heavy with manipulation. To Lynn, Mother's words must have sounded like a hideous promise based on an absolute truth.

Father would never harm Lynn. He never even harmed Carter and me, and we were both boys and older than Lynn.

He abandoned all of us, that was certain. However, he never hit us like he hit Mother. During the worst of a beating he was giving Mother, when Father punched her and the walls until his knuckles bled, even then he would only push us out of the way. In my mind, it just wasn't possible for Father to harm Lynn. Perhaps also because it was one of the few remaining strands of fabric that held what was left of my sanity together.

Carter broke the silence after Lynn spoke. I had not known what to say and could only stare at the top of Lynn's head, while she pulled up her knees closer to her chin.

"Lynn! Mom is lying to you! Now crawl over to Gregg, and get down!" Carter shrieked.

She unlatched her arms from around her legs and began moving in my direction. When she assumed a crawling position, something dropped from her sweater and thumped against the rafters. There was a sudden yellowish burst of light, and then it was extinguished.

A flashlight, I thought. Then it occurred to me that this was the eye. As she continued to move closer, I could see Lynn was trying to hold back deep sobs. Her hair hung down and dragged along, catching little pieces of insulation. Lynn muttered she was freezing, but it came out "fweezing," because she could not pronounce her R's. When our hands touched in order to help lower her down, I felt how cold she was.

"Turn around, Lynn, and back towards me," I said, so I could better curl my arms around her waist. Carter and I worked in tandem to lower Lynn down. When she was completely on the platform of the closet, Carter jumped down and then me. I turned, grabbed Lynn, and swung her down and onto the bedroom floor.

"Damn, you're heavy," I said, but smiling. Elated that Lynn was safe, the three of us got out of the bedroom as fast as we could and away from the closet.

"We'll wait in the living room," Carter said.

When we left the bedroom, Lynn was still clinging to my shirt.

"Yur bleeden," she said to Carter.

"Yeah. Ask num-nuts about that."

This got us laughing. Even so, I saw there were still tears in Lynn's eyes and when she looked up at me, I saw they were pleading and swollen.

The three of us took our places in the living room and waited in agony for Mother and Father to return.

Carter sat in a chair, while Lynn and I sat on opposite ends of the couch. We wanted to sit next to one another, but if our mother caught us too close, we would get in trouble for being too sexual. From the vantage of the couch, I could see enough of the driveway through the filthy curtains to offer up a warning when Dad's Thunderbird pulled up. As if Lynn was reading my thoughts, she made a low whimpering sound. There was a thick feeling of anxiety in the air. Carter would offer up a reminder, every now and then, that we couldn't tell Mother about the attic incident. I looked outside again and saw a bag floating in the wind and lightly skipping down the empty street. It looked like a Holsum Bread bag, and it reminded me of when I ran from the corner store with the large rack full of bread. The driver nearly caught me that day and if he had, he would have really done a number on me. I looked up just then and saw a flash of red outside the window.

I was daydreaming again and forgot to warn Carter and Lynn, which caused them to jump and scream when the front door came crashing inward. Father's eyes were blazing with anger, and with one hand, he held up our Mother by a strap of her bra and what was left of her dress. "Here's your whore of a mother!" he bellowed. We sat frozen. Mother's bright red lipstick looked smeared, but then I saw it was blood that covered her whole mouth and lower jaw. There were thick red lines between her false teeth, which were noticeably cracked – most likely from a solid punch.

Instead of just leaving her at the bar, Father had brought her home to show her children proof that she was exactly everything he claimed her to be – a whore. He rushed into the house, dragging Mother like a marionette with its strings cut – holding her up with his massive fist.

"Your fucking mother tried to screw every drunk in the bar!" our father explained, as if to justify the beating he gave her. Although none of us doubted he was exaggerating.

Mother just stood there, as if in a daze, looking like a rag doll. Father finally released his grip and gave Mother a good shove. She went sprawling forward and fell to the floor.

I was by her side immediately, and then Father's meaty hand grabbed my arm and flung me backward. "Don't help that cunt!" he commanded.

Inside the shoe closet, just off the front door, was a long broomstick. The brush was lost, but it served as a disciplinary tool Mother used on us quite often. Carter ran for it and snatched it in his hands. He stood defiantly in front of Father and was dwarfed by the size difference.

"Swing that, boy, and I'll knock you on your ass!" Father said and then slapped the stick from Carter's hands. It bounced on the carpet and then rolled to rest underneath the couch. We had no phone to call the police. The neighbors didn't want to get involved and didn't care. We were helpless to do anything but watch in horror. Mother staggered to her feet, and Father lunged for her.

Father swung with precision force, crushing the left side of Mother's face with one blow. I got a glimpse of her eye just as it popped from its socket. Her limp body slammed against a huge mirror mural fastened to the wall, leaving an outline of her head. The impact of Mother's skull shattered what was once a beautiful black and white rendition of the Zumbrota Covered Bridge. She then fell to the floor in a slump and did not move. The eye dangled, and I wondered if she could see her cheek.

Father stood over her and continued to swing as if she were still standing. It wasn't until he caught his reflection in the broken mirror that he stopped. He looked puzzled at the face staring back at him, as if he were looking at a total stranger. "Help your mother, Gregg!" Father bellowed, but never looked at me.

He turned to leave, and Carter attempted to tackle him, but bounced off as if he just ran into a brick wall. Father pushed past Carter and simply walked out the door, saying nothing and lighting a cigarette as he left. Moments later, after he eased the car out of the driveway, all that was left of him was a trail of smoke that still hung in the air near the door. That and Mother, who lay dying at the feet of her three children.

Carter ran from the house and down the street to the only pay phone for at least five miles. He knew just to press "0" for help. We had all learned that from past emergencies. Lynn and I waited with Mother. She lay still on the living room floor. Her face was blank and smooth, as if sleeping with her eyes open, but now only one socket was inhabited.

Carter returned from making the call minutes later. Shortly thereafter, the police arrived with their bubblegum lights flashing. They pulled into the driveway and kept their lights flashing the whole time. When they entered the house, they found me kneeling next to Mother, shaking her arm, and begging her not to die. Lynn knelt by Mother's feet, rubbing her legs. Carter stood by the door and looked on as tears streamed down his pudgy cheeks. The three of us begged the police to save Mother. The abused now prayed for the abuser. She was cruel, but she was also our mother.

The paramedics came soon after the police had arrived, followed by a social worker. The police and the paramedics looked like they knew exactly what to do.

One officer wrote things down while appearing to take information from a paramedic working on Mother. Another spoke on a radio that would occasionally squawk loudly, making me jump.

Time had taken an ungainly hop forward.

The paramedic's voice was flat and mechanic, "Fractures: jaw, skull, nose, lacerated *something*, disconnected *something*, … eye." "Vitals: BP, pulse … *something*, swollen … *something*, approximate age, weight, height … *something*, gender: female, alcohol … *something*."

I remember the sense of being in the way and pulled. My left hand was removed from where it was underneath Mother's head by the paramedic. It came away warm with blood soaking my palm. I begged for them to save her, and with every breath between deep guttural sobs, I begged some more.

I do not remember seeing the social worker come in, but I remember her trying to pull me away from Mother. She gently tried to coax me away at first, but when that did not work, she tried more forcefully. Then she would look at Mother's face all busted up and lose interest for a little bit, then sort of snap back, and try to pull me away again.

Between the officers and the paramedics, there must have been a half-dozen people working on my mother. I was not making it easy because I kept screaming for her to breathe and kept yanking on her torn dress. No matter how many times the social worker told me to do so, I would not let go.

With the help of an officer, the social worker finally got me into the kitchen, by mostly pulling and half carrying me. Carter and Lynn were already in there, but I do not remember them going into the kitchen. I do remember not caring about what the social worker had to say; even though she cared enough to get us some water from the sink and kneel down to talk. It was probably something about how Mother was going to be okay, but I did not care about that either. All I knew was that I needed to be in the next room. Next to Mother. The social worker held me while I struggled to get free. Finally, breaking her grip, I ran back into the living room. The thing that used to be Mother was laying with her back flat against the floor, and her arms and legs up close next to her body like she were at attention. The top of her dress was ripped open and her bra was askew, showing too much of her breasts. I remember wanting to cover her with a blanket.

This time, one of the police officers caught me before reaching Mother and lifted me up, pulling me in the opposite direction in which she lay. I remember kicking and squirming to get away and back to Mother. He just kept telling me that it was going to be okay, but he was lying. I knew it. I fought even harder. I fought with all the strength I had left. Carter and Lynn held one another and cried, yelling at me to stop. Not until I saw her whole body jump up from the floor, like something pushed her hard from underneath, did I stop. I stopped dead cold.

The social worker was still there somewhere, but did not bother with me anymore. The police officer that pulled me away had his arm wrapped around my chest, but my feet were now firmly on the floor. When Mother jumped again, I felt the vibration running up my legs. All of a sudden, it was quiet, and right before she jumped a third time, a paramedic in a white and red shirt kneeling almost on top of her yelled something. It sounded like "Clear."

Mother bounced upward and then came crashing to the floor. A paramedic had wrapped her head in gauze, which covered the socket once void of its eye. The gauze was thicker over that socket and I remember wondering if the eye was popped back inside its hole. Mother's other eye, the one that was intact, was swollen shut. The upper and lower skin swelled to the point they pressed against one another over where her eye used to be. *She's blind*, I thought.

Her face, normally skeletal, was puffy and plump beneath the gauze of the head wrapping. I could see the blood soaked roots of her hair turning the white gauze a brilliant red, which had already formed a visible stain on the carpet.

The paramedic pushed on her chest and squeezed air into her mouth with this plastic bag. I knew it was just a matter of time before I would hear this audible crack and his hands would go right through her tiny breast. I watched and waited. But I didn't pray. My head was scrambled, and I could not concentrate long enough to pray. Prayer would come later, as it always did, but for now there was no use in that.

Across the street and peering through her living room curtains was Mrs. Jacobson. The lights and commotion must have woken her up. She had Jessica's phone number from years back and must have called her. The neighbors had gotten used to seeing the police at our house, but not an ambulance. Mrs. Jacobson must have known it was serious. I bet she figured Father finally killed Mother or Mother finally killed one or all of her children.

When they were rolling Mother out on the gurney, Jessica was running into the house. "Get in the car!" she said.

The adrenaline was making me sick, and I vomited twice in the yard before climbing into the backseat of Jessica's car. The dome light was too sharp on my eyes, and I wanted to close them, but was afraid I'd miss Mother waving to me before they closed the two heavy metal doors of the ambulance. She never moved.

Jessica would not drive us to the hospital. I gave the ambulance one more look as we drove away in the opposite direction. Its siren blaring and probably waking up the entire neighborhood. I was both ashamed and afraid.

The street curved around an old dark house I remembered well. I would pass the house each time before the field opened itself up. I never saw anyone around the house. It was always dark. I began to weep.

Raising my head every now and then to look out the window, I saw we were driving past a cornfield. *A good hiding place*, I thought to myself. I did not remember any cornfields near our house. Where we lived was a perfect blend of both suburban white trash and inner city deterioration. However, this was different. It was all green and full of color. Clean. That's what stuck in my mind the most. Everything was so clean.

From the backseat, I asked Jessica where we were going. "My house," she said, then went back to driving. Carter and Lynn sat quietly.

I continued staring out the window at the night lit up by the street lights and watched the lines of the road get real close to the car, then slide away. When we would drive under a bridge, it would get dark and cast a quick reflection of my face in the window. I looked tired.

Obsessed with spitting, it was bothering me something awful not to be able to roll down the window and chuck the glob of saliva building up in my mouth. It was my new compulsion. However, I figured if I spat, Jessica would get mad and maybe even pull the car over to smack me. So I forced the warm goop down my throat and had to fight back the urge to throw up.

As we drove, Jessica suddenly spoke. Her tone was matter of fact. "You know he raped me?"

I thought of what Mother told Lynn before she went out drinking with Dad. I thought about this for a long time and wondered if it were true. I grew increasingly anxious thinking that maybe Mother was right about Dad. Maybe he was going to rape Lynn.

When we reached Jessica's house, all I wanted was sleep. Jessica let me lay down in one of the bedrooms, and I was asleep instantly. I did not awake until late afternoon the following day.

Upon waking, I was disoriented and had forgotten where I was. I climbed down off the bed and went from room to room looking for Mother. The house was empty. I was terribly frightened and called her name, but no one answered. I went back to the bed in which I had first slept and laid down again. Moments later it came back to me what had happened and where I was.

The curtains were drawn making the room dark. Perhaps Jessica had taken Carter and Lynn out for a walk. While laying on the bed much too large for me, the panic began to rise up. I tried to focus on the cornfield, but I kept going back to Mother and wondered if she were alive. A very small part of me found some relief in the fact she might have died. Feeling ashamed, the tears rolled down my cheeks, creating a small harbor upon my pillow. However, shame soon turned to fear when I thought I had caught a glimpse of something black standing at the edge of my bed.

Both very afraid and hungry, I slowly moved under the blankets trying not to look at whatever stood in the shadows at the end of the bed. I drew my knees up, all the way to my chest, and curled into a tight little ball. After pulling the covers over my head and squishing my eyes shut, I eventually fell back to sleep. In the empty dark room, I slept restlessly.

CHAPTER SEVEN

I MUST HAVE SLEPT FOR AN hour or more, when a sudden clatter shook me awake. I was glad for it too, because it brought me out of a terrible dream I was having. All I remember about the dream was that it had to do with Mother and very unpleasant things.

For several minutes, I just lay in the bed and gradually noticed that I was soaked in sweat. When I threw the covers off me, I noticed that I had urinated as well. I was filled immediately with sharp fear that Jessica would get upset for what I had done. Now very still, I continued to lay there. Several minutes passed, and with my eyes open while breathlessly listening, I heard voices. There was movement outside my door.

Unexpectedly, I began to panic and started heaving in-and-out, as if I was drowning. I could not breathe, and my windpipe closed off altogether. The worse it became, the more I fought the feeling I was being strangled. The room disappeared, and there was blackness all around me.

I felt the mattress beneath me and lurched forward. Vomit now covered the large wet pool of urine. Swinging my legs over the side of the bed, the last of the vomit spurted out of my mouth and onto the floor.

I sat on the edge of the bed for several minutes, taking in air and trying to control my breathing. The anxiety slowly subsided and my vision came back. When my breathing returned to normal, I knelt down and used my shirt, tossed on the floor earlier, to mop up the puke. It gagged me, but I fought the urge to throw up again.

Gathering up my nerve, I walked out of the bedroom and followed the voices into the kitchen. In one hand was the crumpled up vomit-soaked shirt.

Jessica took one look at the flakes of puke stuck to my belly and sighed. Whatever scolding she was prepared to launch was short-lived the moment I burst into tears. After a quick rinse, Jessica then gave me one of her shirts to wear, which hung down on me like a small dress. She brought me into the kitchen where Carter and Lynn were, and fed all of us. We were starving and swallowed our food without chewing. After we'd eaten, Jessica laid me back down in another bedroom. Naked underneath while my soiled clothes were washed, I was clean and my stomach full. I eagerly crawled underneath the covers. In doing so, I was asleep in only minutes. This time, I did not dream.

When Carter woke me, it was nearing dusk. He told me the hospital had called and Mother was going to be okay. I crawled out of bed and noticed with great relief I had not peed myself. Carter's face looked tired, like the Mitchell boy who lived down the street when he came back from Vietnam. The same boy whose father had shot himself in the head when his son was off to war.

My clothes, washed and dried, were laid out on the chair in the bedroom. I dressed and walked into the hallway. I saw Jessica carrying a bucket under her arm and away from the bedroom where I had gotten sick. She then disappeared into the kitchen, seeing me but not saying a word. A look of disgust hung on her face. Embarrassed, I looked down. It was midsummer and when I passed the room Jessica had just left, it smelled of cooked vomit.

We would come to find out while Mother was in the hospital that she had refused to press charges against Father. We were not surprised. It wasn't the first time.

Two weeks passed before Mother was released from the hospital. The surgery to fit her eye back into its socket left her with a patch for the next two months. Father had also fractured her skull and broken her jawbone. Mother would be left with a permanent sag to one side of her mouth. When I heard this, I thought of the children's rhyme: "There was a crooked man that wore a crooked smile." Jessica had laughed sarcastically when she made the remark that Mother's mouth would be latched together, so she'd have to drink her wine through a straw until she was healed.

The two weeks we spent at Jessica's were much better than being with Mother. There weren't any beatings or molestations. We ate regular meals and our basic needs were met. However, Jessica did not want us there, and I could tell.

I realized even if we had asked to live with Jessica, she would have said no. Ordinary children would have been a handful, and we were not ordinary children. Living with the experiences of Mother's madness and Father's neglect, Jessica could see it had left us with many issues. Maybe she did not want to be reminded of what she left behind years before.

Jessica was married, but near divorce due to her husband's infidelity – and hers. She had two children of her own from two different fathers. Her home was already in turmoil, and we would only add more problems. I now knew for sure that our only hope of ever getting away from Mother was with Lauren.

It had been Jessica who first put the idea in our heads that Lauren was a possibility. Occasionally, Jessica would stop by the house, and she happened to come by once after Mother had just beaten me. Pinning Mother against the wall, Jessica had threatened to take us kids away. Soon afterwards, we had overheard that Jessica had called Lauren, and they discussed our options. It was the first breath of hope I had in a long time.

I hadn't seen Lauren in a few years. I had been only three when she married and left. Carter had only been five and actually attended her wedding. It was there he drank the alcohol punch and fell down the cement stairs of the church, rendering him a nice gash across one eyebrow needing stitches.

It had been a few years since Lauren had visited us last, and then it had only been briefly. However, I felt this aspect would prove valuable. Perhaps she would not remember us that well. There would be no preconceived notions, no prejudices, leaving the possibility of wanting to help her half brothers and sister. If she really knew us, there would be no way she'd ever take us in. We were damaged goods.

The two weeks with Jessica were over far too soon and she said that we needed to go with her to pick up Mother from the hospital. Upon hearing this, fear struck my heart, and I ran and hid outside. From beyond the screen of bushes that lined Jessica's driveway, I squatted and peered through the tiny branches, watching Carter and Lynn climb into her car. Jessica was already behind the driver seat, and everyone was waiting on me. Her husband would stay with the kids. I knew there was no choice but to go. So I stood and rounded the brush, then slowly walked to the car and entered the opened door. Not saying anything, I slid in next to Carter and shut the door behind me with a bang, which made Lynn jump and Carter a little bit too.

My eyes welled up before the car left the driveway, and the world swayed and waved. I leaned forward and laid my head on the back of the front seat. "Don't get sick in this car," Jessica said. I fought back the growth of puke that wanted to come up and kept swallowing the thickening spit. By the time we were at the hospital, the nausea had passed, but not the fear of seeing Mother.

A nurse wheeled Mother into the waiting room of the lobby, and I did not recognize her at first. She was dressed in a mint-green pajama set with matching slippers. Her head was wrapped with fresh gauze and she wore a patch over the damaged eye. The one that had been popped clean out of its socket. The swelling had completely subsided from the other eye, but a blue-black circle now enveloped it. Her lips were still a little swollen and turned out a bit. The gown exposed a large area of her breast, which was clearly marked with an ugly scarlet and yellowing patch. There was sure to be another one just like it circling and just beneath her ribcage. The paddles had left their telltale sign of rendering Mother enough electricity to jump-start her heart.

I stood just a few inches away from the wheelchair. There was an awkward pause and then I went to hug her. She pushed me away.

Baring temporary dentures, Mother barked, "Watch my head!" while moving only her lips and straining to speak through a jaw wired shut.

Her breath was harsh and rapid, and she glared at me, as if this had all been my fault. Mother continued to look at me. Through me. Her hands were clasped in her lap. I could see the ugly bruising from the needles that left black and yellowing streaks running up her arms, looping around, and disappearing behind her gaunt biceps. The veins protruded from the crotch of her forearms leaving lumpy blue lines of what looked like toothpaste under skin. Somehow, Mother blamed me for what had happened, and I knew when the wounds healed and she had regained her strength, things would go back to the way they were.

The five of us drove home in silence. Jessica helped Mother into the house and onto the couch. Mother looked at the wall mural and seeing the break in the mirror quickly looked away. Jessica left the house soon after Mother was settled. Neither of them saying a word. I walked outside with Jessica and gave her a hug goodbye. She told me to be careful and then left. With the fumes from Jessica's car exhaust still lingering in the dank humid air, I walked back inside the house to begin caring for Mother.

Weeks passed, and I fell into the usual rhythm of catering to Mother's needs. It was somewhat different. Perhaps even a little better. She was too weak to beat me, and therefore most of my days were filled with running errands to purchase her wine. Even better was the fact she had none of the interest in the sex either. I would help change her dressings, and early on when I had pulled away the gauze I saw bloody bits of tissue clinging to it.

Jessica had been right about Mother sipping wine through a straw. "Help me!" Mother would hiss through her fastened-together jaw, and I would bring the straw to her mouth, due to hands far too unsteady to do it herself. I purchased, poured, and helped Mother drink her wine. I got her blankets, propped her pillows, and made her a nice bed on the couch. Mother was not thankful, nor was she nicer during this time, just more feeble, and I knew her strength would one day return.

The day it did was when Jessica came back over; she took Mother to get her stitches removed from her head and the wire removed from her jaw. While Jessica and Mother were out, I took the well-deserved opportunity to play outside. I spent time under the apple tree where it was cool and silent, and I was blessedly alone. It was from under the apple tree I heard Jessica pull into the driveway, and I immediately went to greet her and Mother. By the time I rounded the backyard and passed through the gate, Jessica was already pulling away. I waved and she honked a return.

It felt like there was a hot stone in the pit of my stomach as I walked toward the front door. Something felt very wrong. As soon as I walked inside and pulled the screen door closed, Mother hit the back of my head with something heavier than her hand, and I saw a quick flash of light. I stumbled forward, and my knees buckled. My first thought was, *She must have been hiding behind the front door.*

As I knelt away from her, she followed up with another bash to the back of my head. Something broke apart, sending colorful pieces everywhere. She had used her favorite ashtray – a bored out seashell I always thought had been much too beautiful to put out her cigarettes. Its many broken pieces told me that I would no longer need to fret about that.

"Get me a goddamn cigarette!" Mother demanded. It had been nearly two months since she had last smoked. Father had seen to that by his gift to her in the form of a jaw securely wired shut. Still on my knees, delirious from the hit to the back of my head, I frantically swept my hands around the living room floor looking for her cigarettes.

"I'll show you the works! I'll show you what it feels like!" Mother shouted.

From the gash Mother had opened on the back of my head, I felt warm fresh blood beginning to trickle down my back, following my spine, which then proceeded to blaze a trail down the inside of my pants and into the crack of my butt.

Unmoving and still in a kneeling position, waiting for the dizziness to pass, I tried going into a fantasy. Thinking through the pain was a mechanism I developed. Throughout the abuse, I would concentrate on an object around the room. It was a skill I perfected and had many opportunities to do so. It was always at the ready in my mind. Somewhere hidden and secret, yet nearby.

The blood running down my spine tickled and sent electric waves all over my body. I stayed focused on an object and continued to follow a speck of light, trundling down an endless tunnel. For the most part, it was quiet, broken occasionally by Mother telling me to stay put and not move. I remained staring at the carpet and let the nausea pass. My head was a thumping beat of pain. Although my back was to her I could hear and smell Mother smoking. She had found her cigarettes.

My legs were going numb from kneeling and there was a relentless buzzing echo inside my ears. A thumping clamor coordinated with my heartbeat, followed by a feeling of a thousand razor blades being jammed into my head. Just then Carter came home and, upon seeing me, he shouted, "All he wanted to do was come out and play!"

Carter helped me to my feet and to the bathroom. We passed Mother on the couch and she took a moment to look at us, at me anyway, and then went back to absently smoking her cigarette.

With an old plastic cup, Carter leaned me over the tub and rinsed the back of my head. Thankfully, the cut wasn't as bad as we initially thought. Carter dabbed the cut with toilet paper and poured Peroxide over it, making my head hurt worse. Every time he dumped Peroxide into the cut, it felt as though razor blades filling my head were going to slice through my temples and rip my skull clean apart.

Exhausted, I went to our bedroom and lay down. Carter lay down with me, but before doing so, he got me a blanket from the floor. It was piss-smelling but comforting.

The pain in my head reminded me of when one of my molars had rotted. The decay had eaten most of the tooth, forming a jagged point that kept stabbing me in the cheek. I remember one of my older sisters taking me to the free-clinic and having the tooth removed. The dentist held up the tooth after yanking it from its sick socket and showed it to me. I then received a stern lecture on proper dental hygiene. A lecture meant not for me, but for children who actually owned toothbrushes.

My siblings and I had always been survivors. For example, we learned early that our immediate survival depended upon knowing basic first aid. In time, it seemed only natural to always know where to find a bottle of alcohol, peroxide, gauze, ointments, and rags. Most of this stuff was left over from the time my older sisters lived with us. The house never underwent a thorough cleaning so nothing was ever thrown out. Regardless, we stole food when desperate and a bottle of peroxide was not out of the question.

Rags were always easy to come by. They came from our sheets, pillowcases, and underclothes. We wore them. A shirt quickly became makeshift wrapping for a cut. Anything to stop the bleeding. We learned any cut left without proper attention would fester, because they often did. Knowing this was not the sign of great insight or intelligence. Even an animal will lick its wounds. It was purely instinctive.

Feeling safe next to Carter, I began to drift off to sleep. The pain in my head was going away as long as I did not move it. I thought of a cat I once had – my cat, Sambirdio. Thinking of him always helped me fall asleep. More than a pet, he was my miracle. A gray tiger cat I chose from a litter of nine being given away by a neighbor girl. He had emerald green eyes with gold flecks and a small mouth that always looked like it was smiling. Downy fur, which was soft as cotton, covered his body. Long sharp claws that never scratched me and a mewing that sounded like a musical mumble. I will never understand why Sam made me feel braver; all I know is that he did.

Shutting my eyes and determined to give sleep every chance, I kept thinking of how Sam had recently died. For two years, Sam was my cat and the best friend I ever had. I would think of him often, and weep now almost automatically. At night, I would listen for his motor purr next to my ear on my filthy pillow. He had suffered for several months, but his death still felt unexpected.

Remembering how I came home to find him gone started those razor-blades in my head again. As I thought more about how he died, something rose in my throat and almost choked me.

PART TWO
The Struggle for Life

"Hope is the thing with feathers
That perches in the soul.
And sings the tune
Without the words,
And never stops at all."

Emily Dickinson

CHAPTER EIGHT

THE FIRST NIGHT WITH MY new kitten – the first night in what was to become an endless succession of falling in love, for the first time, with something that would love me in return – I made a promise to myself that I would not let him die.

All day I had kept the kitten concealed. The time would come when Mother found out, but the kitten was far too young, and I was far too lonely to care. She had no idea I had talked a neighbor girl into letting me take the runt of her cat's new litter. While I was over visiting the girl, I peeked into the litter and saw a hairless lump that had been cast off from its mother and lay shivering. Its pink mouth made little suckling motions.

While I sat watching all the other newborn kittens greedily suck at their mother's tits, I became increasingly upset. This kitten would die if I did not do something. I stuck the kitten in my front pocket and adjusted my clothes so it did not bulge out. Carefully taking the kitten home with me, I quickly ducked inside the house and found Carter and Lynn. With their help, we turned an old shoebox into a makeshift bed, laced with tissue paper, old news-papers, and torn fabric from clothes that should have been thrown out long ago. The kitten's new home was complete. Carter and Lynn would not tell Mother. We lied for each other all the time. It was a buddy system based on survival.

Inside the shoebox, the tiny kitten was buried in shreds of toilet paper, and the paper, wrapped around his tiny head, exposed only purple, puffy eyes and a small, pink mouth. He looked like a strange flower.

With an eyedropper borrowed from the neighbor girl and a few easy instructions from her as to how the kitten should be fed, I gently held the tip of the dropper against his tiny mouth and squeezed out one drop of instant milk. The drop of milk traced along the slit of his mouth, but the mouth did not open. I tried again, and this time I pushed the tip of the eyedropper a little harder, forcing the undersized opening apart just enough to get at least one drop of milk down his puny throat.

It worked! The kitten took to the eyedropper as if it was his mother's titty and drank about a quarter of the milk down in only a few minutes. I was elated to have something to care for that would love me back.

Hiding away in the closet below the attic was where I cared for the kitten. Perhaps it was this newfound responsibility, but I was no longer afraid of the attic. A few days later, his eyes opened and it was then I named him *Sam*. Later, I would add "*birdio*" at the end of his name after watching him chase birds in the backyard.

I spent a full summer tending to Sam, and it was wonderful. I recall being there when Sam grew a brownish-gray whisper of downy hair over his little body. I was there when he opened his eyes for the first time and looked up at me. I was there when Sam began to walk, at first with great difficulty and then later when he strode with the agility of a lion. I was there when Sam drank all by himself from a saucer and didn't need the eyedropper anymore.

Sam grew to be both playful and loving. I was happiest when strolling down the street with him darting in and out between my legs, falling behind and catching up again – or through the backyard, while Sam explored the edges of the fence, with the wind blowing in the summer and snow falling in winter.

Of course, Mother hated Sam. She would often chase him from whatever room he was in by pretending to lunge at him with snaring false teeth nearly jutting from her once-broken jaw. "I ought to kill that cat," she would say while sitting back down and lighting up another cigarette. I was careful to keep Sam from Mother, and Sam seemed careful to avoid her.

As often as we could, we would sit under the apple tree together. Sam would be on my lap while I combed his soft fur with my fingers. We would sit a long while, taking in the peacefulness. His breathing would slow and his motor would trail off to a low rumble as he gently fell asleep. I stole lunch-meat and cheese from the corner store to feed him. I also stole cans of cat food, bread, milk — and the always-popular fruit pie, which was for me.

Like me, Sam loved the smell of the lilac bush near the back of the yard. With him nestled in my arms like a baby, I would lean into the bush taking in deep breaths of lilac. My face would hover just above one of the pudgy group-ings of bright pink flowers, sucking in the fragrant air. Sometimes, I'd glance down to see Sam doing the same thing.

Even though Sam possessed long, sharp claws that had never been trimmed, he would not scratch me – not even when I buried my face in his belly and made mumbling sounds. The soft pads of his paws would paddle my cheeks, but never did his claws come out.

As time passed with Sam, something stirred inside me. A feeling that I could not define filled me with a vengeance. The feeling grew stronger as I became older. It also seemed to be hidden until Sam woke it up somehow. When the feeling got to be too much and the tears stung at my eyes, I could reach down and take one of Sam's paws between my thumb and forefinger, giving it a gentle squeeze. This seemed to help, and he would always stare up at me with his usual quiet dignity.

Sam was everything to me. I could, and often would, weep while holding him. Allowing the tears to roll down my cheeks and disappear into his soft coat. I came to see Sam as another refuge. I was never too smelly or dirty for Sam. I was always welcomed and good enough. I was there for him, and he for me.

About a year had passed since I had first brought Sam home. My over-all environment had not changed. As a matter of fact, it had become worse. Still, I did have Sambirdio. The more difficult my life became, the more I clung to my companionship with Sam. I couldn't imagine my life without him and rarely gave this terrible possibility much thought.

It was summertime again, and Sam and I took full advantage of it, spending as much time as we could outside. Sam had been sleeping soundly on my lap when Mother came crashing through the back door of the house and staggered toward the apple tree. There was a faint twitch from Sam, but he did not wake up. I found this to be very strange, even worrisome, but I did not have the luxury of giving the thought too much attention at the time.

Mother stopped short, and for a moment, it appeared that she forgot why she was outside. Then, as if in slow motion, I watched her begin moving again with more purpose than before. Carter now stood at the back door and was watching her. Lynn was playing up the street, and I could hear her calling to Alexis, Kyle's youngest sister.

Mother seemed to advance toward me in a slow plodding motion, and the nearer she drew, the darker her face became. She then reached in and dragged me from the apple tree. When she did, Sam awoke, hissed, and ran away. Now she was above me, looming and hanging suspended. Her breathing was shallow and her eyes glared hypnotically. So close, I watched as they lost their color and drowsily merged, blending into hatred. Then I felt the first sting of her nails buried deep within the soft flesh under my chin.

She pulled me toward the back door. It felt as though my feet never touched the ground. As we crossed over the threshold, Carter reached for me and Mother stopped him short with one smooth slap to the face. He reeled backward, holding his cheek. Whatever courage he may have had before then was now gone.

Mother hauled me through the kitchen and into the living room then stopped. Grabbing my throat, which now felt hard and choky, she demanded to know what I did with her cigarettes. I could hardly breathe nor speak. "Where are my cigarettes?" Mother screamed.

Carter wept in the corner of the living room. Lynn had come in from playing and I saw her now crouched next to him. Mother had most likely smoked the cigarettes or lost them. Her children spent many sleepless nights after the corner store was closed for the evening searching the house for her cigarettes.

I did not answer Mother at first; however, she was excellent at getting things out of me that not only I did not want to tell her, but that were entirely untrue. Therefore, I told Mother what she wanted to hear. "I took them," I said. "I smoked them with Kyle."

There was no reason to get Carter in trouble along with me. As soon as the lie left my mouth, her fist came crashing into it. My bottom lip exploded, shooting a spray of blood down the front of my shirt.

I fell to my knees and immediately discovered that I had both defecated and urinated in my pants. Mother cocked her fist back for another blow and then froze in mid-swing. The streets were silent. An old bible was sitting precariously on the edge of the coffee table, and on the cover was a picture of the boy Jesus. I knelt, waiting for the next blow. The anxiety mounted and I closed my eyes. Using the defensive skill I had perfected, my mind jumped to a safe place. Nothing happened. Her fist did not connect. It was quiet, except for the sound of Lynn crying – a gut sob that brought up a hitch in her throat every now and then. When I opened my eyes, Mother was standing and staring down at me solemnly. She bent, knees popping and sounding like gunshots when they did. She stroked my face affectionately and I could not tell if the oily texture of her palm against my cheek was blood or sweat. Then Mother leaned in and gave me a kiss on the forehead, letting me know it was all over.

Mother returned to the couch. She said nothing. Walking in slow shuffling steps, Carter took me to the bathroom and bent me over the sink where he ran cool water and splashed it on my face, flushed and already puffy. The water hurt and felt good at the same time. First pain, then the pleasure of cool relief. He gently patted my face dry with toilet paper. My lip felt heavy and swollen. I went to the bedroom and found Sam – Lynn must have brought him in from outside when she came into the house.

When I picked him up in my arms, his body twitched and he gasped for air. I wasn't sure what had caused it, but I wasn't focusing well at that moment either. It was safe to cry and so I did. The tears stung my eyes.

I slowly turned and sat down on the bed with Sam drawn across my legs, and he stayed that way, his head hung over one of them. The spot where he lay moments before was still warm from his body. I stroked him, feeling the ripple of his ribs. He twitched again and nearly slipped from my lap.

I continued to stare down at Sam, checking for some sign of whatever caused him to shudder. His tiny slit of a mouth opened, and he thankfully offered up a yawn.

The snot, now caked up in my nose from crying, forced me to hold my mouth open in order to breathe. My bottom lip was throbbing. From the living room, I heard Mother speaking to herself and then offering up a guttering chuckle.

Tomorrow, I thought, *I'll steal some milk for Sam from the corner store. He needs to keep his strength up. He's probably just hungry. That's why he shivered. I'll steal him some cheese as well.*

CHAPTER NINE

IT WAS NOT LONG BEFORE I realized that Sam was truly sick. Only a few weeks into the new summer, he had lost a significant amount of weight. Soon he began to have convulsions that caused him to shiver uncontrollably and then fall to the floor. There was no money for medicine or veterinary care. There was, however, plenty of money for booze and cigarettes.

Mother was baffled and bemused by how much I cared for Sam. It made her angry. Hanging on to Sam was all I had; it was clean fear that I would lose him. Without Sam, I had only the slow gutting of what was left of me, and the long quiet nights after the molestations, where I sat stinking of her in motionless desolation.

Behind the irony of Sam's illness was the fact that I, too, became ill. I was suffering from something that racked my upper torso with agonizing pain and rendered me paralyzed from the waist down. The affliction came on around the middle of summer.

Wrapped in an old blanket, Sam and I would sit together on the loveseat in the living room for hours. Sam's fur was always soaking wet with the sweat that poured from both our bodies. Once, the neighbor girl who gave me Sam stopped by the house. She was a buxom, jolly-looking girl, and wiped her nose incessantly with the palm of her hand in an upward motion. When she saw Sam and me sitting on the loveseat, filthy and sick, she was horrified and questioned Mother – and got a taste of Mother's nasty mouth. After throwing out the neighbor girl, Mother stood at the doorway, calling her a fat whore. I could hear the girl crying as she ran from the house.

Her name was Saffron, and she was a few years older than me. I once asked her for advice about Sam when he first became ill, but she was not much help. She had given the litter of kittens away, and the mother cat roamed and eventually didn't come back. Saffron knew very little about caring for a sick cat and told me just to try to keep Sam warm. The only other advice Saffron gave me was to get Sam to the vet and to keep him away from Mother.

Lynn had been terribly concerned about both Sam and me. I could not move around much at all, and so Lynn would often help me to the restroom as best she could when the time came. However, because of my excessive sweating, it rarely ever did.

I would have to drag myself along the floor with one arm, while Lynn pulled the other arm forward. Getting up on the toilet itself was difficult, but Lynn and I managed. When Carter was home he would help us too, but he spent more time away when I was sick. Lynn would not leave with him during my illness. It must have been difficult for Carter with a drunken mother and a sick brother in the same house. There would be long, monotonous successions of me just sitting there on the loveseat holding Sam, along with Mother's undeviating assortment of complaints about me being sick. Like me, Carter was limited to the boundaries of being a kid himself and I couldn't blame him for wanting to leave.

Once when Lynn was helping me down the hall, Mother jumped from her chair and gave my legs a hard kick. I felt nothing, but went rolling briskly to one side of the hallway. She kicked again and again, while Lynn begged her to stop. I noticed Mother's eyes were dreary throughout the entire ordeal. Her face had shown nothing but a lackluster expression – unexcited, dry, and lifeless.

So much of my time was spent on the loveseat when I was sick. While Sam lay with me, wrapped in a blanket in my lap, he would breathe in short shallow rasps. I would occasionally lick my finger and touch his small mouth to be sure the air was moving in and out. The same way I would check Mother when she passed out.

Ironically, I had learned this trick from Mother when she checked on one of her regulars as he slept. His name was Red and he lived on the same block. He was what you would call a 'freebee', if it were not for the cheap wine he exchanged for sex.

Sometimes, he would be passed out in her bed, a hump under the covers, and not even the bedsprings were moving. Therefore, Mother would suck her finger, pulling it from her mouth, making this popping noise, and hold it under his nose. "Son-of-a-bitch is alive," she would say and slap him hard across the face to wake him up.

One morning, while Sam and I sat wrapped in the old blanket, I remember how he stirred, but did not open his eyes – too weak even to preen his fur. Suddenly, he felt like dead weight. His belly no longer moved up and down. "Sam!" I shouted, but he was completely limp.

"Stop fucking with that cat!" Mother screamed.

Without hesitation, I screamed back, "He's dying!"

Nothing reveals courage more than desperation and I was desperate. At the mercy of Mother, I had never even come close to this level of courage until Sam became sick. It was a blind and stupid bravery that was barely within my reach most times, but I grabbed at it frantically.

Lynn jumped up and ran to me. Mother didn't move from where she was sitting. She only watched as this awful scene played out, with the usual stupid look upon her face – dim-witted and faded.

"Sam! Don't die! Don't die, please!" I pleaded.

"Don't talk back to your mother!" she said to no one in particular. It was as if she were responding to a conversation held long before now.

"Same old shit!" Mother went on. "You crying over the fucking cat. Crying and carrying on like a little, queer cocksucker."

Her words went unnoticed as Lynn and I worked on gently moving Sam out from under the blanket, in order to get a better look. I felt distracted because of the panic – sick and hazy.

I looked up at Lynn, kneeling on the floor before me, vigorously moving the soaked covers out of the way. She moved graciously and robustly at the same time. I watched her hands. Unlike mine, they were healthy, calm, capable hands, doing the duties of caring for a cat she loved as well.

"He's breathing! Gregg, he's breathing again!" Lynn shouted, which came out "*bweathing*."

Mother lunged toward me, shoving Lynn aside. Now, standing directly in front of me and glaring downward, she rocked back and forth with a drunken sway, but said nothing.

I did not look up. I continued to check and re-check what Lynn had shouted. That was all that mattered.

When Mother finally spoke, her voice had a menacing smoothness to it. "I'm going to strangle Sam when you're asleep. When you wake up tomorrow, he'll be dead." I saw she was smiling, satisfied with herself.

"Please don't, Mommy. I'm sorry." I said, but that only seemed to make her angrier.

In an instant, Mother sprang for me. I had just enough time to move Sam to one side. Even then, I marveled at her physical strength, while she pulled me upward by the hair and then let go. Without any muscle control in my legs, I came crashing down atop the coffee table, bounced upward again, and then fell to the floor. My eyes never left Sam, who was now looked lifeless on the loveseat only a few inches from me.

"Here's your fucking sorry!" Mother bellowed directly into my ear. "Here's your fucking sorry!" she screamed again, and the smell of alcohol-saturated breath filled my face.

I continued to lay still keeping a close watch on Sam. Done in, my head felt like it weighed a thousand pounds; I simply gave in and let it fall to the floor, waiting for Mother to stop screaming into my face. When she did, Lynn helped me to my knees and eventually back on to the loveseat. After making sure I was settled, she placed Sam on my lap. Like me, he was wet and shivering.

My head hurt something awful, and I could see Lynn's eyes were raw from crying.

"Sam's okay," I said and pulled his body closer to my stomach.

Looking at him now, I couldn't believe he was the same kitten. His face looked desolate, almost blank. I couldn't bear the thought of being without him and tried to cry as quietly as possible. Mother was only a few feet away, and although she seemed to be drifting off from drinking, she was capable of coming out of a stupor in a matter of seconds. Sometimes, as she sat there staring at us, her face would seem to change shape, and would go from lifeless to alert. From tranquil to dangerous, and we knew she was about to go into a rage. I couldn't let that happen again. Not now – not with Sam so sick. He'd die for sure without me.

As I laid my hand under his paw, letting it rest on top of a couple of my fingers, just for a moment I felt something strange go through me. The feeling had something to do with why I was fighting so hard for Sam.

I ran my fingers up his back and stopped where there was a collar around his neck. It was something I had made, a green ribbon laced through a St. Christopher medal I had stolen from Kyle. Months ago, I had slipped the decoration over his lovely face onto his neck. It was a perfect fit. However now, it was far too big, and if Sam could have stood on his own, it would have hung all the way to the floor.

I faintly stroked the downy soft hair under Sam's chin. Mother had gone into one of the bedrooms and passed out. Lynn had fallen asleep in one of the chairs, and the house was uncommonly quiet. From outside, through a crack in one of the windows, I heard the wind. It sounded like a high-pitched, haunting laugh.

CHAPTER TEN

FALL WAS APPROACHING AND WITH it school would follow, and with school, more shame. As I looked out of the window, there was an ache in the small of my back – a place that, up until this moment, had been nerveless. It passed, and my attention was drawn to Sam again where he was cradled like a baby in the crook of my folded arms.

Revolting thoughts began racing through my mind in increasing numbers, and Sam was among them. I tried not to look too closely, but they were drawing nearer in clarity. Hope was growing faint.

Suddenly, I became aware that Mother was standing at the end of the dark hallway.

"I knew you were faking it, you little cocksucker," Mother said furiously.

I realized immediately what she meant. I was standing. The ability to do so had come back so suddenly and unexpectedly that I did not realize I had stood up with Sam in my arms.

Mother quickly moved the down the short hallway and pounced. I half-threw, half-dropped Sam onto the loveseat. The blanket he was wrapped in broke his fall. My arms were flailing in order keep balanced, but it was no use. I had not walked in several weeks, and my legs were weak. I spun around and was yanked backward, forcing me into a kneeling position, facing the same window I was staring out only minutes ago.

From behind me and snatching a lock of my hair, Mother snapped my head backward. I saw Sam from my peripheral vision, and he seemed to be convulsing under the blanket, his movements jerky.

Mother shouted, "Faker!" –and walked back into the bedroom where she had probably left her drink. Forcing myself to kneel upright again, I felt sharp pains in my legs and back. Sam was no longer convulsing. His eyes were only slits. His mouth closed. His head lay over one paw and dipped slightly. I could see his belly moving rapidly up, in, and out. I gathered him up in my arms, blanket and all, and sat back down on the loveseat. I put my finger to his small chest and felt his heart was pounding as fast as mine.

The paralysis was gone. The pain in my legs told me that. I looked at my hand, and it was bleeding. It must have hit the sharp corner of the coffee table.

My eyes grew heavy. Mother would be back soon, Sam was getting worse, but I was so tired. I looked again at my hand and fell off to sleep.

Just before school started, the paralysis had ended. Sam was getting worse. I would rush home from school to take care of him and would spend much time sitting with him asleep on my lap. Fall turned into winter, and there was a chill in the house. The utility company had shut off our heat, claiming they had not received payment from the State.

Near fall, the house was always cold and in the winter, it was freezing. The kind of cold that hurts all the way down to the bone. The wind blew in from outside and all over the house. You could hear it whistle and moan. We would stuff shirts and towels around the windows to keep out the cold as best we could. Sometimes, Mother would turn on the gas oven and open its door. My siblings and I would huddle together on the kitchen linoleum floor, before its black mouth agape and hissing, and relish in its warm breath.

Sitting Indian-style on the loveseat with Sam on my lap, I pulled the blanket up around my shoulders. Sam stirred and made a wheezing noise. While holding him, I looked out the small living room window and noticed there was a fresh dusting of frost that covered the ground like a white apron. There was also frost on the window. Evening had set in, and I remember the warmth between me and my kitty compared to how cold it looked outside.

An icy Midwestern wind was blowing, and I began quietly singing. "Mary had a little lamb, little lamb, little lamb – Mary had a little lamb. Its fleece was white as snow." It was a tune I learned on an old player piano we had in the basement. While singing, I continued looking out the window, watching moonlit snowflakes beginning to fall. "Everywhere that Mary went – the lamb was sure to go."

It was really snowing now, and there was already a small curve of powder built up at the base of one of the bottom exterior panes. The window appeared to be smiling at me. Afraid Sam would get too warm, I moved the blanket off of him. My eyes would go from the window to Sam, and back again – watching for some sort of movement. Some sign of the life he used to have. I suppose it was hope I was looking for.

I knew he was dying. At the very least, I wanted to be there when he did. I began to feel lately that even this would not be possible. It was a fear that came from a bottomless place, deep within my heart.

Winter passed. Spring was here, and it would be summer soon. This meant I would be able to spend all day with Sam, nursing him back to health. He had survived the winter, which meant there was a chance he was going to make it and I had survived another difficult school year. Once school was out, he would no longer be left all alone with Mother. Every day I would rush home from school and find Sam exactly where I had left him on the loveseat. I had returned to feeding Sam with the eyedropper, as I did when he was just born. Eventually he stopped eating altogether, and the convulsions became more prominent and longer lasting.

On the last day of school, I ran all the way home without stopping to catch my breath, even though my lungs burned. Although Lynn shouted for me to wait up, I did not listen. I cleared the two porch steps and ran through the front door relieved to know with school out of the way, I could spend every day caring for Sam.

The blanket he normally was wrapped in was there on the loveseat, but Sam was not. Mother sat on the couch drunk, and it was how she looked at me that I knew something was wrong. Mother's singular practice of lifting the booze cup to her mouth seemed difficult. She was extremely uncomfortable from the outset, and her voice shook as much as her hand holding the cup. I thought for a moment it was the sickness coming on, but then I again looked at the empty blanket, and before she mouthed the words, I said them aloud. "Sam's dead" – and forgetting her rule about showing emotion, I wept in front of her and would go on weeping until my chest ached.

I remember the dull ignorance on her face, and how Mother's eyes looked more guilty than ashamed or sorry. There were long pauses in between each question I asked and each was the same. "What happened to Sam?"

She seemed to ponder the question seriously as if it were not the same question I had just asked, but she did not answer me. Mother just went on staring at the floor and sipping her wine. Then she regained the balance of power that always served to place her world back on an even plane. Mother took back control and quickly dismissed me from the room with one angry threat. There could be little doubt something terrible lied beneath the surface of what happened to Sam. I would never know, and the only creature that made me feel just a little safe was now gone.

I lay on my bed and cried, desperately wishing Mother was just playing a cruel joke and Sam was hidden somewhere in the house. He was not. Not knowing how he died made it worse. It was important to me that he did not suffer in the end. It became difficult to keep Sam within my thoughts without the anger interfering and pushing away the images of his playful character. Several nights were spent lying awake and trying to remember him. Daydreaming about what he once was by closing my eyes and concentrating. I would hold the image of him for a few seconds, and then it would disappear, but not before I glimpsed his small face slipping slowly away in front of mine.

PART THREE
When I Was a Child

"Where does one go from a world of insanity?
Somewhere on the other side of despair."

T.S. Eliot

CHAPTER ELEVEN

I LEFT THE CORNER STORE, WALKING past the first house and toward home. The flesh on my arms still burned from the lit matches tossed at me by the storekeeper. He was a stout old cuss. Most of the time he was businesslike, but he had caught me stealing again. I tried to drop the booty in my pants pocket when I thought he wasn't looking, then I casually walked up to the counter and asked for a piece of penny candy as a decoy. But he figured the bulge in my pocket had not been there when I walked into the store. As I stood there waiting for the penny candy, he grabbed a box of wooden matches, and with hands like a skilled surgeon, he dragged one match after another across the striker, lighting and throwing them in one smooth motion.

The matches cleared the rubber change mat lying on the counter, doing tiny flips in the air, igniting and then landing painfully on the exposed flesh of my arm. Most of them just stung a little, then bounced off. However a few stuck to the skin and burned.

By the time he waddled around the counter to give chase, I was already out the exit. He always stopped short at the end of the parking lot, so once I crossed the street connecting to our block, I was home free.

When I got closer to the house, my stomach was grumbling in anticipation of the hard-earned fruit pie in my pocket. I noticed as I got closer to home that there was an unfamiliar car in the driveway. *Mother must be entertaining*, I thought, and continued past our house and down the street. It had been a year since Mother had been in the hospital, and she now operated back at her normal speed, bringing the men in and out regularly.

I walked with my head down, keeping to the middle of the sidewalk, pretending either side was a steep drop into a fathomless chasm. When I reached the end of the block, I looked up momentarily to cross the street and headed for the grouping of trees and undergrowth we referred to as "the field." Turning slightly to the left, the ground beneath my feet went from asphalt to willow brush and eventually, green grass. Leading to a storm drain was a narrow river. I watched the swirling brown water carry away a smattering of small twigs and buds where they would disappear into an iron mouth, making me think of the fruit pie in my pocket. Apple, my favorite.

I stood on the metal plate and listened to the water dump into the drain. Stamped beneath my worn sneakers were the words *Water and Sewer*. I stepped off the drain and walked further into the field. As I walked, the grass became thicker and taller. The trees grew larger and closer together. The air was cool, almost chilly, and I felt more at peace.

Only a few minutes before, I had narrowly escaped with the fruit pie. The son-of-a-bitch storeowner was a mean bastard, and I knew he would have hurt me worse had he been able to catch me. The old man was slow, but he had a double barrel shotgun hidden behind the counter. I knew this for a fact because it'd been pointed at my mother a few times when she got to cussing him out if she thought he cheated her out of a couple bucks. She'd just go on cussing at him, waving her arms all over the place as if he wasn't standing there with a loaded gun in her face. I'd beg her to leave, tugging on her arm. The old man had this thick Hungarian accent and would bark, "Listen to ya boy, friggen whore, and move on." This went on about every couple weeks, but he kept selling his booze to her and Mother kept buying it.

The wind started to pick up, and the sky turned a little darker. I kept walking on through the field. I thought of turning back, but I knew it wouldn't be safe. Not that it ever was, but if Mother had a man in her bed, I didn't want to be around. The shame was unbearable. I had learned that, when the men came over, things got worse than usual. The thing to do was to get the hell out of the house. Then, if I took a beating for not being around to skim their wallets, it was better than watching them lay on her and make those awful grunting sounds. I still couldn't tell time or tie my own shoes, but I was smart enough to know trouble when I saw it.

The sky was now completely black, and by the time I reached the trees, it was as if it went from day to night in only a few seconds. It was going to storm, there was no doubt of that now, and I had no place to go. I settled next to a thick oak and waited for the rain.

In the distance, lightning lit up the clouds, then thunder rolled. I was told that you wanted to steer clear of a tree during a lightning storm. I jerked and curled into a ball. I could smell electricity in the air. Another snap of light shot across the sky followed by a crash of thunder so loud it made me scream. Suddenly, the rain came, and it felt like needles against my skin. Thunder cracked again overhead and the wind blew harder. More rain needled and stung my face. It came down so hard I could not see anything in front of me. Nothing but wet blindness and hard cold rain.

I was now completely drenched and freezing. The lightning strikes grew farther apart, but the rain was coming down harder than ever. Several small puddles formed all around me. *I'll wait out the storm*, I thought. *Just like with Mother.* It was both relieving and heart-breaking at the same time.

I didn't want to get hurt anymore. But I didn't want to leave Mother. Yet she tortured me. She let Sam die and the rage against her for this boiled inside me, mixed with bitter confusion. The rain continued to fall, and I wondered if I was going crazy. I closed my eyes and wondered if this was finally the end.

It was a fear of mine to go completely insane. A fear Mother would perpetuate by telling me that I was already very close to total lunacy. "Your grandfather went crazy, you know?" she would say with a glint in her eye. "He lost his fucking mind and died in a mental institution. You know your grandfather had to wear one of those straight jackets because he would try to dig his eyes out and punch himself in the balls."

At this, she would swing at my genitals and sometimes make contact, causing me to fall to the floor gasping for air. She would then lean over me and whisper, "Gregg, you look just like your grandfather."

I once saw a picture of my grandfather when he was only a boy. It scared me something awful, because she was right. I looked just like him.

When the rain slowed to a drizzle, I got up and began walking back home, forgetting about the fruit pie in my pocket. Escaping to Lauren's didn't seem real anymore. It had been over a year since the option first came up, but nothing had progressed. Yet I never lost the will to survive. Not because I was courageous or brave. It was simply because I knew nothing else.

As I passed the houses, I could hear the pinging and rattling of the rain against the gutters. About halfway home, I noticed the unfamiliar car was gone and hoped that Mother was content with what the man had paid her. It would be even better if she were passed out, and I could sneak inside and quietly change into dry clothes. My hopes were soon replaced with agony when I saw the screen door burst open and Mother step out onto the porch. She eyed me immediately and stared without saying a word. Her mouth was a thin line. Her arms crossed. My only hope now was that both Carter and Lynn were home. However, it would not have mattered if they were.

I continued walking along the sidewalk toward the house. The sidewalk was not steep, but it felt steep to me. My legs became heavy with dread. In front of me was a puddle, and I sloshed through it without care not to get my shoes wet. I was already sopping wet, anyway.

I passed the house next to ours. There was a dog as wet as I was, hitched to a stake in the yard. It looked at me distrustingly when I passed by, and I instinctively put my hands in my pockets in case he jumped forward and nipped at my fingers. My impulse proved correct. The dog put its ears back and showed its teeth, then barked, and jerked its head. The distance closed between me and Mother and my fear increased.

I walked further along the sidewalk, slowing my pace. My head down, I then turned right and into our front yard. In my mind, I tried to think of the field and how it stretched outward, away from the houses, becoming open country. How the blue of the sky was more prominent over the vastness of the field. It helped a little, but not much. I could feel Mother's eyes glaring down from the porch on me, and something caught in my throat.

The protection of the field was behind me. *I could turn back and run*, I thought. I could run until I reached the trees of the field and keep on running. On the other side of the field, I thought there must be a better place.

Where I could start again. Like when we fouled up our turn during a game of tag and asked for a "do-over." Yes. That's what I needed most. A "do-over."

Before nearly reaching the porch, Mother started for me. I realized that I should have stayed in the field, despite the storm. I had been safe there. I was no longer moving, frozen in place, expecting the worst. There was a loud bang, which I thought was more thunder, but then the left side of my face exploded. What followed was a grand sweeping of landscape before I came crashing to the ground.

She pulled me up by the hair and dragged me a few feet over to the porch. I was forced down hard, and upon smacking my tailbone, a series of electric jabs went shooting up my spine. Mother remained absolutely silent. No yelling. No cursing. She sat down next to me and looked out over the yard. When she finally spoke, her tone was calm. "You're lucky to be alive. The lightning could have killed you." She then turned her face toward me and whispered in my ear. "This isn't over, goddamnit." Mother got up and walked inside, her voice moving away as she did.

Mother was the crazy kind that you saw coming at you staggering, shouting obscenities and flailing her arms, but she was also the crazy kind that was calculating and manipulative. This made her the most dangerous kind of crazy there was.

Worse than when you saw it coming was when you did not. That was when Mother was planning the beating in her head. She would sit on the couch, always with a cigarette smoldering next to her. Always with a drink in her hand or within reach, staring at nothing, and then she would fix on me.

Sometimes, she would start off in a conversational tone with a question that didn't make much sense: "Gregg, whose side are you on?" Her voice would be dry and clear without a trace of awareness.

"I'm on your side, Mamma," I would reply, and then she would just go on looking at me. She would then tell me that she loved me, and I believed it, because I was afraid. I was willing to believe a lot of things, especially when I desperately wanted them to be true.

Then she would tell me to come and sit next to her, and I would. Our arms and legs would be right up against one another, and sometimes we would both be wearing shorts and no sleeves. Skin against skin, which made me ashamed and sick in my stomach.

Mother would then turn and look at my face, and sometimes she would kiss me on the mouth. I would get a sick feeling. Then her hot and dry hand would come crashing against my cheek, and I'd be drowned in brilliant purple light, hidden behind a curtain of both surprise and heart-wrenching fear.

Afterwards, she would tell me to go away from her and sit down on the floor. Looking at her, you would never know she just slapped me if it were not for the cords standing out in her neck. Mother would go back to looking at nothing, sometimes with this peaceful smile, and I would try really hard not to cry and make her mad.

I had honestly began to wonder if the alcohol destroyed Mother's brain and made her crazy, or if she had been that way before she started drinking. If she had been crazy all along, maybe she had gotten it from her father. Then that meant it could happen to me. It terrified me more than the abuse did. Mother could pass on her insanity to me. I wondered with genuine fear if crazy was catching.

There was a brief moment while sitting on the porch when I allowed myself a fantasy about heading back toward the field along with its defending grove of trees. The moment passed. I got up to go inside. The fear and hatred for her grew stronger. Rage burned inside of me, but yet again, I would obey Mother. I was caught somewhere between two worlds: hatred and helpless devotion.

By the time the screen door banged shut, I was yanked to the carpet. Mother shouted, "What is your name?" It was just another trick question. One that I would never get right and would provide her with the minimum justification necessary to carry out what she was about to do. "Your name, goddamnit! What is your name!"

I said nothing, knowing that any answer would prove useless. A hard slap and then another – both landing to the side of my face Mother had struck only minutes before when I first stepped into the yard. She was directly behind me, holding my head upright by a clump of my hair. Another slap and another, and the last caused me to twist and pull something in my back. She landed another blow to the same side of my face. Cupping her hand slightly, Mother hit me again, forcing a suction around my ear – driving the air inward. The pain was excruciating. Something popped inside my head, and the sound of her voice suddenly changed, becoming muffled.

Multicolored lights and starbursts danced inside my head. My ear rang, drowning out her shouts. I just closed my eyes and concentrated on the field. I concentrated and waited for her to stop. The thought of losing my mind came rushing back. *What if she gives me brain damage?* I wondered.

Mother had been holding her cigarette pinched between her middle and forefinger in the hand pulling my hair. As she rolled her knuckles forward to get a better grip, the cigarette rolled forward as well. The lit ash, now tangled within my hair, burned at my scalp and I frantically slapped at my own skull. Mother stopped. Perhaps, my display of self-abuse had caused her to do so. She did not sit down on the couch. Instead, she left the room and headed for the bedroom where she had recently been with the stranger. Mother was probably making sure the money she collected was still there after the bitter exchange of drunken sex.

My body ached all over. Using the coffee table as leverage, I pulled myself up and went over to a chair to sit down. Once sitting, I laid the right side of my head down on the armrest. The left side felt twice its normal size and hurt. My mind drifted off, looking for some sort of foothold on reality. I thought about Lauren again. It gave me some comfort and got my mind off the pain. I began thinking that it wouldn't be a silly plan of escape or fantasy any longer – I'd make sure of that.

I forced myself to get up from the chair and go to the kitchen to find some ice in the freezer. I shoved a few cubes in one of my socks and made an icepack for my face. I snuck out the back door and went over to the apple tree. I had to fight the dreadful feelings of remorse when they crept up inside my head. Settling down on the old crate with the sock filled with ice against my cheek, I let myself fall into one of my favorite make-believe games of being a soldier. Sometimes I'd act it out with a fake rifle, scurrying around the field or construction site behind the corner store. Other times, I would sit alone and just imagine. Especially under the protective cover of the apple tree.

But I knew deep down that I was not a soldier. I followed Mother's orders blindly, and I was a soldier in that regard. I also bled and therefore I was like a soldier. I was not brave, but I did not believe all soldiers were. I believed, like me, a lot of them just followed orders and hoped they were not hurt or killed. Yet hard-boiled into them was all that training, and I had none of that. It was just make-believe for me, and not real like the pain in my cheek. I was not a solider at all. I was only a kid, and the fantasy of being a soldier was fading and funneling away.

I raised my head in order to look out through the thick growth of leaves. There was a single line of apples hanging neatly across one of the branches. Looking down again near my feet, I noticed an arc of sunlight. I thought, *If Sam were here, he'd be staring at it and every now and then swat at it with his paw.* This made me smile, sending a jolt of pain across my entire face. I watched the arc of sunlight grow narrow, thin to a mere slit, and then fade away entirely as a cloud drifted by briefly. Rising slowly, I walked through the natural opening, stooping as I went, and stood up when I reached the outer skirt of the apple tree. My back protested and made random popping sounds – already beginning to stiffen.

It was cool, and for a moment, it felt as if fall was coming. Summer would be over soon, and I would be starting school. It would be my last year attending elementary and then on to junior high. I was not ready for the higher academics and suddenly felt embarrassed. But this meant nothing to me now compared to what my life was at home.

I would walk back to the field tomorrow and find a quiet place deep within the trees. Far away from where the older kids hung out and smoked their joints.

I knew Mother would be angry when I returned home. She would give me that craning look when I walked into the house, and her jawbone would be slowly working over the butt of her non-filtered *Kools Menthol* cigarette. Her eyelids would be half-lowered and working me over slowly too, like her cigarette. Still, I hoped maybe she'd be passed out and wouldn't notice when I came home.

I headed toward the back door. She still needed me, I knew that, but not the way a good mother needs a son. As I reached for the screen door, this fresh and liberating feeling came back to me, stronger than ever. It did not matter if Mother needed me. I began to realize I did not need her.

CHAPTER TWELVE

THROUGHOUT THAT NIGHT, IT FELT as though my heart was frozen. There was no love and no hate. My mind walked into and out of all those things that once kept me resolute in my decision never to leave her. I was close to breaking free. Closer than I had ever been before. Freedom was within reach for the first time in my life. I could feel it. It was as if I was breaking through a new-formed crust of ice into a pool of cool, fresh water. I lay down and fell fast asleep thinking of leaving Mother for good.

Morning came, and with it, her rage. Mother had found the scratch paper that I had written my master plan upon: "Call Jessica frum corner store. Tell her com git us. Go live with Lauren." I had put the words down over a year ago and read them over and over. They gave me a goal, something to live for without Sam.

My head was still on the pillow when her hand came down and busted me in the nose. I tasted blood running down the back of my throat, making me gag and swallow rapidly. I could see she was holding my plan in the same hand that crashed into my nose. She was past comprehension and far from restraint. She was screaming something, but it rang hollow against my ears.

Mother climbed on top of me, pinning me down. This always struck me as peculiar because I never fought back. She grabbed my lower lip and pulled hard. The pain pushed me into a dark tunnel. All of a sudden, my testicles felt as though they were on fire. Mother had reached back, taken hold of them, and squeezed. In an instant, day turned into night and everything stopped momentarily. Mother climbed off me and left the room.

Carter suddenly ran into the bedroom and to my side of the bed. His voice came from very far away and sounded crippled and broken. I was curled into a fetal position, holding my testicles and struggling to breathe. Carter's voice was raspy and echoes of his voice were ringing in my ears, but I could not move. I could not see. For several agonizing moments, I found myself trapped between sleep and wakefulness.

Carter sat down on the bed next to me while I gasped for air. Gradually, the ache in my groin subsided and the air again moved easily in and out of my lungs.

"I'm all right," I told Carter; however, when I swung my legs out onto the floor, the room swam temporarily. "I'm going for a walk," I said and thankfully was able to sneak out the front door while Mother was in the kitchen, pouring herself another glass of wine or whatever rotgut she was drinking. My testicles ached as I walked down the street and toward the field.

The warmth of the sun felt good. My plan was to first rest a bit in the field, and then later I'd cut through the old apartments on the other side of the block in order to avoid my house on my way to the corner store. In my pocket was thirty cents, enough to purchase a soda and fruit pie, and I was relieved to know I wouldn't have to steal this time. Back in the trees, I would eat and sleep.

Upon the reaching the field, I hummed "Mary had a little lamb," as I walked, allowing my hand, palm down, to brush the tops of the Indian Grass. Once on the smooth green blades that led up to the taller weeds, under the bright sunshine, I stopped and closed my eyes, enjoying the warmth on my tender nose. I left the soft weeds and they whispered against my shoes as I headed for the trees. For now, I would sit against one of the tall oaks and rest. The sky was a beautiful bloom of bluish white.

I had spent the whole day in the field, leaving only once to get the fruit pie and soda. It was growing darker now, and realizing I had spent a considerable amount of time away from Mother without panicking or fretting to the point where I would go running back to her, filled me with surprised joy. Along the darkening street, I made my way home. My heart became stiff and cold the closer I came to the house.

There was a chill in the air that told me I would catch hell, and remembering Mother had found the note with the plan written on it enforced this belief. I'd still have to pay for my disloyal behavior with more beatings. Apprehensive about going home, I walked on the opposite side of the street. Closer to the house, a phantom pain shot through my groin, and I suddenly halted when I saw Mother sitting on the porch, smoking a cigarette. I could tell when she took a drag because the tip would glow very bright and then subside. *She is waiting for me*, I thought.

A car turned the corner, and I ducked behind Kyle's house and hid away for a second. With all the strength I had, I walked across the street and out of the shielding darkness. My tongue probed the raw split in my lip nervously. When I reached the steps of the porch, Mother flicked her cigarette into the yard and got up to go inside. I knew that was the signal for me to follow her in.

I waited until she shut the screen door before I opened it. I then went into the house. It was dark, but Mother lit a match to ignite another cigarette. When she did, the glow cast a shadow of her head against the wall, and I thought of the paper cutout of an old style portrait we had once made of ourselves in school. There were two profiles depicting the left and right sides of my head. They were facing one another within a folded piece of paper. Mother tore it up in front of me saying it was a queer thing to do. It had been a gift to her on Mother's Day.

"Come here," Mother said and stood up. She reached out her hand and told me to take it. I was led down the hallway and into her bedroom. She told me to strip down, climb onto the bed, and get under the covers. They stank of sex. Mother followed after me. The metal springs under the mattress squeaked as she climbed in the bed. When she slid next to my body, I could feel she was naked, and her skin felt cold. "Take off those goddamn underwear," she whispered.

She leaned to one side and hoisted herself up, resting on her elbow facing me. I pushed my underwear down to my ankles and used my feet to kick them off the rest of the way. Mother was still smoking her cigarette. Taking one last puff, she crushed it against the headboard. It was pitch-black, and I could hear her exhale the last of the smoke that filled her lungs.

Her hand moved to my genitals, and cupping them whole, she squeezed. Although she did so much more gently than before, they still ached, and I felt the sickness rise up in my throat, choking me. "You're not going to leave Mommy, are you?" she said.

I could hear her breathing quicken. Without a single utterance and while she forced me to please her sexually for what seemed an eternity, in my heart I answered her.

The molestations had been going on for years, but they seemed worse for me as I got older. My mind was not able to justify, nor comprehend, what took place in Mother's bed. Reason stopped dead against a wall of shame and confusion, and there was no punching through it. No answers to any of the abuse as to why. Only a sharp reminder, every time she raped me, that I was one more step closer to complete and total insanity. Soon, I thought, a trapdoor deep within my mind would be raised, and the horror I'd kept locked up all these years would climb through.

In the corner of my mind, there was a mirror, and the reflection was not my face, but something distorted and angry. It took great effort to push the sight away; however, the rage building inside of me was becoming even more powerful. What was once love became hate.

I was running out of strength. It was nearly used up. Leaving me too was the desire to help my siblings. I knew one day it would be gone. I knew I had to act soon. I would figure out a way to escape this place. All I had to do was convince Lauren.

The sex acts became more frequent and brutal. Mother then got it in her head that she could up the ante on prostituting herself if she got the teenage boys in the neighborhood involved. She did and they came and went.

The teen boys were more particular when it came to a mate. More so than the old comely drunks Mother usually attracted. Therefore, doomed by her usual appearance of being grotesquely skinny and generally unwashed, Mother resorted to an inventive array of other sexual practices. Those that did not involve penetration.

The boys that took part in this disgusting ritual would tease me when we passed on the sidewalk, "blow jobs and hand jobs…the only job your mother has." During their taunts, I also learned that apparently it was the same price for both.

There was no cause for the increase in the molestations, except maybe the fact I was getting older. However, they did increase and it was not just with Mother.

He was a short and fat man. One of Mother's regulars. I had been sitting under the apple tree, blissfully alone. The ground, kept cool from the shade of the branches, was soft under my bare feet. I took in deep breaths and let them out slowly in order to calm me down; something I did often. I leaned against the trunk of the apple tree and closed my eyes. Before long, I was asleep.

The sound of the back door slamming shut woke me. Peering through the branches, I saw the fat man with beady little eyes, balding and always wet with perspiration. He was walking toward me. How could he have known about my hiding place? And as if to answer, from the open kitchen window, floating through the air, came the haunting sound of Mother's laughter.

"You must be Gregg," the man said on his hands and knees, pushing through the foliage. I immediately scooted away from him, putting the trunk between the two of us. He had on a red-and-white striped shirt that was too tight, and bent over with his gut hanging down he looked like a fat candy cane. "Your momma and me want you back in the house," he said, suddenly lunging for me. I squirmed out the other side of the tree, scraping up my arms on the rough bark of the branches and ran. By the time I reached the sidewalk, I was crying, but didn't stop running.

When I thought it was safe to return home, I did. The man was gone, and Mother sat drinking. She didn't say a word, but I knew she sent the man out to see me. And I knew why. What I didn't know was how much he had paid her.

That night, Mother went to bed and told me to stay up. Confused at first, I simply obeyed, taking it as a good sign she wasn't making me go to bed with her. About an hour later, there was a soft knock on the door. I went to the window and looked out. It was the candy cane man, and he was wearing the same striped shirt. I stood frozen, and he knocked again. It was no use. Sooner or later, I would be forced to give him what he had already paid for. I unlocked the door, opened it slowly, and he limped inside. I realized I had not noticed the limp earlier that day.

"Please, mister…" I begged, crying.

He leaned down and whispered to keep quiet. Before the man shut the door, I stole a look outside as if to run, and he gripped my shirt with his free hand. It was cold outside. The night was clear. The stars were out.

With his arm around my shoulders, the man led me over to the couch. He sat down and pulled down my underwear, which was all I had on. Grasping my buttocks with his hand, he then knelt in front of me and began sucking at my limp penis. I prayed it would not get erect, and my prayers were answered. This didn't stop the man. It didn't seem to faze him at all. He pulled out his own penis from his pants, which was big and stiff. With his mouth on me, he began rubbing it up and down with his other hand. By now, I was sobbing, my sight blurry with tears, but I tried to keep quiet. Both fear and shame overwhelmed me. Moments later, the man shot a stream of goop. He hurriedly wiped it up with his shirt. "Don't cry," was all he said and quickly and quietly left the house.

The house was dark. A thin slit of light came from the place where the curtains came together, where Carter and I often stood staring out the window and waiting for our father. I could still feel the man's saliva wet and cold on my penis and testicles. The embarrassment was too much to handle, and I wept for several minutes. With what little strength I had left, I got up from the couch, pulled on my underwear, and walked down the hallway toward the room I shared with my brother. Upon passing Mother's bedroom, came the haunting sound of her laughter.

PART FOUR
The Passing

"Although the world is full of suffering, it is full also of the overcoming of it."

Helen Keller

CHAPTER THIRTEEN

A FEW WEEKS LATER, I WALKED down the street with my arm slung around Lynn's tiny shoulders. Carter was walking along beside us. The small display of affection made Lynn uncomfortable. We weren't allowed to touch one another – Mother's rule.

The hot sun. The tacky houses of the neighborhood. The three of us walking and not saying a word. Our heads down. Not knowing where we were going. Believing there was no place to go. And coming to understand fully that there was nothing left except to escape.

I shared with my siblings what I'd recently overheard when Jessica had been over – something that had filled me with new hope – or more accurately, what seemed to be our last hope. "Jessica said she got a hold of Lauren," I said. "All we have to do is call Jessica if Mom beats us one more time."

"Fuck man, that won't take long," Carter said and added, "For fuck's sake, Jake . . . that's a fact, Jack."

Lynn giggled and pushed my arm off. I could see a flash of hope in her eyes when she turned to do so. "So what do we do?" Lynn asked while we kept walking. Walking further away from the house and toward the field. I knew I'd miss the field, but that was all.

"All we have to do is wait for next time," I said.

I didn't have the nerve to share my plan with them. I'd draw Mother into a beating frenzy. I'd then run to the store and call Jessica. It didn't matter Mother found my note because she'd play right into it. She'd have no choice. There was no way Mother could stop herself from two things:

drinking and hitting me. This time, I was going to use them to get us out of here.

Suddenly, at the end of the block, before it began the gradual curve to the left, Lynn stopped. "I don't want to live with Mom anymore," she said and started to cry.

The strain was too much, and I yelled, "Shut the fuck up!"

Carter was quick to defend her: "You shut the fuck up, Gregg! I'll kick your ass!"

Normally, I would have let it go, however, things were different now. "Fuck you, fatso!" I said and stood my ground.

Carter landed the first punch squarely at the tip of my shoulder. My arm went numb, but I found the strength to swing back. By the time we dropped to the ground, punching, kicking, and biting one another, Lynn was halfway home. Carter pushed himself off me and ran after her, more afraid she'd inadvertently tell Mother what just happened, as opposed to making sure she was all right.

I pulled myself up and headed for the field. When I swung around again to see if Carter and Lynn might have come back, I saw they were gone. Maybe they went inside the house or ducked in the backyard. I didn't care. My arm hurt like hell, and I kept swinging it back and forth to work out the charley horse.

The pavement ended, dropping off slightly, and turned into dirt. The sensation always made me feel better. It told me I was close. Casting a golden light across the field was a late afternoon sun. I grunted and pressed forward. My arm hurt. But I had something to preoccupy my mind. I had a plan to carry out.

Just before the lip of the tree line, before the first thicket of oak and maple, I saw something that turned my beautiful haven into something degenerate. Something so awful that I would never again be able to enjoy the peace this coppice of trees once gave me. Aside from the molestations I had been forced to endure from Mother and strangers, it was the most horrible sight I have ever seen.

Her name was Marla. Prepubescent beauty enveloped her. Long brown hair and eyes to match. She was a classmate of mine, and I had a crush on her from the day I saw her beautiful smile on the playground at school.

She was not smiling now. The neighborhood twin boys, both older than Marla by five or six years, were hurting her. Although she seemed to partake in this revolting ordeal, I could see the anguish in her face. I knew it well. It stared back at me in the mirror.

The twins wore shirts and no pants. Marla was completely naked. They took turns. One boy held her upright while the other would thrust his hips between her legs, spread apart by his brother. She made small groaning sounds and looked up at the sky. There was nothing but a blank expression on her face. I didn't run for help. Who would I tell? Who would care? Instead, I sat low to the ground and watched the rape unfold before me. I did nothing. I said nothing. I was not a hero. Only a stupid boy.

The first twin uttered what sounded very much like a growl, and on his face, he bore an expression of what appeared to be pain. He switched places, and the second twin mimicked the first – in much less time. The twins hurriedly got dressed and ran away laughing.

Still frozen in place, I watched Marla use a pair of crumpled panties to wipe around her crotch. Upon seeing this, I fought the urge to puke by repeatedly swallowing the acid that raced up the back of my throat. She then got dressed, but much more slowly than the twins. Her movements were mechanical. She wasn't crying. Afterwards, she walked directly toward the spot where I was crouched down in the thick tall grass, and turning slightly toward the neighborhood, she missed me by only a few feet.

I breathed a sigh of relief when she passed by. She didn't seem to notice me, and I thought she probably would not have seen me if I was standing directly in front of her. I waited until she left the field and rounded the corner of the block. I had no idea we lived so close to one another. When Marla disappeared out of sight completely, I stood and walked toward home. The trees no longer symbolized the magic they once held. My haven ruined. What good was it to me now?

The apple tree had been spoiled by the stranger who liked little boys. The grove of trees tainted by the rape of a girl I knew. Sam was dead. Leaving this living nightmare was the only solution.

On the way home, a horde of birds flew overhead, seeking the protection and tranquility of the field and its trees. I felt a pang of regret stab me in the gut and thought of Marla.

My thoughts went to the reminders of sex I tried to bury, but they always surfaced. I pushed hard to keep them away, but the thoughts would push back and come in a rush.

Mother, the sex, and then the floodgates would open. The stranger's mouth on me. The babysitter with her underwear around her ankles, kneeling and sucking so hard it hurt.

We were often left alone while Mother was out drinking with one of the many people in the neighborhood that drank as well. Although it never seemed to me that they drank as much as her. Sometimes, when Mother was at Mrs. Dowling's, her youngest daughter Sachi would come over to the house. She would say that Mother had sent her to check on us, but I knew better. Mother would have never cared enough to have anyone come and check on us. She never would have even thought of it.

Sachi was probably sixteen or seventeen. A plump girl who liked to wear shirts cut off just under her breasts with no bra and her belly hung over the front of her jeans like a muffin-top. Carter would tell me in private that he liked her boobs. He would say, "I like them titties. I like them titties a lot."

She would put Lynn to bed. When he got tired, Carter would trundle off to bed as well. Sachi then would coax me into staying up and say she would get me something from the corner store just down the street, like an ice cream or sweet cake. She would, too, and bring it back to the house. I would eat it fast before she could take it back. Afterwards, Sachi would just start looking at me funny, sort of with her head down and her eyes looking up. I remember thinking it was kind of cute in a way. She would then get really quiet and slide down her pants and then her underwear, if she were wearing any. Sometimes, she wasn't.

I would see the deep red cris-crossing lines around her stomach where the skin was all bunched up because her pants were too tight. It looked painful. I'd look away because I didn't want to see her naked and also because I knew what was going to happen next.

She would then get on her knees and take down my underwear. Usually, I was wearing only a pair of underwear and an old t-shirt. Sometimes, she would giggle, but mostly she just put her mouth over me and made sucking sounds. The pain was enormous, but I would not cry out. If I did, Carter or

Lynn might come out of their bedrooms. They would see what Sachi was doing and that I was not stopping her.

More strangers. Faceless men and women. Men Mother would bring home from the bar. Women who visited from the neighborhood and drank with Mother. Shoving my hand inside themselves while wiggling on their backs, moaning and laughing at the same time. Their breasts sagging like their bellies. And Mother always within only a few feet away, hidden in some other room. Sometimes she would be with a man and sometimes alone, but she always knew when to come out – after they had finished. When it was all over, she would collect the money. And I saw, she would collect the money from the ladies too.

With the thoughts of Marla still lingering, I was nearly home. By the time I reached our house, I really started to doubt Lauren was going to take us in. As a matter of fact, I never really believed Mother would have let us go without a fight. Not out of love, but out of spite.

"Come here, Gregg!" Mother was standing with her hands firmly against her hips. "Were you and Carter fighting?" she said in her most righteous tone. "I don't tolerate fighting in this house!"

For a long time I did not answer. I just stood there looking at the ground and listening to her breathe really hard through her false teeth. I did not know what to say. There was never a good answer. We were fighting, and if I lied Mother would see right through me. If I told the truth, it would be the same fate. So I just stood there and waited. I waited for what she had already set her mind to do long before I came back from the field.

She continued to stand on the porch with her hands on her hips and staring down at me. The last light of the day was fading. "Get in this goddamn house," she said, turned and walked inside.

I followed her, stopping on the small dirty and peeling square of linoleum just past the door. With what strength I had left in my voice I squeaked out, "I'm sorry, Mamma. We were just wrestling." It was a lie, but panic set in and it was all I had left.

Lynn was wrapped in an old winter coat and sitting on the floor. Carter was sitting on the couch. Mother stood only inches from me.

"Don't you say another goddamn word," Mother said and grit her teeth so hard I could hear them grind together. "I'm going to beat you black and blue."

"Mom, no," Lynn whimpered.

When Mother grabbed for me, I threw my hands instinctively in front of my face and then let them fall to my side. The life had run from me, and I felt I no longer even had the strength left to protect myself.

Suddenly, she stopped. It was Carter that caused her to pause for a moment by letting out a killer scream that filled the house. It sounded as if the roof had been ripped off. That was all it took for her to change direction and now focus on him. Carter was at an age when he was coming into his own. He just looked at Mother with an expression on his face that was both anger and something that could break your heart. He clenched his fists, and he too grit his teeth. If not for the little beads of sweat at his temples, you'd think he was not afraid, but he was. Mother looked confused as if her only ally betrayed her – like they had some sort of secret bond, and Carter just broke it. Mother then walked to the couch, sat down, and told us all to get out. We quietly filed one by one out the front door. I was filled with relief, but I knew it was only temporary.

When we reached the sidewalk leading to the porch, we heard a loud bang, and the door was shut and locked behind us. Although it was still summer, the nights grew cool. Lynn was still wrapped in the old winter coat. The sleeves dangled empty. Carter and Lynn were not wearing shoes. The three of us stood in the fading orange light, looking at the ground and wondering what to do.

"We'll sit under the awning in the back," Carter said. Again, one by one, we rounded the corner of the house, passing the old wooden gate, and found our places under the awning. We sat on old lawn chairs and at a broken picnic table. We did not speak. There was nothing to say. We just had to wait until Mother let us back inside.

Normally, I would have been peering through the kitchen window in order to check on Mother and make sure she wasn't trying to burn the house down or commit suicide. But at first, it didn't seem to be in me anymore. However, it was still there a little, and I felt the twinge of fear creep inside me and tell me that Mother was probably cutting her wrist right now. Yet I was so tired.

The twinge in my gut told me that at least a part of me was lying. Despite my realization that I could live without her, I still couldn't let go. Although I was tired, I still loved her. It had been eleven years with Mother. It was the love part that forced me to get up and walk to the window on the side of the house and peer in.

I shimmied up the wooden gate and leaned over, bracing myself on the small ledge of the window frame in order to look inside. When I did, my blood ran cold.

Mother was sitting on an old bench behind the kitchen table and facing the window. She was just staring at a knife and turning it slowly in her hand. I went to slam my fist against the glass and plead for her to stop as I had done so many times before, but before I did our eyes met. Mother saw me looking, and it was then she put the point of the knife against her breast. She had been waiting for me. Expecting me to look through the window. The sham was uncovered.

When she saw me just staring and doing nothing to stop her, she threw the knife at me. It clattered against the glass, making me jump and lose my balance. I fell to the ground, and before I could get back up, I heard her angry voice calling me inside.

Carter and Lynn were behind me now and followed as I walked toward the front door. When we rounded the side of the house and turned to walk up the steps of the porch, we saw Mother standing in the doorway.

"Not you two fucking bastards – him," and she pointed her crooked finger at me.

I walked inside and was rendered a hard slap to the back of my head, as a prelude to what lie ahead. Carter and Lynn stood at the bottom of the porch, quietly pleading with their eyes. When Mother slammed the door, I caught a glimpse of Lynn and saw she was crying.

"Take off your clothes . . . all of them."

Mother spoke in a low angry tone, but you could also hear the excitement in her voice.

"No, Mommy," I said, but was already pulling off my shirt.

Mother's face reminded me of Jonny Noost. He was a boy from down the street, who I had once watched stick a pin in a toad's leg. His eyes danced with excitement as the toad limped around. It made me sad when I saw the toad hop and the leg with the pin in it sort of drag behind, trying to catch up.

Mother could not wait, telling me to hurry so I removed the last of my clothing as quickly as I could. I now stared at the carpet, cupping my small genitals.

"Let me see that winkie, you little queer. Let me see what the men suck," she said grinning, and I could see her false teeth were jutting slightly out of her mouth. Then, using a sucking technique, she righted them underneath her gums. Before I could move my hands out of the way, she rendered two rapid slaps to my groin that forced my own hands to slam against my testicles. There was an arc of light that flashed behind my eyes as the pain shot down my legs and then up into my gut like hot lead. I fell to the floor feeling sick and all done in. Drained and worn down, I only wanted the pain to go away and this to be the end.

"You have a little winkie," Mother whispered, now hovering over my body, as I lay curled in a fetal position to one side.

"How can you put that in a woman?"

She then put her arm under my neck and pulled me upward into a sitting position. The room swam and I nearly fell backward again, but she jerked me forward and held me upright.

"Cross your legs like an Indian." Her words swam in and out of my head like the room.

She continued to speak quietly.

"Have you had enough?" she said sweetly.

"Yes," I answered, still reeling from the sickening pain in my belly.

"No. No, Gregg, you haven't."

And with one hand squeezing my shoulder to keep me straight, she reached down with the other and grabbed hold of my penis with her thumb and forefinger. "Move your hands out of the way . . . Mommy is going to see if you're okay."

Her voice never lost that sweet pitch to it, which made it sound even more crazy. She didn't pinch, but instead gently pulled the loose skin forward and backward. It was worse than the hitting and slapping. I pushed her hands away. I could not go through with it.

My defiance enraged Mother. Letting go of my penis, she landed a slap across my face, knocking me backward to the floor. Compared to the rape, the slap actually came as a relief. Again holding my genitals, I rolled to one side. Taking a handful of my hair on the back of my head, Mother twisted my face toward hers with one quick jerk. Leaning into me, our mouths almost touching, Mother whispered, "I'm going to kill you tonight."

I did not say a word. I just kept hoping that she would not touch my genitals again. The alcohol was thick on her breath, pungent and sickening. Our mouths were so close, her breath became my own. My stomach lurched and a puke burp escaped my throat, causing Mother to back away from my face. She stood up kicking me once, telling me to get up and go to bed. I did, and later that evening, when Carter crawled into bed next to me, the shame was so great I pretended to be asleep.

With my eyes squeezed tightly together, I lie very still and awake next to my brother. Minutes later, I listened as Carter's breathing slipped into the familiar pattern of sleep. An hour had gone by, maybe two, and I was still awake. Carter grunted as if dreaming and rolled over. I held my breath and waited for him to settle again. When I felt it was safe to open my eyes, I looked around the dark room and watched the moon shadows dance along the walls and ceiling. I watched with eyes wide open. I watched and waited for Mother.

I did not have to wait for long. Mother came to the door and stood, saying nothing. What little courage I had earlier to push her hands away had left me. I understood completely and crawled quietly from the bed not wanting to wake Carter. We walked in silence to her bedroom with me following closely behind. Mother had told me she was going to kill me this night – and in a way she did.

CHAPTER FOURTEEN

THE NEXT AFTERNOON, I HID inside the old closet leading to the attic and smeared lotion on my raw genitals. The lotion stung my penis. I wanted to stay in the closet forever.

There was suddenly movement in the bedroom, and I stopped dead with my hand greasy from lotion, cupping my groin. I was scared to death I would be caught in this position, but I was too afraid to move. Through the rickety door of the closet, through its broken slats, I watched Mother step into the bedroom. I backed up as far as possible, pressing my body against the far wall and continued peering through the slats. Mother was clad only in a pair of worn underwear. Her breasts sagged and were terribly wrinkled. In her hand was a bottle – half-empty. She appeared to be waiting for someone. I kept perfectly still. Seconds later, in walked a stranger.

"Don't fuck with me!" Mother shouted to the man.

"Here! Here's the money!" the man said and forcibly shoved a wad of something in her free hand. His speech was as slurred as Mother's.

Mother set the bottle on an old dresser, and they both fell into bed. I turned and looked away as she pulled off her dirty panties, throwing them to the floor. Afterwards, I could hear them both thrashing around. The man was grunting.

"Hurry up!" Mother demanded, and the man's grunting intensified. I covered my ears with my hands, but could not shut out the noise. My head was bent down and I saw that I still had not pulled up my underwear. Too afraid to move, I just closed my eyes. Closed them hard. I was faint and fought back a nauseating feeling.

"Get the fuck off me!" Mother said after the man apparently had finished.

"Fucking whore," the man grumbled and pulled on his pants.

There was an exchange of curses from both of them, and the man left the room. I could hear him push past the battered front screen door, which banged hard against the side of the house. A car door slammed. Then, there was the sound of a car driving off, and soon afterwards, Mother shouted to the room, "I've been raped!"

Despite the hint of false terror in her slurred words, had I not been in the closet, I may have believed her. I would have at least tried. It would have been easier to do so. Knowing she was lying made what had just taken place much worse.

I sat perfectly still. Too afraid to make a sound, I knew if Mother found me in the closet with the lotion and my genitals exposed, she would beat me into unconsciousness, accusing me of spying on her sex act with the man. I waited, and although it seemed like hours instead of minutes, Mother finally left the room. I watched as she slipped back into her underwear, grabbed the bottle off the dresser, and staggered out of the room.

I listened and heard Mother finish dressing in the living room. Where she had allowed the man to undress her, not caring if her children walked in on them. I listened until I heard her walk through the kitchen and then out the back door. I heard the scrape of metal against concrete as she fell into the lawn chair under the awning in the backyard. I listened. Leaned forward and nearly vomited, and then, I listened some more.

Pulling on my underwear and a pair of Carter's too big for me hand-me-down swim trunks, I gently opened the closet door and slid off the small platform, and down onto the bedroom floor. The room smelled of sex and decay. The man's cologne hung in the air and mixed with the smell of Mother's scent. A scent I could no longer seem to wash completely off my hands.

Quickly walking from the bedroom, I made a beeline for the front door in the opposite direction of where Mother was in the backyard. Before leaving the house, I popped on my tennis shoes near the door, not bothering to try and tie the laces. I wore an old tank top and no socks. Standing in our front yard, I could hear the faint musical sound of the ice-cream truck one block over behind Kyle's house. It would be rounding the corner soon and my empty stomach grumbled in protest.

Kyle was in his front yard setting up their sprinkler and waved for me to come over and I crossed the street. The temperature was screaming hot and I thought the water would feel good, especially on my sore genitals from Mother's rough sex the night before. Kyle turned the squeaky water faucet counter-clockwise until it would not turn any more. There was a low groan from the exterior of the house and the hose attached to the sprinkler swelled. Then came a hissing sound as a horizontal row of holes across a silver oscillating arm suddenly shot thin streams of water into the air. Both Kyle and I screeched with delight.

Bracing for the cold water, Kyle and I were readying ourselves to sprint through the vertical threadlike jets, when the ice-cream truck came lumbering down the street clanging loudly. Mrs. Jacobson surprised us by coming outside and offered up a whole dollar for Kyle and I to share for ice-cream. In no time at all, Kyle and I, red faced and already getting sunburned, were standing shy of a few other kids at the window where the man in white would exchange the dollar for treats.

I remember Kyle handing the man the dollar and quickly shoving the change in his trunks, and I remember the ice cream cone I got, but not the flavor. Then I shot around the front of the truck, having only licked the cone maybe once, and a car that had been driving past the truck hit me. It clipped my left arm, the one holding on to the ice cream cone, and spun me around like a top. I forgot all about the ice-cream that went flying out of my hand and landed someplace a great distance from where I was standing. I hardly remember the car hitting me, but I remember the suddenness of it and wailing like a banshee. And how I almost passed out right in the middle of the street, cradling my left arm that already felt twice as big as my right.

All that I had wanted was to eat the ice-cream before it melted. Before my siblings saw I had gotten one. Before Mother had seen, most of all. I hadn't bothered to look before running into the street and had not seen the car until after it struck my arm. The sound of tires screeching did not register in my mind until afterwards. Until after the earth began to spin much faster, and then, there was the hot ache in my left arm, and the earth went on spinning.

The driver had stopped and jumped from the car and ran to me while I slowly pulled myself up in the bright June light. He was frantically feeling my body and apologizing. He looked very afraid, and his head kept darting around as if trying to find someone. I ran from him crying and toward our house. I do not know when Mother had come from the backyard, but she was now standing on the porch. She did not run to me, only stood there.

When I bolted past her, she moved slightly and let me go inside. From inside the living room, I heard the driver just outside the front door apologizing to Mother. She mumbled something and he left. Mother came inside the house. I was sitting on the loveseat holding my arm and trying very hard to stop crying. She told me to lie down, and I did. On my back, I let my badly swollen arm lay across my chest giving myself a one-arm hug. It felt heavy.

The sun was going down, leaving slanted shadows of purple light across the living room, giving it a sense of summer shade. I tried to will the fingers of my swollen arm open, but the pain was too great, causing me to writhe, and white light flooded my brain. I was within an inch of screaming and bit down hard, sucking in air through my clenched teeth. The tears ran from my eyes, slipping down my cheeks and into my ears, tickling and making them pop. I never imagined I could sleep with pain like this, but I was wrong, and soon I fell blissfully asleep.

When I woke, Mother sat in a chair, regarding me coldly over a lit cigarette, holding a glass of wine. Carter and Lynn sat side-by-side in another chair with worried faces.

Carter spoke. "You were hit by a car."

Sharp stabs of pain pricked at my left arm.

Lynn was talking now. "Gregg, you were hit by a car."

Then I was falling asleep again. Going. Going away from the room. Mother was still watching me and smoking. Quiet. Too quiet. Lynn was crying. Carter looked worried. I was listening to the wind outside. It sounded like blowing rain. Lynn was talking. Talking. Talking. The drummer in my head beating louder. Mother sitting and staring, smoking one cigarette after another, drinking. And then everything was blotted out.

Again, I awoke. I was so hot. Turning my head slightly toward her, I saw Mother get up from her chair and walk over to me. She balanced a glass of wine in one hand while a cigarette jutted from her fingers. It struck me odd both the glass and cigarette were in her left hand. *She's right handed,* I thought and again went away. Falling. Falling.

I was drifting in and out of sleep, and when I awoke again, Mother was kneeling next to the loveseat. She rubbed my leg with her right hand and looked into my face. Suddenly, she turned toward where Carter and Lynn were sitting and sent them to bed. They left the room and waved when passing by. I watched them go and took a deep breath. My swollen arm, still lying across my chest, moved and felt as if it would split open.

"Your arm is just bruised," Mother said, smiling, and I saw the lipstick caked between her teeth. It looked like blood. She got up and looked toward the bedrooms. Waited a moment, then turned, and knelt down beside me once again. Placing her glass on the floor, she casually plopped her cigarette into what was left of the wine, which produced a short hissing sound.

Mother then unexpectedly cupped the hand that once held her glass firmly over my mouth. With her other hand, she gripped my swollen arm and squeezed hard. I recall the taste of tobacco on her palm, and then there was nothing but pain. Pain followed by peace. Falling. Falling, and then finally gone.

CHAPTER FIFTEEN

A S THE WEEKS WENT ON, our interaction with Kyle, Louis, and Alexis dwindled down to almost nothing. We rarely ever saw them, even though they lived right across the street from us. On one level, the isolation bit deep and left me angry, but there was also the relief of hiding away and not having them see me. The older I got, the more aware of my situation I became and the more ashamed. As I grew older, shame turned into rage. The more I thought about the abuse, especially the sex, the more the rage built up inside me. It strangled me and clawed at my skin.

Kyle's parents stopped their children from even playing at our house. Mrs. Jacobson, once warm and friendly, now seemed distant and cold to me, Carter, and Lynn. Mr. Jacobson was no longer tender and polite. He seemed cold as well.

We were giving up. Mother was cutting away at our will to live. Even Carter began to lose weight at an alarming rate. His clothes, once snug, now hung loose. We wore our poverty in plain view and did not try to hide it any longer. We were victims of Mother's great and terrible energy. We were alone with a monster in the house, and every moment with her became a fight to get my breath back. I missed playing with Kyle. Time spent was always with Mother, and the best of these times was when she was not a monster or a mother – the best times were when she was asleep. But this was no longer enough.

I was alone in the backyard. "One more time she beats you," that's what Jessica had said. "One more time, and I'll come and take you away from her."

Jessica would have taken us away that same day if I had broken down right there on the spot when she made her promise. However, I was a child and thought like a child. I took her words literally and believed I had to wait for that one more time. In addition, I had grown so used to hiding my feelings away that I couldn't come totally clean with her. It would have meant telling her everything. I could have told her about the beatings, but not the sex. I just wasn't able to do that.

Another part of me felt that even telling Jessica about the worst of the beatings would not have been enough to convince her. I had grown so used to the lies that I was afraid if Jessica did not see fresh blood from some ragged, wandering gash across my face, she was never going to help us. I had been beaten repeatedly since Jessica's promise, but I did not call her. I just couldn't get up the nerve.

I was in the backyard standing next to the lilac bush. It was in full bloom and normally I would have taken in the exotic scent and found it both pleasing and relaxing. Instead, the smell rose up in my nose and filled my throat, making me gag and eventually vomit.

As I stared at the fresh pool of vomit on the grass near the lilac bush, I knew I had to draw the beating. I knew it was time.

My nerves were on edge, and I vomited again while hanging on to the cyclone fence that separated our yard from the neighbors. I recall thinking dully that I hoped they were not home. Another dry heave told me there was nothing left to throw up. I buckled over from the gut-wrenching act and folded my arms across my belly. Then, standing up slowly, I unfolded my arms and let them dangle by my side. Breathing in and out deeply, I reached inside the front pocket of my pants and felt the two dimes I had been saving to call Jessica. I turned and abruptly started for the back door.

I'm going to do it, I said to myself. *I'm going to make her mad and draw the beating.* I went into the house. It seemed the only thing left to do, and even then, I waited for something to stop me. A sign of sorts that would tell me I didn't have to do this. Nothing came. Only Mother was in the living room. Carter and Lynn were not home. Now only the two of us. Again. Mother was leaning to one side of the couch and mumbling when she saw me. My eyes were fixed on her. She made no pretense of listening to what I was saying.

"Mom, why do you drink?" I said again. This time louder and still just above a whisper. I had no breath left in me. My mouth was dry, and it quivered. She heard this time. I could tell by the way she stopped mumbling and stared right through me. I panicked and nearly took it all back. Almost begged for mercy and recanted what I just said, but it was too late.

"What the fuck did you just say?" she asked abruptly. I stood silent, looking down at the floor.

"How dare you question me!" Her voice squeaked when it reached an unbelievable pitch, quavering just a bit. She was in utter disbelief and still trying to get her mind around the question. Moreover, the fact I would ask it in the first place. It was the perfect question, and one that came to me only after entering the room seconds before. I knew it would cut deeper than any other.

"Come here, you little cocksucker!" She was literally shaking with anger, ready to explode. At first, she only sat on the couch, screaming at the floor. Suddenly, she stopped screaming, looked directly at my face, and glared. Then unexpectedly, in one smooth and fluid motion, Mother lunged, clearing the coffee table and hitting my chest with full force.

I fell backward, and my body smacked the floor, absorbing our combined weights. There was a quick flash of light and the sound of rushing air escaping my lungs. Straddling my body, Mother positioned herself directly above me, slapping at my face. With every slap, light and dark wrestled with one another behind my eyes as if watching a torch fall down a long dark well. We were crotch to crotch, Mother bending forward slightly, while she continued slapping at my face. Left and right. Back and forth. Over and over. Every now and again, raking her cigarette-stained nails across my cheeks. I felt the scratches on my skin and both Mother and I were sweating. The sweat ran into the fresh scratches, making them sting and causing a deeper ache.

Thankfully, Carter came home, and seeing Mother, he shouted for her to get off me. His voice was harsh and throaty. Standing bent over and directly behind her, he then immediately locked his arms around her small shoulders and tried to pull her off. Mother instantly snapped her head back, rendering Carter a solid butt to the nose, causing Carter to squeal in pain. A covet of blood shot from his nostrils and onto Mother's back.

Carter continued to shout and pull at Mother, turning his face from side to side in an attempt to avoid more of her head butts. "Run!" he shouted.

Mother's weight kept me pinned down with my arms locked to my side, and I could not move. Carter lunged backward while holding tightly onto Mother and managed to pull her off me.

"Run!" Carter shouted again.

This time I managed to wiggle free, and knowing he could not hold her for long, I desperately struggled to stand. I managed to pull myself to my feet, hung my head over them until the world swam back into focus, then half-staggered, half-crawled to the front door.

Once outside, the sun burned the cuts on my face, and my head was throbbing. I looked toward the corner where the pay phone was. *I can't make it,* I thought and started to cry. I dropped to one knee and tried to catch my breath. I knelt in the yard for a moment, gathering myself, and then rose to a standing position. I again headed for the pay phone.

Suddenly, through the haze of pain, I heard Mother burst through the screen door. I turned just in time to meet her wide-open gaze.

"Get the fuck back in here!" she shouted.

This got me moving again. I headed toward the corner store as quickly as I could.

Mother shouted threats, and I heard them even as I crossed the street at the end of our block. I remember looking both ways, but could not see because of the tears standing in my eyes and they were nowhere near letting up. So, as best I could, I hurriedly crossed and hoped a car would not come along and hit me. I reached the edge of the small parking lot and on unsteady legs, I walked over to the bright silver *Bell* pay phone.

Sobbing violently, I reached inside the pocket of my pants and was immediately filled with dread. The dimes were gone. I tried the other pocket. Nothing. I again switched to the pocket I was sure I had placed the dimes earlier that morning. On a few occasions, I had come close to spending them on sweets, and even though my stomach gnawed at itself when thinking about it, I did not.

After shoving both my hands as hard as I could into both my front pockets at the same time, I finally happened upon the dimes. They were in the pocket I had placed them originally. With unsteady fingers, I dropped the first dime into the slot and dialed Jessica's number. She answered. My throat locked and I could not make a sound. She hung up after saying hello two, maybe three times.

One dime remained for one more call. Dropping the second and last dime I had into the slot, I dialed carefully, and Jessica answered again, obviously irritated by a crank caller. I managed a few broken words and then heard only silence, followed by dial tone.

Placing the phone back into its cradle, I gathered what strength I had left. While clutching at the air in order to breathe, I walked to the rear of the store where there was a garden hose attached to the building. The keeper used it to rinse the small asphalt parking lot. Not caring if the keeper came outside, I turned the knob and waited for the water to gush from the nozzle. There was a bad moment when the water did not come, but then eventually it did. After a whoosh of air followed by a few spits of spray, a steady stream of water began to run from the hose. I waited as the water went from warm to cool. Holding the hose, I watched the clear water rush past and brought it carefully to my lips. I drank greedily. I drank the cold water until my belly cramped.

To ease the pain in my beaten-up face, I splashed a handful of cool water over it. Afterwards, I turned the faucet clockwise until it locked into place. I thought for sure the keeper would come running from his store as soon as he heard the high-pitched squeal of the water being pinched off in the pipe. He did not. I dropped the hose, which made a hollow clinking sound on the asphalt, and began to walk toward home.

I slowly walked past the silver *Bell* pay phone and over the small square of asphalt that made up the parking lot of the corner store that was only able to fit maybe three or four cars at the most. Across the street and past the first three ticky-tacky houses, and there I stopped. I stopped short of a line of shrubs and hid, peering around just enough to catch a glimpse of Mother still standing on the porch. Not sitting. Standing. She was intent on finishing this.

Lynn must have come home while I was at the pay phone calling Jessica. I watched Carter and Lynn walking away from the house and toward me. When they got closer, I stepped slightly into view so they could see me.

"Mom wants you home," Carter said.

I saw in his face that he was just delivering the message, but did not feel it should be honored. His nose looked twice its normal size and it was beet red. There was dried blood on his chin and the front of his shirt. Carter's blue eyes were wet and shiny.

"Mom said we're both in big trouble," Carter said.

I figured he avoided a beating for holding her down just long enough to come and fetch me. I was pretty sure he was going to pay later.

Lynn was by his side. "Tell me we're going away, Gregg," Lynn said, and the tears ran down her cheeks. "Tell me!" she pleaded, and I broke from the weight of regret. My plan failed. Believing the call never got through to Jessica, I was consumed by remorse and took my anger out on Lynn.

I replied, "Fuck you!" – and immediately felt the terrible weight of even more guilt for responding this way.

Lynn recoiled from the outburst, but stayed next to Carter. Still hidden by the shrub, the three of us waited. By the time Jessica's familiar car rounded the corner behind us, we were all weeping uncontrollably.

CHAPTER SIXTEEN

JESSICA ROLLED TO THE CURB and from the car told us to meet her at the house. With one look, she knew whatever had happened had started with Mother. I wiped the snot from my nose, and the three of us started walking home. When Jessica turned into the driveway, Mother darted in the house. We watched as Jessica got out of her car, walking briskly and bent-over with her fists pumping back and forth as she went. She strode with a purpose, and I was filled with a mixture of joy, terror, and sorrow.

By the time the three of us walked into the house, Jessica had Mother pinned down on the couch, and it looked like she was choking her with her own collar. Mother just looked up at Jessica, as if in some sort of stupor, and pretended she did not understand what was going on. I do not remember all of what Jessica said, but I do recall it involved a lot of cursing. Mother just sat there the whole time, quiet, watching Jessica's face. Every now and then Jessica would pop Mother in the mouth with her hand, and I would flinch. That was the first time I saw Mother take guff from anyone. Dad was ten times Jessica's size and Mother would fight him. However, she did not fight Jessica. Mother appeared to be somewhat afraid, but mostly docile and shockingly apologetic. It looked like all the fight had finally gone from her – as if she had finally ran out of all the hate that made her strong all these years.

Then Mother just started laughing with this detached look on her face. Carter, Lynn, and I just stood off to the side and watched with confused horror. None of us knew what to do, and I was actually afraid for her. I was relieved when Jessica finally let go of Mother's shirt, but then suddenly, with split-second timing, Jessica hauled off and landed a hard slap across Mother's face.

"Don't hurt her!" I screamed.

Afterwards, I was afraid Jessica would get mad at me for sticking up for Mother and just leave, but she did not. Instead, she just kept yelling at Mother, letting loose all those things pent up inside her for far too long.

Many of the things Jessica said I had already heard from my older sisters – usually right before they stormed from the house for the last time. However, some of the things Jessica was saying I had not heard. Some of the accusations I wish I had never heard. Like how Father had raped Jessica and Lauren, and how Mother had allowed this to take place. That made me think of the stranger – and Mother in the next room, laughing when I passed by.

Jessica told us to go outside and wait in the car. I pleaded with her again not to hurt Mother. She did not respond to my plea, instead just said that she would be right behind us. Silently, my siblings and I walked from the house. I did not realize it would be the last time.

Carter went first, followed by Lynn, then me. I was staring at Mother the entire time. We descended the crumbling steps of the porch and into a thick smell of gasoline coming from Jessica's old car motor that was still running. We climbed inside the backseat, and I watched the day end its life through a stained red sun slipping beneath the horizon.

We waited anxiously for Jessica while I secretly hoped she would not hurt Mother. Minutes that seemed like hours went by, and Jessica finally came outside. She climbed behind the wheel of the car and put it into gear. As we backed out of the driveway, Mother walked outside and stood on the porch, folding her arms as she did. I breathed a sigh of relief and heard Carter do the same. The car swung into the street, and Jessica changed gears. Mother smiled, lifting an arm to wave as we drove away.

From the backseat of the car, in between Carter and Lynn, I turned and faced out the back window as we continued to drive away. Mother was still standing on the porch and waving. I slowly lifted my hand and waved back. We rounded the corner, and she was gone.

Now facing forward, I stared down at a pair of hand-me-down shoes, much too large for my feet. Laces undone and hanging past the worn rubber soles. It was dusk, shadows were thickening, and I could see the first face of a bloated moon. My cheeks burned from the cuts left by Mother's nails.

Beside me, Lynn is crying. Carter stares out the window. I attempt to speak but cannot find my voice. My throat is hard and dry. Jessica looks at me in the rearview mirror, shakes her head in disgust, and then turns her eyes back on the road. On we drive toward Jessica's, where the next day we will leave with Lauren. Behind me is a past that is still not done. Behind me is Mother. Alone.

We drive without speaking to one another. I struggle to gather up all the force I have left to fight the impending panic that threatens to suffocate me. The day's events rush in and out of my mind. I try and cast them aside, only to have each ugly event come back even stronger than before. I examine what I've done and start crying. Jessica pulls the car over and drags me from it. I can only stop crying long enough to choke up the vomit that had been boiling in the pit of my belly.

Back in the car, I'm freezing. I roll into a ball and try to become invisible between Carter and Lynn.

As we drive further away from Mother's, the air seems to soften. I speak, but uneasily now. Stomach acid stings the back of my throat, and I have to keep swallowing to ease the pain. We pass more tacky houses and eventually the railway tracks, then on to the highway. The windows are down, and a warm wind blows. Holding my face up toward the open car window, I let the wind dry my eyes and breathe in slowly.

We hurry faster down the highway. Picking up speed. Jessica wants to get home. She wants this night to be over. The moon is blurred by passing clouds. I'm growing more anxious. We hurry.

The warm wind blows. Inside me, there is something familiar stirring. Longing. I now know what it is. At last, it comes to me while we hurry away.

I want to go home. Mother needs me.

Book II
1975 – 1985

God Must Be Sleeping

For Sarah, who is with me to the end and waits for me in Mousatonia.

The world is a dangerous place to live, not because of the people who are evil, but because of the people who don't do anything about it.

-Albert Einstein

CHAPTER ONE

The Most Terrible Light

"In the far corners of resting and wakefulness, there is a puny, abject, shuddering figure, distorted of visage, deformed of shape, disheveled and unkempt of appearance. Perchance I knew then that this was me."

WE HURRY FASTER DOWN THE highway. Picking up speed. Jessica wants to get home. She wants this night to be over. The moon is blurred by passing clouds. I'm growing more anxious. We hurry.

The warm wind blows. Inside me, there is something familiar stirring. Longing. I now know what it is. At last, it comes to me while we hurry away.

I want to go home. Mother needs me.

At the point we rounded the corner of Jessica's street and her small wooden-framed house was in view, only a few miles from where I lived with Mother for the last eleven years of my life, I realized it was too late to change what I had done. By now, the weight of guilt was overwhelming. I jammed the small stubs of my fingers hard against both my eyes to stave off the tears. I made every effort to run down the events over the past few hours, but they kept coming back in fragments; except one. I had betrayed Mother. I used her rage to help orchestrate the escape and this made what I did feel like a trick. Using her weakness against Mother was indeed trickery. Just another form of deception. Manipulation at its rawest and what made it worse was that I became exactly like Mother in order to execute my plan of getting away. I was too young to understand that it was the only way we would have survived, but being only a boy –a lie was a lie.

Upon rolling into Jessica's driveway, I gave up trying not to cry. Jessica barked something and soon my brother, sister and I were filing into her house. No one spoke. I had also given up believing my siblings and I had a chance.

The elation of opportunity, which once burned inside me, was now dead. I wasn't interested in finding that hope again, now gone from me, somewhere within the limits of nothing more than a fleeting thought. I had hunted for a way out for the past three years and discovered now that the planning of our escape meant more to me than actually realizing it. Within minutes of finding a dark corner of the living room, I sat down and waited. Waited for my next move. Waited for someone to tell me what to do.

"There!" said Jessica aloud, straightening her shoulders and belting out a jagged laugh. "It's done. You're rid of that goddamn bitch!"

From the other side of the room, Carter was turning the knob of the television making a *ker-chunk* sound with each successive turn of the silver dial. I don't remember if the sound was on or off. Lynn sat next to me grasping and un-grasping an old doll she must have taken before leaving Mother's. I felt sick and beaten. Lifting my head wearily, I made sure to offer Jessica up a smile so she would not get upset, then let my chin drop against my chest.

"Goddamnit, Gregg Tyler!" said Jessica. With a burst of audible self-satisfaction, she instructed me to appreciate what she had done for my siblings and me. "What in the fuck do you have to cry about? You're out of that house!"

Then pointing only to me, she bellowed, "Do you want me to take your selfish little ass back to that lunatic of a mother?"

Here she stopped short of saying something else. There were several moments of embarrassing silence. Still her finger pointing accusingly at me, Jessica added bluntly, "You better get your fucking shit together before Lauren gets here tomorrow. She doesn't need your bullshit crying over that fucking cunt you called a Mother."

"That's all right," said Lynn, with a quiver in her tiny voice, as she looked down at her doll. Even at nine years old, Lynn knew everything was different, but in many ways, still the same. We were so afraid and our nerves shot. Completely unaware what lay ahead. The abuse didn't just go away overnight. It lingered and held on – a vice squeezing the life right out of us. And that's how it would be for years to come.

For now it was another night huddled in a strange place with strange people even though we were with family. It was like muddy water in a tin cup you have to drink or die of thirst. You drink it and choke it down because somewhere in that cup there is life. This is how it was for us that night before Lauren would come and get us. With no idea of whether we were going to live or die. No idea if it was going to be better for us or worse. Just choking down that muddy water and hoping it would be better, while we gagged on all that fear of what would come next. The unknown. A small part of us knew it was a chance at survival. And, a bigger part of us knew we were still choking on all that fear.

As we sat in Jessica's living room, something seemed to come to me like a skeletal hand reaching for my throat. For the last eleven years my home was with Mother and more than once I had told myself that life away from her would be impossible. More deeply than ever, this thought came to me tonight because Mother had become a huge part of me. Lonely and sick at heart, I felt the sympathy, and fear too, of Mother creeping into me, grieving with me, pleading with me to change my mind and return to her. With each minute that passed this night, and with each day and night that would follow, Mother would be alone to hurt herself. The fear of this became more real and it painted a picture of her dying.

Making it worse was our uncertainty of how Lauren and her husband Tim would react to us. The years Lauren had been gone must have changed her. Furthermore, the years had changed Carter, Lynn, and myself as well, and not for the better. Each of us felt very strongly that Lauren did not really want us.

Making it worse for me was that I had forced the issue of Lauren taking us in, using every manipulative trick Mother had ever taught me. This, compounded by the fact I was telling the truth. We were really being abused. I was really being prostituted out. Death was possible and as real as the cuts and bruises on my body from past beatings and molestations. The red soreness around my genitals even more proof.

It had been a bad eleven years for me, nine for Lynn and thirteen for my brother. That's thirty-three years of abuse combined and had I known how to read and count back then I would have been playing with the math like I started doing years later. "We all fall down," the nursery rhyme went and I knew the rhyme pretty well. We sang it in school. I hated the part when all of us kids had to hold hands and then literally fall down on the ground at the end of the song. I always felt like I was dying and I always felt strange holding on to another kid's hands. I'd be yanked toward the ground and it always hurt like hell because I was frequently sore from the beatings.

I watched my brother click away at the TV and Lynn fumble with her doll and all I could think about was Mother, praying the whole time in secret she was okay and not dead. I started to get really scared because maybe what happened was going to push her over the edge and she'd not fake killing herself this time but go through with it. It'd be all my fault and even Jessica, who hated Mother would blame me. I let it all get away from me. The plan seemed perfect but not anymore. It seemed so fucking stupid and harmful to the only person I loved most in the whole world. Mother.

"Time for your baths!" yelled Jessica. "Gregg, you go first and wash your face! There's no use bellyaching anymore about what happened and remember what I said!"

She spoke angrily, trying to scare me even more, but Jessica didn't need to try so hard. I was scared shitless. Trying to make Lynn feel better, I told her she could take her doll in the tub when it was her turn. She looked up at me with a pale face and just dropped her head with a sigh.

"There's no way I'm taking a bath in Gregg and Lynn's dirty water," Carter said.

"They'll drain the tub, Carter! Now shut up and wait your turn! And, stop fucking with that goddamn TV!" Jessica snapped.

Carter did as he was told. He settled on a channel and sat back staring at the floor. Still, no sound came from the TV. Just shows I did not recognize because we never had a TV. It didn't matter. I could not have enjoyed them anyway. There was no feeling inside me other than fear and sadness.

I was sick. Not sickness of the ordinary sort. It was in my brain —that's where it was. Eleven years with Mother, and never a glimpse of freedom until maybe now. Eleven years without adequate food, water, and shelter. No love. No hope. Eleven years of just the dead, gray world of abuse with the awful decadence and perversion of strangers taking advantage of me. Their touches and groping hissing inside my head every night like snakes and leaving a black-like emptiness in the pit of my stomach. I knew for sure the sickness in my head would kill me. But not before I suffered a long time in a mental institution like Mother said. It would come after all. I hadn't escaped. The insanity came along with me. It was going to stay inside me until I was nothing more than a crazy boy with mental problems. There was so much truth to this and it was at the core of my fear. There might be death at the end of me losing my mind, but that's all. I was doomed all right and no one knew it but me. Not Carter. Not Lynn. Not my older siblings. Not even God.

Locking the door behind me, I entered Jessica's bathroom. I had not realized I locked the door until I was nearly undressed. It was something which was not allowed at Mother's. It would not have mattered because the only bathroom in Mother's house did not have a lock. It used to. However, after years of Mother kicking in the door, the lock was ripped from its place and was nothing more than twisted metal.

I hurriedly began preparations to take my bath. If I took too long, Jessica would be upset. There was even the fear of her breaking through the door and yanking my naked body from the tub. It was not a real fear, but even imaginary fear was still real enough to suffocate me and leave me gasping for air, clutching my small chest, while the world – like the water in the tub – swam by.

My tub now full, I quickly undressed and climbed into the warm water – not cold like the baths Mother had forced me to take. I lowered my small body into the water and immediately began urinating. It was instinctive. The fear still with me. Still inside me. My tub water was always cold.

Mother once told me the bath water was always cold because Father did not send money to pay the bills. However, the water in her baths was always warm, almost too hot. Forced to watch her bathe, I would stare at the steam coming from the rush of water as it ran from the faucet. It was better watching the water and not Mother undressing and readying herself for the bath. Made to sit on the crooked toilet seat while she took her baths, I would fix my eyes on the hot water gushing into the stained and chipped porcelain tub. Rather this than see the grotesque body of my Mother naked and so vulnerable. The hot water made her body squishy. I hated how my tiny hands would sink into her flesh down to the bone, constantly dragging her upward after she had dropped into the water, having fallen fast asleep.

Submerged in the warm tub at Jessica's with the faint scent of my own urine rising up with the steam, I closed my eyes and thought of nothing but Mother. What I'd give to know she was okay, for just a moment's touch of her hand. I was still so in love with her. Knowing she was safe would drive out this fear, I thought to myself. The loneliness was stifling —a sort of slow torture and it was splitting my heart in two.

"Hurry up!" said Jessica, banging on the bathroom door and startling me so bad, I jumped splashing water up and over the side of the tub. The jolt got me thinking again of Lauren. Got me thinking of what might be coming. Only one more night and I would be even further away from Mother. And then I thought of what new life I would be entering. Wondered if I'd be able to enjoy it because I never had anything like this. No longer Mother's caretaker —what would become of me? There'll be no more saving her. She'll die for sure without me. I believed this with every part of me. I thought maybe I could write her letters, but Lauren would never allow me to send them. I did not write so well, but I knew how to write the words I love you. I miss you.

I waited a little longer in the tub and then sat up. Waited some more. My heart was heavy and I began to cry again. Mother isn't safe any longer. She was kept safe by me and only me. Adding further to this belief were the memories of the many times she nearly died in the tub. Just like the one I was now sitting with my legs tucked up against my chest. Another thought passed through my head. It would be so easy to drop beneath the water, take in a deep breath, and drown.

The next morning, a long time before anyone else got up, I awoke and knew that I was no longer in the bed once shared with Carter at Mother's. There was not the familiar smell of piss and shit. There were not cockroaches scrambling from massive nests under the mattress. There was not the odor of alcohol mixed with cigarettes and sweat in the air. There was only me and a hot lump burned in my throat. Although the bed was clean, I felt strangely uncomfortable because it was not mine. When I opened my eyes there was also no longer Mother standing there quietly watching me sleep, ready to pounce the second she saw me awake. A small bit of sunlight came in under the window curtains. It was day. The day Lauren would be here. This was not the only reason I stirred and awoke. It was because I thought of Mother and how she was alone, probably dead. All of the things that happened the day before came back to me. The plan leading up to leaving Mother, of anticipation, fear, and then longing as we drove away.

I pulled myself out of bed and choked back a cry as not to wake anyone else, but it danced on my lips all the same and made them quiver. I half rose to my feet and then dropped backward. The room swam and I laid crossways with my back to the mattress and my feet dangling over the edge. Touching my shaggy hair, I felt it was slick and greasy, forgetting to wash it when bathing the night before. I poked at my ribcage that protruded from under the oversized shirt used as a sleeper. And, a thought kept coming back to me.

It's my fault.

It's my fault.

The words struck upon my heart with a chill of horror. And then I thought, *They'll find Mother dead, and it will be my fault.*

I could not get the thought out of my head that Mother was dead, and I was as good as dead when they found her. Not just because it had been my fault, but because I still loved her. The line between love and hate was then from time to time an evil made stronger by Mother's abuse. How awful was her voice upon the innocence of a boy's frail shoulders. So, listen carefully. Because it is likely you too will hear me crying. Oh how I wept, in the midst of my own silent screams, my own lonely nights. Weeping and praying, I sang the song of both hope and death. Of which, either would have been my salvation.

Jessica walked past the bedroom door and yelled to the house it was time to get up. It was a cold invitation, lacking warmth or sympathy, and I felt that she wished Carter, Lynn, and me had stayed with Mother. We were a burden to everyone. When I walked from the bedroom and found Jessica in the kitchen, I tried to voice my gratitude and at the same time hide my sorrow. Jessica was looking down at me as I stumbled for the words, and I was sure that she wasn't really paying attention by the look on her face. She just waved it off absently and told me to get ready, leaving the kitchen, with the words still in my throat choking me.

Lynn came wobbling out of where she slept. She walked like a dying old woman, and I noticed her eyes were puffy and red. She was so tiny, and her small thin hands shook as she held them out to me for a hug. I nodded, not saying anything and gave her a squeeze. Coming in behind Lynn was Carter and he brought with him a foul odor even though he bathed the night before. His armpits were stinky. Actually, even though we all bathed, we all still stank and were starving. I did not use the bar of soap in the tub and I'm sure Carter and Lynn did not either. We never had soap before when living with Mother.

Jessica came back into the kitchen finding the three of us together and again told us to hurry and get ready. I quickly forgot my hunger. My pulse was beating quickly. Sensations filled me which I had known for years. I saw Lynn's red eyes fixed on mine, looking up, and I turned my face to escape her questioning, painful gaze. Carter was rummaging through the cupboards. Beyond the kitchen, somewhere in the house a wooden floor creaked, and then we hear the wail of Jessica telling us one last time to get ready. It came to us now as an exasperated sort of sound.

My horror increased when Jessica said Lauren would be there soon. I went to the bedroom to dress in my only pair of presentable clothes, an old Cub Scout uniform. Father had purchased the outfit years before, but I never could go through with attending the meetings held just around the block from where we lived. I couldn't bring myself to be away from Mother. Father never knew. Had he come back home, he would have.

I wanted to make a good impression when Lauren came to pick us up. After dressing, I looked in the mirror and for the first time took notice of myself. I was lame and sickeningly weak. The uniform purchased years before hung on me although I was older and a little taller. Turning from the mirror and leaving the bedroom, I was filled again with a strange uneasiness. I was sure Lauren would not recognize me, and that it would be reason enough to refuse my siblings and me a place to live. I was afraid and shivered visibly from the fear. Too weak to put up a fight, I would simply go back to Mother. She would seize me by the arm the moment I walked into the house, and in a guttural angry voice, just before the beating, there would be an inhuman taunting triumph.

"Didn't think you'd come back, Gregg!" she'd jeer.

"Well, you did, and I've been waiting to get you alone ... remember what I said if you ever left me?" Mother would ask warningly.

"Remember?" she'd say and then rolling a leather belt into tight loops around her bony hand, she would nearly whisper, "Now take your pants down and show me that winkie."

I was convinced that my brother, sister and I didn't stand a chance with Lauren. She wasn't prepared to take us on. How could she? I thought maybe it was better to be sent back to Mother, regardless of what lay waiting for me. It almost seemed easier to take than the anticipated rejection.

Lauren's household would be full already with her husband and their only son. Adding to this lot would be two preteens and one teenager. All of which were carrying a load of emotional and mental baggage. If I knew of my own disturbing problems, then surely Lauren must have her suspicions. Perhaps she fully understood what lay beneath the minds of my siblings and me and had accepted we were damaged goods. *Of course she must know*, I thought. It was obvious my own tics, day-mares, and uncontrollable bedwetting were visible to everyone. Even more apparent was the fact I could not read, write, or tell time. I even struggled to tie a shoestring, never making it past the first loop.

My siblings and I were sick with a strange illness in our heads. At times, even I was convinced I was going insane. It was painfully obvious to me, so Lauren must know this as well. I struggled with understanding how she could take us into her home. How was I to know we would be unwelcomed houseguests from the start. Six years had passed since we last saw Lauren and she was rarely brought up by Mother. If Mother did mention her name, it was to ridicule her. This was common with regard to how my mother spoke of her children, so I didn't pay much attention.

I witnessed my own disorders repeatedly, of which I was an obedient servant. Locked inside a fantasy world, too afraid to come out, I waited on the footstool for the moment when Lauren would take one look at me and refuse to take us in. Folding and unfolding my hands, trying to find the right position, I sat there quietly.

Where are Carter and Lynn? I thought. Suddenly, I realized that I had situated myself on the footstool in the center of the room. It was not like me at all to draw attention to myself like this. I was always more comfortable in the back and often ended up there anyway because I never measured up no matter where I was. Hidden and kept quiet. Unseen and unheard. This had always made me feel so alone and ashamed. Too stupid. Too ugly. Too short. Too smelly. Too fucking strange to be accepted by any group. My family was no different. My brother, sister and I were left with Mother by all of our older siblings. All of whom had gone out of self-preservation. I did not blame them. How could I? I too had left for the same reason.

I scooted the footstool to the edge of the room, trying not to move. Not much longer now. The anxiety and weakness was again upon me. I found it difficult to breathe, and with great effort, dragged the air down into my lungs and pushed it back out. It seemed now as though all ambition had left me and that even the fighting spark that started all this was becoming disheartened. As I waited, a gloom darker and more somber than that of the previous day after leaving Mother was falling about me. The earth seemed to drop away from under my feet and I began to tumble downward.

I'm slipping into a day-mare, I thought. And then there came the panic that if I did, Lauren would see this and refuse me for sure. I pinched my arm hard and it worked, stopping the plunge with a terrific jar. I wanted to cry, but did not. I heard a voice, then two, three, many of them, it seemed. My dazed eyes caught glimpses of dark objects floating in front of them. I knew what they meant. I had fallen into these stupors many times before.

Jessica repeated Lauren was on her way. She would be here soon. Hearing this, I turned my face toward the wall. Something rose up in my throat and choked me as I squeezed my hands together until they hurt, fighting the panic.

"Pull it together, Gregg!" Jessica suddenly cried.

Carter and Lynn were now in the room and Carter moved to stand and look out the window. It reminded me of how he waited so many times before while looking out the window at Mother's – waiting for Father to return.

The stool on rollers wheeled easily on the wooden floor and I spun it toward the front door. Even though I was still sitting, I nearly tumbled from it. Lynn had now joined Carter at the window where they stood together, staring at the driveway through a window that needed washing. It was another one of my many tics. I would fixate on anything dirty or grimy and desperately wanted to clean it. I once stole a sponge from the boy's restroom at school left on top of one of the sinks, and after getting home, I scrubbed the kitchen counters. I remember the anticipation of using the sponge and how excited I was while cleaning.

A faint flash of sunlit chrome shot through Jessica's window and I knew Lauren had just pulled into the driveway. "Lauren's here!" Carter yelled.

"She's here!" Lynn repeated.

"Stop your goddamn yelling!" Jessica said from behind all of us. Followed by, "Sit your asses down!"

Carter and Lynn quickly sat on the couch. Like game show contestants, the three of us sat gazing at the front door waiting in anticipation. I almost puked and stared at my feet fighting the urge. The stinging acid taste lingered in my throat for a few seconds, then died away.

Focusing again, I went back to looking at the front door. Minutes later, Lauren, her husband, and their five-year old son were moving swiftly through the door and into Jessica's living room. Once inside, the room was dead and silent for what seemed an eternity. All of us just staring at each other.

It didn't surprise me in the least Lauren looked upon me, my brother and sister with disdain. So many others from superior environments had done the same throughout our lives. Although I had grown used to this particular look, it continued to sting each time. What little relief I felt from the absence of my mother's abuse was destroyed with that look. I thought we must have reminded her of what she'd run from in the first place. Lauren probably spent the last six years forgetting her past and pretending it never happened.

I tried to call out to Lauren words of greeting, but I had no tongue. My mouth opened wider and the movement drew a sharp exclamation of pain from my jawbone. It was the first real sound I made. Lauren saw it plainly and suddenly I was ashamed. She looked down at me for a moment, her dark eyes and oval cheeks framed between two great sweeps of blond hair, and said nothing. Her skin was so clean and scrubbed that it shone brightly.

Jessica, standing near finally spoke, and directed the three of us to wait outside. Like the condemned, we filed past our two eldest sisters and out the front door. Minutes later, we were sitting in the back seat of Lauren's car. Her husband, Tim, was in the driver's seat. His shoulders were broad and he sat as straight as a tree. His head set and quietly staring directly ahead. Tim's silence was unnerving. A terrible hand gripped at my heart and it felt as though it would stop beating. Like when I was only a few years younger and I had a recurring fear that my heart would stop. I ran frantically everywhere to get it racing again, so that when I put my hand over my chest I could feel its thumping.

I sat motionless, cut into two equal parts. One wanted a chance at this new life and the other wanted to be with Mother. The choice hung over me like a stone. I made an effort to sit up straight, like Tim. From the passenger seat, Lauren motioned goodbye to Jessica. There was a flicker of animation in Jessica's face while she stood on her porch waving. I saw it plainly, her squinting dark eyes looked like they held back a secret.

I did not dare move or breathe in fear Lauren or Tim would change their minds. Sitting next to me was Lynn and the skin of her arm touched mine. Instantly, it gave me some comfort as it always did to be near her. My little sister, who cared for me when I was semi-paralyzed by helping me to the restroom, was always there for me and I for her. Sometimes, I wondered about the four other siblings I may have had, but they died. They had died at birth, two younger and two older. There lived only seven, but what mattered most was Lynn.

Sitting in the car, though next to Lynn, I felt terribly worried. It was death to stray from Mother; hers and mine. However, it was death to stay with her as well. I had spent the last eleven years of my life filled with horror that I would never forget. Lynn was often at my side, but not during the really bad stuff. The molestations, rapes, and prostitution. During these moments, I would keep quiet but for the low moaning sounds of grief that came from me. I did not want Lynn to hear, and afterwards, I would hobble silently to my bed.

Outside the car, the sun rose warm and golden. A summer air blew and I could hear children playing somewhere down the block. Occasionally, there would be a cracking noise and then cheering. At last, the car began to move as we headed toward our new home. As we drove, Lauren sat near the passenger door in the front seat with their only child in between her and Tim. He was only five years old with blonde hair like his mother and was a beautiful little boy. Seeing this, I felt a pang of jealously and anger. We drove in silence, and with each passing agonizing mile, I was driven further away from Mother.

This was the loneliest journey in the world. The trip to Lauren's was a solitary mind-beating heart-wrenching experience. The excursion had but one rival –actually driving toward Mother's instead. Being with Mother or leaving her I discovered was the same feeling. It was the most terrible thing in the world –loneliness. *I will die from it*, I thought. *I will go insane first and then I will die.*

The gloomy truth of this rang true and the panic engulfed me as Lauren's husband guided the car over the roadway. I was afraid for Mother and for me as well. I prayed that Lauren would see my fear and offer some kind words. She did not speak. She did not need to. I could see in her eyes that she found us to be nearer dead than alive.

My eyes were raw from crying and this made Lauren uncomfortable. Blood red showed where there was once a bright green. I had a touch of strangeness about me I could not hide, which is why I'm sure she kept her child from me. From us.

On our way we drove and I wondered if I would have a warm and clean bed. Would we eat on a regular basis? I wondered this as well. Would I be forced to use the restroom in a hurry, as it was when Mother watched and whipped my legs with a belt if I could not urinate or defecate quickly?

My heart was filled with terrible loneliness. My head was filled with mad worry for Mother. I could not sort any of this out. It had happened too fast. The plan. The execution. The abandoning of Mother. There was not just worry for myself, but for my brother and sister as well. I worried about everyone, and the disquiet, like the sickening loneliness within me, grew until it was suffocating. The love I had for Mother was coming back and pushing around all the fear. Pushing it to the side and replacing it with the sweet tenderness of a boy's love for his mother and the tears came into my red swollen eyes once again.

If I could see Mother one more time, I would confess to her that I had made a terrible mistake and I would never leave her again. The loneliness continued to wrestle for a position with the madness of leaving her. I would tell Mother I loved her still and would forever. In my mind, I saw this pleasing Mother and she would change. It would make her a different person. A better person. A good mother. My mother. Upon which this opportunity would be worth the risk of my return and I wanted to tell Lauren to take me back, but I did not have the courage in which to do so. I could not tell Lauren I had changed my mind. Neither was worth the backlash and I knew this to be true. Altogether, returning to a loving mother was always a fantasy of mine, one that would play itself out for years to come. It was a powerful fantasy and my favorite. Worthy of the effort it took to recover from the realization it would never come true.

We reached Lauren's house and being offered no encouragement to leave the car, we did so without being told. It would become a badge of honor for Lauren and her husband to have saved us from certain death at the hands of our mother. In return, we were put to work immediately. Lynn helped Lauren clean the house and prepare dinner. My brother and I began washing the car, sweeping the garage, and weeding the garden. I did not mind. It allowed me time to collect my thoughts. At times, while doing chores alongside Lauren's husband, I tried to make up some sort of conversation. He listened with the lifeless stare of someone who is contemplating an exit at any given moment.

The first night at Lauren and Tim's I slept on the floor. Lauren had put down blankets, and within minutes of spreading out on top of the makeshift bed, I was asleep. Lauren's husband was mesmerized by my sudden unconsciousness and lifted me up by one arm, dangling me for his wife to see. He was laughing and lifting my limp body up even higher. His laughter suddenly stopped after seeing the urine dripping from the crotch of my pants onto the sheets and through to the carpet beneath.

He let me fall with a slump and walked away in disgust. Lauren snapped at me to wake up and shower. When I returned from rinsing off wearing a pair

of shorts far too large borrowed from her husband, she was scrubbing frantically at the urine-soaked carpet wearing rubber gloves. Having just arrived, I
had already shamed myself and felt all hope of earning Lauren and Tim's love
and respect had disappeared.

The next day was no better than the night before. It was the beginning
of summer and to my bewilderment we would need to meet with a lawyer.
There would be a child custody hearing. Mother wanted her three children
back. Lauren, along with the attorney, explained the plan was to prove
Mother was unfit. I had no idea what that meant, but it sounded bad. It also
sounded dangerous for my siblings and me. We would have to testify against
her in a court of law. However, before that, we would have to be questioned
by the attorney. This struck a whole new chord of fear in me. I would have
to tell everything. The prostitution. The molestations. I could not. It would
not be possible. Therefore, I intentionally spoke only of the physical abuse,
poor living conditions, neglect, and starvation. I would concentrate on these
things and speak not a word about the sex.

From the first time I began talking to the attorney I was handicapped by
my inability to sound convincing enough to leave some things out. I was terrified if I did not tell the attorney everything, we would be sent back to
Mother. However, if I did tell him everything, I would die of shame.

For weeks, the attorney picked away at our stories and wrote them all
down on several long thick yellow pads. He searched for signs of weakness and
anything that would give Mother an edge in court. From the first conversation with the attorney, I began to give up what little life I had in me. Any calm
I had tried to find by wandering around the neighborhood those summer days
was vanquished by the attorney's questioning. He was so intense and I cracked
with every question. He would stop long enough to gather his thoughts and
then begin again, and Lauren was always in the background listening, watching, and grinning. She would finally be given the chance to take down the
beast – the bitch that bore her and it was a long-running vendetta.

Blazing over my head screaming was the apprehension that Lauren and
Tim, along with the attorney, would soon find out about the sex. The things I
did with Mother and the strangers. So powerful was this fear, it rifled through
my heart like pistol shots every time I thought the attorney suspected anything.

The new life I had hoped for seemed so far ahead. The days were filled with hours with the attorney and between those lines of his yellow pad there was no life for me. No words of faith. I was reliving the abuse each and every day.

My greatest wish was for all of it to end, and after each session with the attorney, I was filled with a strange and uncomfortable emotion to hurt myself and those around me. I was accustomed to loneliness, but not this feeling of rage. Even when Mother beat me, I would never become angry. However, during that summer there seemed to be something about me that was changing for the worse. Something I had never felt before and it wormed its way deep down into my soul and made my heart beat faster. I was changing from a spectator to a participant. I was turning into my mother and father.

That summer Lauren introduced us to reading. It was and would become the single most influential act she had committed in the building of what would become my educational foundation. From which, all other possibilities became reality. It began at the public library where I along with Carter and Lynn were instructed to check out as many books as we wanted. I could not read. It was a huge embarrassment. Therefore, my first book chosen was *Green Eggs and Ham*. I struggled with each word. However, before long a picture rose slowly in my mind and the words began to make sense. It was the chance I had been waiting for. I was finally fighting a great fight I could win. I was no longer dying of the mental and emotional sickness that comes with loneliness – and appearing for the first time out of the gloom, I saw a picture of hope.

Reading took away the pain of the conversations with the attorney. I could lose myself in fantasy; something I knew a great deal about. New fantasies. A mental and emotional escape. I did not care if the reading was building my mind. All I cared about was it was saving my heart from breaking. I still saw Mother's face and hoped against hope she was alive. But she had failed me and I began to see this too. Perhaps it was written in the pages of the countless books I struggled to read with a dictionary on one side and a thesaurus on the other. Or, perhaps it was something new growing inside of me that was once dormant. Something better than the anger and shame. Something amazing. Someone other than me.

With the attorney's questions now over, soon the court battle would begin. Mother was granted permission to represent herself, which was explained to mean she could ask me questions; any questions she wanted. This filled me with dread, but the chance to see her again after so long filled me with excitement as well. The love for her had still not gone away.

The silence of the room at the courthouse where I now waited was frightening. My hands were wet and clammy and I kept rubbing them on my slacks. If someone shook my hand they would know for sure I was afraid by the wetness.

"They'll need you in a few minutes," Lauren said, when stepping inside the room where Carter, Lynn and I sat. Then she promptly left. After she closed the door, I gave out a loud sigh.

Lauren had spent a lot time with the attorney preparing, but would not have to testify. When I asked her why not, she said it was because the case had nothing to do with her. That was all. The bailiff entered the room and spoke calmly to Carter, Lynn, and me. Something about which hand to hold up and which one needed to be on the Bible. Covering these rules was the only love and kindness I had been shown. He was gentle and I almost burst forth in a sobbing breath because of it. Suddenly, he was gone and outside there was a restless bit of moving. The door opened and the attorney entered.

"It's time," he said, and we followed him out of the safety of the holding room. As we did, all three of us sighed heavily.

In the outer hallway were many hearing rooms, leading to the one where I would end up. The one where Mother waited. Not until I reached for the bench where I was asked to take a seat by the attorney did I notice how my hands trembled. A bit of the sunlight shining through high windows blinded me for a second, but then the glare passed, and when it did, standing only a few feet from me was Mother. I quickly sat down and took several sips of water from a glass on the table in front of me. I was shaking so badly, I needed two hands to steady the glass.

"The judge will enter in a few minutes and we all stand," the attorney urged to me, softly. Apparently, we were supposed to speak quietly while in this room.

I stole another glance at Mother and saw the look in her eyes. Her face was so white and thin that she might have been taken for a corpse if it had not been for the dark glare in her sunken eyes. I was close enough to Mother that I could smell the odor of mildew coming from her clothes. She then said something to another person in the courtroom and I could hear the irritation in her voice.

I quickly looked away, bent forward, and took another gulp of water. The wooden chair in which I sat was hard and much too big for me. For an instant, the room swam and I folded my arms nearly laying them on the table with my head down upon them. The bailiff cried out, making me jump, and the judge entered the room.

"All rise!" the bailiff shouted.

All together, the room came to its feet, and there followed a sound of chairs groaning and cracking.

"Be seated!" the bailiff shouted.

We all sat down, followed by the same sounds coming from the furniture.

The judge read some things into a microphone that sounded important, legal, and cold. A strange, broken cry squeaked from me when my name was mentioned. A few minutes later, I was walking toward where the judge sat high above the court and was then directed by the bailiff to the chair in which I would sit. There was a pounding of the judge's hammer as I was placed inside my wooden cage, where the words would come grief-stricken from my lips, and in spite of the fact they were true, they were most assuredly ugly.

Throughout the testimony, my feverish face would look at the floor, and the judge often reminded me gruffly to look up and speak into the microphone. There was no alternative for me, or for Carter or Lynn, but I regarded myself no better than a thief and a liar. The advantage I took of Mother in order to survive filled me with repugnance, and I prayed for when this would all be over. It brought back fresh heartbreak and despair. Lost in the oblivion of confusion and dread, was my reaction of uneasy fear. The actions of the guilty. There was something in the air that choked me. A terrible loneliness oppressed me. It was like a clammy hand smothering my heart in its grip, and it made me sick. I looked up from my feet and at Mother and knew now that there lay between us a gulf that an eternity could not bridge. Nothing would fix what I had done.

I shuddered and gripped my hands underneath the witness booth and looked again at Mother. She was staring directly at me and my eyes were drawn to her glare. I've returned to Mother, that was true, but not to save her this time, but to do harm by telling the truth. In the moments before my testimony began, the feeling of her presence seemed to add to the smothering weight on my heart. I waved to her from behind the microphone and offered a weak smile of apology. She only glared back at me. There was stifled laughter in the courtroom and someone was crying.

Boxed inside and trapped on the hard wooden chair, before me were far too many people; including Father and his attorney, and of course, Mother. She was alone and seemed so small behind her long wooden table. She had the same kind of writing pad the attorney had when questioning me. My duty to her was now destroyed and she knew it.

From the table in front of her, she lifted her long thick yellow pad of paper and a pencil. And for more than an hour, Mother worked steadily on making me out to be a liar. Step by step, she mapped out her defense and wrote things down every now and then. I did not know if she were actually making notes or pretending to. Mother would then place the pad down on the table and ask more questions. It was a bitter struggle, without rest, with the most horrible specter that ever hovered within the courtroom. A struggle that drew Mother's cheeks in and put deep lines in her face; a struggle of wits in which Mother was winning.

More than once, Mother ground me down exceedingly small, by her questions and accusations, and then, in more terrible moments, she seemed to be convincing. The minutes of torment lengthened into hours. To the bottom of my soul I suffered, because I understood what it all meant for me. The distance growing broader between us, while the old terrors gathered swiftly, and the grief and shame enveloped me.

Occasionally, Mother would fall silent for a few minutes, gathering strength for the next round of questioning. During these times, I choked back my weakness. She moved swiftly from one end of the table to the next asking questions. Mother looked sharp and spoke fluently without any trace of a drunken slur. I was confused, having never seen her like this. It disarmed me and soon I was uttering incoherently and weeping. The lights grew very bright and the clicking of the wooden chair was the only sound I heard except the faint, hissing monotone of Mother's voice demanding I tell the truth and take back all those lies I told about her.

My heart was filled with a sudden throbbing pain and I remember telling her I was sorry. Afterwards, the judge turned to me, smacking his hammer, and telling me to just answer the questions. Shivering, I tried to answer her but she was lying. In place of sound there came that clacking of my chair again and I could see Mother's mouth move but nothing came out. There was a moment's silence. The room seemed to tremble with it. Then, Mother regained herself, slamming down the yellow pad, and the room, was again, filled with her voice. A voice that was terribly cold. I grimaced every time she asked a question. I don't remember my answers and could no longer see anything in the courtroom –just Mother. Her eyes upon me fully, she seemed too close to where I sat. I could smell her odor and wondered if anyone else could smell her as well. Mother seemed more emaciated than before. Her sunken eyes watched me with a rat-like glitter, and her hands looked like claws.

More and more I was losing my ground and feared I would be told Mother had won the battle and I would be going back with her. Ahead of me the space between us closed to nearly a few inches from our faces. I was broken and she knew it. The smile on her face gave it away. Weird whispers came with her voice. Like a special language only I could understand and she was aware of the fact I had tricked her once, but I would never trick her again.

It was the thought of returning to live with Mother that pulled me from my trance, and after a few seconds I returned to Mother's cross-examination. She rose with her arms folded and looked down at the yellow pad. New and strange thoughts had come to me, and among these was the wondering why Mother had never been this composed. This sober before. I had dreamed of her being normal, being happy. These boyish visions filled me with happiness. And now, here she was proving that it was possible. A thousand times I fantasized about Mother picking me up in her arms and hugging me. I sat on the witness stand wondering why she could not have used the power she wielded today for goodness.

"I love you my little one," she would say in these fantasies, saying it over and over – each time followed by a kiss on the cheek or forehead. My heart leapt exultantly, but then when Mother unfolded her arms and looked up from her yellow pad directly at me, the fantasy was abruptly over.

By the end of the first court day I had become numb, but the dagger of accusations and questioning still chipped away at me little by little. Mother continued to ask questions while looking at me blankly. I answered the same question a hundred times and was too afraid, too tired, and too sad to comprehend most of what was being asked or answered. It was like a painful nightmare during a deep slumber in which I could not awaken.

In the glow of Mother's eyes, I saw how angry she was at me for tricking her. Her questions took me as far back as my own memories would go and were twisted as if they happened another way. According to Mother I had somehow made a terrible mistake and was being cruel. This was part of her defense in addition to absolute denial of any wrongdoing. The seriousness in which Mother asked her questions added validity and I looked like a liar in every word. She could relax and look vigilant, while I looked like a cruel and stupid boy. There came, every now and then, a violent reaction from her, but Mother would then pull herself together and resume questioning. And that one terrible thought that drove out all others kept coming back –she would win the custody battle and I would return with her.

Mother continued to argue her case another day sober and her sobriety further proved I was lying. At this, my heart burned a suspense that was suffocating. In the hours Mother questioned me, there came the inevitable reaction of oppression and gloom. I had never seen Mother as I saw her now, having so much control, dressed appropriately, her appearance clean. I wanted to cry out she was a liar, but the look on her face held me silent. My cheeks were flushed and my lips burned an unnatural red. I looked the part of a liar myself. Mother's eyes were glowing with strange fires that made her look smart and earnest. When she sat down after cross-examination, Mother would sit slowly, deliberately like a lady. She did not stagger back and drop into the chair like she had so many times before at home.

Afterwards, it was Father's attorney who would question me. His words were dry and sterile. They crushed me. His face was stern, and at the same time, uninterested. I would swallow hard before answering a question and the sound was magnified by the microphone. My hands trembled and putting one hand over the other did not help, but looked even more suspicious. Like I was trying to hide my guilt.

I once looked up while Father's attorney was asking questions and I saw a light leap from Mother's eyes after hearing my response. That light was always followed by her whispering that she would kill me. I could see the quick rise and fall of her bosom. I do not remember the question, but my answer like so many others was simply, "Yes." There was a demand in Mother's face, her eyes, her parted lips. She would sit motionless clasping her hands tighter under the table, and I could hear the swift beating of my own heart. I never thought I could tell the story of what happened in so few words, leaving out the sex stuff, yet I did, with more and more of that glaring hateful light creeping into Mother's eyes.

Once I stopped breathing when Mother seemed to touch upon the molestations during her questioning. She was right on the edge, but then decided not to go further. Her questioning changed direction and she stopped. There was something terrible in the query of her eyes more so, but something seemed to rise up in Mother's throat. I saw her effort to stop and it rattled her just a bit. It startled Mother, and in an instant she had regained her composure. But in her eyes it was like she wanted to in order perhaps to clear her name. At first while seeming to contemplate the question that hovered around sex, Mother did not move. No sound came from her tight-drawn lips. She then covered her face with her hand and stood for a moment, and in that moment all the force of the hovering question nearly brought tears to her eyes. I saw them shimmer and we both seemed to nearly drop dead of shame. However, a new line of questioning came forth, and like a tigress, Mother leapt back into action. The pleading in my face may have stopped her or the fact that if she uttered anything about sexual abuse, prostitution, or otherwise, it would have had to be explored. Mother had done wrong and knew it, but she was also cunning.

A tiny moan may have escaped me and I swayed a bit in the chair. I scarcely remember the next few minutes of questions or the explanations given. I do recall nearly doubling over and vomiting. I also remember my vision impaired by the tears and the blackness that danced around my eyes making the room dark. My head sank, rose laboriously, then sank again. When I looked at Mother, she was filled with horror. Her voice almost a scream when she saw my reaction. She was dying and the first chink in her armor began to show. At one point, the judge asked Mother something, she shook her head, and then she went back to asking questions.

My answers continued to come in low moaning sounds and the judge kept having to ask me to repeat myself. My face was flushed with fever and my hair was a disheveled mass from twisting it. I saw how Mother's dark eyes burned brightly seeing me touch my hair. She never allowed me to do this, though for what reason, I never understood. Perhaps for no other reason other than Mother feeling she was the only person allowed to touch and rip the hair from my head.

Mother's strength may have waned a bit when nearly asking me about something to do with sex, but her strength was back now. She had no more fear and glared into my face. She picked up her yellow pad, read some notes, and put it back down again.

She's composing herself, I thought. Then from Mother sprang another question, demanding, and fiercely upon me. With the quickness of a cat, the next question was being asked before I could finish the last. I wrung my hands and the anxiety came down upon me like a sickening thud with every beat of my heart. I was groping blindly at the answers while sinking further into a pit of blackness. I kept waiting to finally pass out. Normally it scared me terribly, but this time I wanted to. It was an escape.

Mother continued cross-examining me and I felt as if she continued I would die. Most times, I was speechless, would gasp, struggle, and then answer her. Answer the court. I sat helpless and knew everyone could see the twitching of my throat, the quiver of my lips. Any moment I waited to faint and actually struggled to fall into the darkness of unconsciousness. My head grew heavier, but I would not pass out. Instead, I brushed the hair from my face, caught what breath I had in my lungs, turned toward my accuser, and wept.

Suddenly, Father was weeping too and the judge slammed the wooden mallet against its small round block. Father lifted his head once and looked at me then lowered it. He withdrew whatever case he had. His lawyer spoke for him while he looked down and continued weeping. In that moment, I could not have loved Father more.

The judge said something again and I finally realized he was speaking to me. "You may step down," he said. "You are finished."

Mother was furious and seemed to be approaching the place in which I was sitting. Then, she stopped short, grabbed up her yellow pad and marched toward the exit. However, on her way out of the courtroom I thought for a second she turned and looked at me. Before she left for good, I wanted to cry out one word to her –at least one, but what came instead were the choking sounds of a sob I was trying to hold back. I sighed heavily and left my wooden cage. Mother was now gone and I realized, this time, the parting was final.

The bailiff escorted me from the courtroom, down a long hallway, and into another holding room. Where I stood looking out of a long window, wept silently, and waited.

CHAPTER TWO

A Memory Unforgiving

"I seek confinement, protective bliss from a memory long unforgiving and unremitting. There are many like me. Because blame is for God and small children."

WHAT PASSED AS CONVERSATION ON the way home from the court hearing was Lauren rambling on about how we won. How we finally had taken Mother down. I did not know who she was referring to as 'we'. I did nothing but stammer and stumble over my words and pissed myself just a little. Not enough to notice, thankfully. But I knew and I bet Mother knew as well. I bet she could smell what little urine squirted into my pants from where she was standing.

I thought over the events of the day and remembered how, in the space of silence that followed waiting for my turn to testify, I sat in a holding room. I was trying to remember what the attorney had instructed, but whispered words from Mother came to me instead along with a terrible realization of the crisis I now faced. The thought of surrendering to my first impulse and not testifying filled me instantly with a terror of the retribution that would surely follow. My hands were clenched so tightly that my nails dug in and hurt my palms. I began practicing telling Lauren that I could not testify against Mother, but the words died in my throat.

To tell Lauren how afraid I was, to make her know the truth, that Mother was stronger than me and more powerful, might have angered Lauren so much that I would be sent back to Mother. So, I had decided to keep quiet. I could not have brought myself to speak these words to Lauren regardless. I was not brave enough. Nothing would have stopped the hearing from continuing. Nothing would save me.

In the end, Lauren would never know how close I came to not going through with testifying against Mother. I remember how Lauren's eyes lit with power when realizing she had a chance at taking Mother down. It meant a great deal to her for reasons I did not understand. The whole ordeal seemed like a dream to me. A dream where I remembered everything that happened, and as hard as I tried, could not forget. Convincing me that these terrible things were done to me were the countless hours of pouring over the details with the attorney. If necessary, I thought of telling the court I did not remember, and would have done so if anything came up about the molestations, prostitution, or sex of any kind.

Out of the window of Lauren's car, I could see the house approaching slowly. It took form in the shape of a box. The yard was mowed and neat. Lauren and her husband Tim took great effort to ensure appearances were up to standard. Their home was kept this way inside and out. It was another reminder I would never measure up.

I was exhausted and the court appearance took from me the last dim shadow of what would pass as longing for Mother. One after another, the memories of my life with her were falling away. What I did not know at the time was that these memories would never leave me for good. They would lay dormant waiting for a sound or smell to remind me. Waiting for someone to break my heart and then all the memories would come rushing back in a flood of pain, confusion, and one day –a raw form of rage.

For now, I was still only a boy with the mind and emotions of a child much younger than me. Underdeveloped in every which way. Even my height was stunted and I still looked much too thin for eleven. There was something appalling in my appearance. The lack of confidence in myself made me more ugly and vulnerable. Anyone could take advantage of me. I would not protest. It was not in me, and instead, I would obey. That is what I did best.

In the quiet looming of my mind, I was no more than a servant. I could no longer hear the motor of the kitten I had once had, Sambirdio, to give me peace. Within reach of my grasp was nothing more than desolation. I would walk slowly and with my head bowed going about the business of doing exactly what Lauren and her husband told me to do. Behind me was the ghost of Mother and I was oblivious to what would pass the time of a normal pre-adolescent.

We were not allowed to watch more than an hour of television per day and there wasn't anyone to play with in the neighborhood. So, I read. I sat silent for hours at a time staring into the white pages filed with words I still did not understand. Picking over each one and sounding it out. One word at a time, I began to form complete sentences, and from these sentences, paragraphs. But they were still children's books and I was ashamed because I was no longer a child.

A week or two had passed since the custody hearing. Summer was closing and the weather was turning cool. Lauren's husband was an avid hunter and promised he would take me and my brother hunting with him. I did not want to go. I did not want to be with him. He frightened me and the idea of Tim having a gun was even more frightening. Then there was the daily regimen of household chores Carter, Lynn, and I were assigned. They varied from one thing to the other; including detailing one of Tim's most prized possessions –his motorcycle.

Lauren stood opposite me in the kitchen only inches from my face before she spoke. "Did you and Carter do something to Tim's motorcycle?" She gritted her teeth when uttering the question. Tim could be heard in the yard cursing.

"No!" I said. "We washed it just like Tim told us to."

"Well, he can't start it and he is really upset!"

Lauren never cursed. Ever. No matter how angry she became. It was unsettling not to hear someone curse every now and then. I grew up with cursing and it was a normal part of my vocabulary. By holding back from cursing, Lauren appeared a bit off to me. Crazy-like and disturbing. It was as if she were hiding something. Something dangerous that could hurt me.

Tim came crashing through the kitchen door and it gave me a jump. It even scared Lauren. She noticeably backed away from where I was standing.

"Carter! Get in here too!" Tim yelled to the house. Carter was soon standing in the kitchen near me.

"What in the fuck did you two do to my motorcycle?" Tim's question was followed by his fist crashing into the side of the refrigerator.

"Nothing!" I pleaded. Carter just looked afraid and remained quiet. Tim's rant was unshakable. He had already worked himself into a frenzy before entering the house. While he kicked at the kitchen chairs and pounded the walls Carter and I just stood there waiting. Waiting for the beating. Tim did not hit us. Not that day. He beat the shit out of the kitchen and swore up and down, but he did not hit us. "Don't ever touch my goddamn motor-cycle again!"

"You boys are stupid and you fucked it up!" he said, and then pushed through the kitchen door where he went back to examining his motorcycle.

Lauren excused us abruptly from the kitchen and told us to go work on our list of other chores. We did so, gladly. Out of earshot, I whispered to Carter, "Well, at least his fucking motorcycle is clean." We both giggled.

Something strange began to happen to me. The remark came from an unfamiliar place. A place of confidence. It felt good. It felt like in a very small way as if I was fighting back. Fighting back was new to me.

Testing the boundaries a bit more and digging deeper into this untapped resource of strength, I said to Carter before striding out the front door of the house, "Fuck it."

Carter replied back, "Yeah. Fuck it."

At the very sound of Lauren and Tim's voice, I was still afraid. Regard-less of a budding confidence inside of me, I still did not talk back or refuse them in any way. Sometimes, with the sound of Tim's voice came a low cry from my mouth I did not realize I was making until Lynn pointed it out to me one day. He, along with Lauren, could stop me in my tracks with a look. And that look came often enough to do a lot of stopping. They were angry and it was obvious to my siblings and me that we were unwelcomed guests. I tried to love them both like I tried to love Mother. But like Mother, they seemed not to notice or simply not have time to notice. Too busy, I suppose. With three ready-made screw-ups like me and my siblings and one child of their own, I guess it must have been pretty tough. Still, I always wondered how they found the time to love their only child, but seemed to run short when it came to us.

As summer closed in and the school year was to begin soon, I frantically read more and more. The fear of shame was extremely motivating. Christ! I was barely out of Dr. Seuss and I would be expected to read at the 7th grade level. And this was just reading. I still did not have the most basic math skills, and as far as my multiplication tables, "Fuck it."

We did not have presentable school clothes, so Lauren took Carter, Lynn and I shopping. Not far from every comment was how she was spending a fortune on us. We were told to pick out three outfits each; pants, socks, shirts, and a pair of shoes. My siblings and I had no idea how to shop for clothes and none of us knew what the hell "sizes" were or meant. Lauren ended up just grabbing up what clothes she figured we needed and piled them in our arms. With one hand trying to grip the wad of new clothes and the other dangling a pair of shoes, I filed to the register with Carter and Lynn. We looked like refugees.

For a moment I was unable to move or speak and just listened to the 'ding ding crunch' of the cashier banging the keys of the register. Every time she'd smack down the fat Enter key, I'd jerk and wince. Suddenly I saw something in Lauren's face that stuck me with a chill and I knew it was loathing. A word I did not know but one I felt just the same.

When the cashier called out the total, all I could do was stare at her in speechless astonishment. In all my years with Mother, she had never spent that much money on her kids. I felt guilty as hell and Lauren played off this guilt. It worked. On top of the fear I had inside me was the pressure of having to earn everything Lauren and Tim were doing for us. I took it all on myself like I always did. I couldn't really live the words, "Fuck it" – not yet anyway. They gave me momentary relief but I'd go right back to working like hell to prove myself or be what someone else wanted me to be. It was a goddamn tiresome thing.

The great big frightened eyes looking back at me while Lauren paid the cashier told me that Lynn was feeling the same way. I knew that look and thought to myself I'd never be able to pay Lauren back. It'd hang over me like a stone. I had come used to recognizing the feeling inside me as guilt. Born into it and suffered by its ugly and heavy hand for years, it was a feeling that was always at the forefront of my emotions.

Lauren paid and we all left the store. I bowed my head and carried my clothes to the car. When we were all inside and Lauren behind the wheel, I heard my voice in a half-sob say, "Thank you." Lauren did not say anything in return. Only nodded.

The time passed quickly and school was upon us. I don't remember the first day. What I do remember was that the world, yet again, had fallen upon my shoulders and with each passing minute of classroom instruction I felt more and more stupid. The tears shone in my eyes a few times during class, but I quickly pulled it together. I was filled with pain every time I could not answer a question and felt worse when I was called on. Seven hours. Seven different classes. Seven failures and I hadn't even made it past the first week. I got lost just trying to find my class and once there, I'd be lost academically until the bell rang.

I had now been away from Mother for nearly four months and I could still feel her bony hands choking the life out of me with each panic attack. I felt so young, so childlike that in the pale glow of my face I told all my classmates how weak I was. My features were more like a girl, and with my eyes, mouth and small chin, if I let my hair grow out I'd look like one. It did not take long before I was called names like 'faggot' and 'homo'. My actions were hesitant and unsure. My voice quivered when I spoke and was too high –almost squeaky. Without a doubt, the classes were harsh, but lunchtime was a horror all its own.

"Whatcha eatin' faggot?" the tough kids would tease.

"You suckin' any dicks today?"

Keeping my face lowered and staring at the food I no longer wanted, all I could do was wonder in agonizing disbelief, *how did they know?*

The line between the bullies' teasing and the reality of actually believing they knew about how Mother molested me and prostituted me out to strangers was blurred. At times it would disappear altogether and I was convinced somehow the other schoolchildren knew about my sordid past. It haunted me and made me angry, but the anger was always subdued by the dull and heavy weight of guilt. I couldn't defend myself because it was true. It didn't matter if none of it was consensual. The teasing bad boys were right. Mother was right. I was a little cocksucker. And with this realism came with it the drawing of myself inward.

Sometimes, not often, I would hear the teasing and there would be a slight glow of defiance in my eyes. The boys doing the chiding would seem to take a step back, but then I'd show again how much I feared them and would not fight for myself. I was dead inside and they knew that too. I'd slink at their feet, and there would be a gleam of naked courage in their eyes. What they did not realize is that I had died now twelve years ago.

Days turned to weeks and by the first marking period, I was failing all of my classes. Lauren scolded me every chance she got for letting her and Tim down.

"We expected more out of you, Gregg," she would say disappointingly during one of many lectures.

"Carter and Lynn aren't as smart as you."

"You really let me and Tim down."

Worse yet was the fact I was still wetting the bed. There were many long lectures about how this was unacceptable behavior for a boy my age. Hell, I could have told Lauren that. She could have saved her breath and jammed all those long lectures up her ass. I agreed that it was unacceptable, but I couldn't help it. I just couldn't stop. She'd look at me grimly and terribly after stripping my bed of the urine soaked sheets and there would be this ghostly radiance that fell upon her face. She would push her chin down on her chest looking at me, but saying nothing while the clothes washer bumped in the background accusingly. Lauren would see the pathetic droop in my shoulders and know she had a captive and pliable audience. Sometimes I'd be crying, yet this didn't seem to dissuade her from hammering the shame home. In that moment of total annihilation, she would have this thrilling warmth spreading all over her face and the glory of total humiliation left me mute.

I was failing school, pissing the bed, and getting my ass kicked pretty much every day by the school bullies. To me, school was all that is terrible. The pitiless loneliness of my life had placed me in an environment that could totally exploit every weakness. It was a continuation of the abuse. Before me was more desolation and humiliation. The code of things was that only the worst of mankind survive and all that the innocent dream of and love is smothered under the weight of their hatred.

Tim made good on his promise and purchased a shotgun for me and Carter. The shotguns were a model Ithaca 4/10, single shot. He would drive us to a cornfield and we would hunt bird and small game. The feel of the gun and its sound made me nervous. I couldn't shoot straight. The harder I tried, the more I missed, and Tim's angry instructions were difficult to follow. It was as if he spoke another language.

"Use the goddamn bead, Gregg!" he yelled.

I'd think to myself, *what the fuck is a bead?*

Other colorful commentary came in the form of,

"Your pattern sucks!"

"What the fuck are you shooting at?"

"Pop your goddamn barrel."

"Shoulder that fucker!"

Pure nonsensical speak. Shit, most of the time I figured he was making it up and just trying to sound crazy to scare me.

Failing school carried with a threat of not going hunting and I often wished Tim would ban me altogether. But he'd change his mind at the last minute and I'd end up having to go. Maybe he honestly thought Carter and I enjoyed hunting. I would have if he wasn't so damn upset with me all the time when I did something wrong and I always did something wrong. I would need my whole hand to pull back the hammer of the shotgun where Carter and Tim needed only their thumbs. My little fingers could barely pull the trigger. Aiming at some rabbit was tough enough and I'd always miss. Hitting a bird flying through the air was impossible. I would have been better off closing my eyes when I shot, and often, I did just that.

In a way I knew Tim was trying but his frustration got the best of him most times. Seeing he was actually hoping to turn me and Carter into sportsmen, I cut him some slack and tried to look past the anger. And yet, I kept going back to wondering why he was so mad at me and Carter. We were really trying our best. Neither of us ever hunted before and it was only recently I could actually spell the word shotgun.

My devotion to learning was unquestionable. It was born out of the fear of humiliation. I tried to be a good hunter for Tim and a good student for both Tim and Lauren. I just did not and could not measure up. I even tried going out for an intramural basketball team and was benched. This was after I went out for the 7th grade varsity basketball team and did not make it past the first cut. I was starving for acceptance and the only way I could see achieving this was through learning. Filled with the desire to rise above my situation, I pressed on. Crumpled and exhausted against boys and girls smarter and better than me, I still would not quit. I had visions of achievement that kept me alive. Kept me trying, but I wasn't built for success. I had to start from nothing and make something of it. It was a losing battle, but a battle it was and I knew that.

I was going it alone and this made me both tired and angry. When I reached out to Lauren or Tim for help with my schoolwork they would try sometimes, but other times they would get very frustrated with me because I did not understand the lesson itself.

The bullies were relentless and building inside me was this burning anger of failing and being a failure. I was pegged from the beginning. I couldn't carry the load of schoolwork, being ass-whipped during lunch, and constantly humiliated by the limitations already present based on my upbringing. I pushed forward blindly. Stripped of any self-dignity. And, at night while alone in my room, the strangers would come inside my head and tear me down again. I could imagine and actually feel them placing me across their laps. I hid this shame from everyone. Still, no one knew and I would die before they did. Late at night, in my bed I would stop, listen for the strangers, and stifle a cry by covering my mouth with both hands, because they always came.

The days grew warmer and summer was approaching. I was still failing school and taking a beating three to four times a week from the badasses. At times, I would attend a school dance and thought there were moments when I was falling in love. But I was always too shy to speak to another girl and did well to hide my happiness at the sight of her. *She will only break my heart*, I thought. The presence of the girls reminded me of Mother and the love I still had for her. But also the manipulation possible with their words and actions. Weary of rejection I stayed away and only watched them from a safe place. I found girls to be oppressive in nature. Always wanting to command the boys.

Control them. It would have been easy for them to do this to me. I would let them, but not this year. Not at twelve. My shyness protected me from certain heartbreak that would come soon enough.

Left with nothing but fatigue by each day's end in spite of the few triumphs I had academically, I was still incredibly far behind the other children. Dragging me downward with each minor success was always a major failure. If I got a "C" on a report card, I would still end up with a "D" in the class. Now and then, I would try and bask in the elation that I was improving, but it felt like a lie. I could feel Mother behind me telling me I would fail. I could hear Lauren and Tim tell me that I was failing. The sound of their voices were a low and echoing doom. I wanted to burst forth with great courage but I did not have what it took to do so. I did not measure up. My desire to accomplish something continued to whistle ahead and I often wondered how I would be able to keep up the pace of dragging every ounce of perseverance from myself. My heart sank every time I failed a class or did not do exactly what was asked of me by Lauren and Tim. Now and then, I'd pause to think of Mother, but the thoughts were more and more fleeting. The load was just too heavy on my heart.

I held out for a better day and kept pushing ahead with my schoolwork. I moved through the hallways between classes, uneasily toward each anticipated failure. I pressed myself against a losing battle and drew upon what little strength I had deep inside. I resumed my way across the unfamiliar territory of my new life. What were familiar were the physical beatings I took most days from the bullies at school and the emotional beatings I took from Lauren and Tim. In both cases, I said and did nothing. Even though my blood sometimes ran fierce through my body and my hands trembled with anger, I held these things from my abusers. Once or twice early on I almost lashed out and said something to Lauren or Tim when they were browbeating me, but I held my tongue. And, once or twice I almost fought back against the bullies but my feelings always remained submissive. Mother had trained me well.

As the prospects of ending my 7th grade year with at the very least a "D" average drew closer, a long-awaited summer was about to begin. Free from the bullies. Free from the pain of humiliation and being tagged as one of the dumbest students in my classes. When I walked from the school to the bus, the boys would still call me ugly names but there was a light wind that lifted my spirits a little and fell across my face. It reminded me of the apple tree, and most of all, it reminded me of my cat Sambirdio. In my mind I could still see his furry face raised to my lips, while I looked into his big green eyes. Lately, I thought a lot of being under the apple tree and away from Mother. Where the timber of the branches protected Sam and me. I wished we were under the apple tree again. My weakness began to show to all that could see. My fear, fragility, and loneliness. My cheeks burned all the time with shame.

Shaking off what I could and pressing forward was a case of pure survival. I still hadn't thought of suicide, but that would come later. For now, I kept trying to wash away the remnants of each day's humiliation and keep moving forward. Study. *Feed your head, Gregg.* That's what I thought. It felt more than right. It felt perfect.

Right before my first year of junior high school ended, I met a girl. She said she liked me. My heart immediately filled with joy. The boys found out and beat me harder still during lunchtime. She watched and wept while they did so. I could not look at her afterwards so I ignored her in the hallways and it broke her heart. Mine too. Before the first beating in which she witnessed, I had a chance to hold her hand. We held hands between classes, hiding the public display of affection from the teachers. I couldn't let go of it when we separated. Aware of my first chance at affection, I clung to it and would not have broken up with her had she not seen the humiliation in my face after the beating. Afterwards, I told her that we could not be together and she cried softly. It was sweet and heartbreaking. It was the first time I had ever broken someone's heart. It made me draw away from her even more. I cried too, alone and in my room, slinking close to my bed in case Lauren or Tim barged in like they always did – I could pretend I was rummaging for something underneath.

My heart whined against the impending loneliness and when alone I would make a low wailing sound. Damn it! I cried all the time when alone. Soon, this would turn to rage. The nightmares were coming back even worse now. Spending so much time alone, I talked to myself. And what I heard was only the sound of the sad songs Mother would sing, and behind her voice –only empty and dry laughter.

CHAPTER THREE

Crooked Passages

"Constantly losing my way, faith was drawn from resilience."

TWO WEEKS BEFORE THE END of the school year and still one more year remained where I was stuck in junior high. However, I felt this was still better than high school. I was a lost cause and subjected to ridicule at the pre-pubescent level. I wouldn't allow myself to imagine what horrors high school would bring.

Finals. A series of unspeakably difficult examinations culminating a school year of knowledge crammed into a single event. I would have seven to take and seven to fail. I studied as best I could. A useless endeavor when you consider I still had no solid grasp of reading. Lauren and Tim would remind me often that I better not fail my subjects. They claimed too much time and effort had already been spent on grooming me. Once when studying, Lauren pushed her way into my room and put upon an already heavy burden of fear that if I failed I would have to repeat the 7th grade. For a few moments after uttering those words she stood silent listening for my reply. What came instead was the sound of low moaning, perhaps which came from a place inside me she knew to tap. To exploit.

"You're not trying hard enough," Lauren said.

I was sure that I had heard it before or at least something very similar. I did not understand. I looked at her while she stood in the doorway, and she at me, while sitting on the chair before my desk. She was gazing steadily.

"I said, you are not trying hard enough."

The words frightened me because if this was not trying, I thought, I was sure to fail. In the background Tim was bitching at the television. My throat seized up and made terrible sounds –embarrassing me. Lauren left closing my door behind her. When positive she was finally gone, I let myself cry.

Now clutching my throat, there was both terror and grief in my heart. For an instant I felt like passing out. I understood the feeling washing over me. It had been there so many times before. My mind ready to give way to the awful strain of fear. It was times like these I felt more like a helpless child.

I am so tired, I thought.

I am so very tired.

And useless.

And so stupid.

I went on studying but the fear now was so dense I had to re-read my textbooks and class notes over and over. I would again think of the apple tree, where in the winter, it would form a shelter from both snow and wind, and Mother only a few feet away in the house. With a thick lump in my throat I pushed harder to try and retain the information, quizzed myself repeatedly, but could not remember what I had just studied. I was stupid, and would prove it, yet again, when I failed my exams. My only relief was that the grades would not be read aloud in front of my classmates.

The books and pages of notes in front of me were spread across the table I used to study. Piled high were even more books I had not yet begun to read in preparation for final exams. Looking at them was depressing and struck a nerve deep inside me that felt the same as when Mother would degrade me during the beatings.

"You'll never amount to anything," she would bark.

"You are a waste of my time."

"A useless little cocksucking queer."

"Worthless."

"Hopeless."

"A germ I should have killed at birth."

In the glowing light of my desktop reading lamp, I poured over the words scribbled frantically on the pages of the notebooks before me. The textbooks yet to be opened next to me were as high as my head. No fuel within me to press onward, I tried to do so running on empty. The blaze of achievement now vanquished. It was hidden or had fallen asleep in the flame of Lauren's warnings of failure. For the next few hours, I dragged myself through the pile of study materials in readiness for final exams. Soon it would be late and I needed sleep. In my dreams, the nightmares would come and in them would be the odor of Mother's sex and the putrid sweat mixed with cologne of the strangers.

The next morning, I awoke to the alarm, dressed and looked at my notes of which would be my first exam. It was as if I had never seen the words. Never heard them spoken by the teacher and did not remember writing them down. Throwing everything into a book bag, I left my room and greeted Lauren. It was more of a dutiful thing where I would receive the day's instructional lecture and be reminded of the chores that needed tending after school.

"You kids aren't going to just sit around this summer," she continued to tell us as summer approached.

"There's work to do."

There was always work to do in Lauren and Tim's household. Even when there wasn't work to do –there was always work to do. No one was idle except Tim. He would smother his chair smoking a pipe commanding the servants. Lauren was always busy as well. Relentless in her own endeavors. Always rushing. Rushing. Rushing. And, complaining about something.

As I hurried off to catch the bus, I heard Lauren tell me to do well on my exams.

"Good luck!" she said cheerfully.

My mind would always twist at the phony gesture of intent in her words and actions. I knew she didn't mean it, but she'd say things like that nonetheless. I knew what she really meant. She meant, "I hope you fail because that would make sense." A puny little bastard like me was destined to fail. Born to achieve failure. Turn it into an art form. So far, I had been pretty goddamn successful in doing just that. So far, I had yet to let anyone down. Sincerely meeting all of their expectations. Yeah. Yay for fucking me.

I waited for the bus with the other kids but did not speak to them. We had nothing in common. Nothing to share. Boarding the bus, I sat down in the back. It was warm now that summer was here. Too warm. I smiled at whomever was sitting next to me and went back to staring at my shoes. Finally learning to tie them but no longer excited at this accomplishment.

Sometimes I would see a cute girl and stare at the back of her head. Marveling at how her hair tumbled about her shoulders, rippling and glistening in the sunlight. It would sometimes be long and fall loosely about her. I would watch in absolute adoration and amazement as some of the young girls with long hair gathered it between their fingers, divided it into shining strands, and pleated it into a thick braid. With my eyes fixed upon these innocent but erotic scenes, I would feel a sensation in my groin, and in doing so, would quickly look away.

Stepping off the bus, the one friend I managed to make that year greeted me.

"Hi Gregg!" he said, and I replied, "Hi Greg!" in return.

We both marveled at our common names; albeit different spellings. He was waiting for me where the big yellow school buses would line up in the morning and also in the afternoon. Seeing him standing there waiting for me always made me feel happy inside. No one had ever waited for me other than Lynn and it was generally under dire circumstances where we were both riddled with fear.

Greg was my first friend since the boy my age who lived across the street from Mother. Greg or Gregory was his formal name and he was much smarter than me and a better athlete, but he never made me feel inferior. He was also a talented musician and adopted into a wealthy family. His father was a former Naval Flight Officer where he met his wife in Germany. Greg, along with his sister, were both adopted but not related. He had a great home life, was good looking, smart, and talented. It was easy to have a fair set of bragging rights among his peers. I often wondered why he would want to be friends with the likes of me.

"Are you ready for finals?" Greg said confidently.

"Nope." I replied. And then added, "Fuck no."

The two of us were in only a couple classes together, one of which was wood shop. I was flunking that as well. Greg would produce these works of art and was easily able to complete the woodworking assignments. I needed all the help I could get and Greg was always willing to lend a hand.

"Well, good luck!" Greg said chuckling

"You too!" I said, although he didn't need any.

"See ya at lunch," he said, and ran off to nail what would be his first "A" of the day –followed easily by six others. Not me. I would end up barely passing each of my classes.

Greg's mention of lunch sent shivers down my spine. In addition to the humiliation of failing my classes, I would have to undergo more teasing from the bullies and another beating. It was customary and a ritual that now took on epic proportions. It seemed as though every asshole in junior high was getting in on the action. I had earned a reputation of being a pushover and weakling. A common moniker when referring to me by some of the boys was, "Weak Tittie." I once begged the wood shop teacher to let me eat lunch inside the annex instead of outside in the courtyard. He refused even after I told him the other boys were beating me up. This seemed to make him even more upset and he just bellowed, "Get out there with the rest of the kids!" I obeyed and took yet another ass whipping.

On the first day of finals, I had three exams. Two before lunch. Bombing them with ease, I reluctantly went to my locker, grabbed the brown paper lunch sack, and headed for the courtyard. The depression of failing and fear of what was to come was just too much. I ducked into the boy's bathroom and hid inside one of the stalls. Feet up on the toilet, I ate my lunch in silence. Suddenly there was a banging on the stall door and the goddamn wood shop teacher commanded me to exit the restroom and go outside in the annex. Obviously I wasn't the first to use this trick of concealment and he was wise to it. Sheepishly I exited the stall and eventually found myself in the courtyard. Like a sheep to slaughter, the beatings began almost immediately.

Greg always did his best to tell the boys to stop picking on me, but he was afraid as well. Once he tried to intervene and was punched in the stomach. That ended any future attempts of bravery. I did not blame him and it most certainly did not hamper our friendship. He stuck up for me and that was all that mattered.

The boys lined up and took turns pushing and shoving. Sometimes a boy would crouch down on all fours behind my legs while another rammed me from the front. I would go flying backwards, smacking my head on the ground so hard that I saw stars and little dancing white dots. Just like the ones I saw when Mother beat me. And just like Mother, the boys were cruel, wanting nothing but to bring pain for no reason.

Maybe it was the flash of shame I saw in the girl's eyes I once was sweet on, and honestly still was, while watching me get bullied. Or, maybe it was just the events of the day that were no more than a culmination of years that brought a windfall of disgrace down upon me. Whatever it was that caused me to pull myself up off the dirt and glare at the boy who just pushed me down, it was a real as the numbing sting in my head, and the blood in my mouth from biting my tongue.

I saw Greg standing behind the boy who pushed me. Out of the danger zone. On the bike rack behind me were the girls who sat on top and flirted with the cute boys. I was not one of these lucky few. Thin and awkward. No self-confidence. Always looking down and nervous. Traits that would never win me a date with the prom queen. No teachers about. Just me, the bullies, and the scrambled mass of pre-pubescent students huddled in their respective cliques.

"Fuck you cocksucker." That's all I said, not just to the boy who just pushed me, but to all of them. A simple sweep of my head let them know it was a general acknowledgment to the group. No fanfare. No burst of emotion. Just a conversational tone that carried with it a simple but effective toss of the gauntlet. And, now that I had thrown down the hammer, there was no going back.

"And fuck your mothers too," I said in the same quiet manner of speech. It came out so nonchalant, I could have been saying, "Hello."

This got the bullies moving. Jokes about someone's mother always got a reaction. The boy closest to me nodded as if he was still trying to understand what just happened. I could see his little brain working it over, and every now and again, he'd wince as if in pain. While he struggled to grasp the idea that his punching bag for the last few months seemed to be standing up for himself, another boy simply lunged. I felt a hot flash against the side of my cheek and then an agonizing pulse that shot through my whole face and head. Knocked down instantly, I scrambled to my feet. Wobbled and almost fell. The laughter all around me cut through the air and hurt worse than the sucker punch. I smiled while the tears rolled down my face. The cheek that was struck already felt numb and swollen and I could not feel the tears on that side of my face.

The same boy came in for another blow and was already in mid-swing. I took one step back and he missed me completely. The boy fell forward and when he did, I rifled my balled up fist into his ear. There was a wet smacking sound. Then the blood began to trickle down from his battered ear to his neck and disappear into the collar of his shirt.

I was still smiling and crying at the same time. The nausea in my stomach was replaced with what felt like hot coals. The boy grabbed his ear and screamed. The laughter turned to mumbled excitement and shouting. Looking like a familiar drunkard from the old neighborhood, the boy staggered and looked dazed. I stepped in front of him and brought my fist down, sweeping from high to low, with a solid cuff which slammed into the lower part of his eye socket. Another wet popping noise and I could feel something give a little just below his eye and above his cheekbone. This time, the boy folded in half, dropped to his knees, fell to the ground and lay writhing in pain.

The crowd had dispersed and kids were running everywhere. Some went for help. Others just stood with gaping mouths. Most of them just continued to shout. I stood over the fallen boy and noticed I was no longer crying or smiling. I was just staring. Watching and waiting for him to do something other than shriek and twist in the dirt. I noticed the other bullies did not advance on me or defend their friend. For the first time I also noticed something else. My penis was hard as a rock.

It was the shop teacher, of course. He now had every interest in me whereas before none was given when I came to him pleading for sanctuary. He grabbed my arm and began pulling me toward the school. Before long I was sitting in front of the vice principal. I don't even remember walking through the halls on the way to his office. The vice principal sat behind his desk looking at me over his glasses. He then reached inside one of the desk drawers and pulled from it a folder filled with papers.

"You're flunking your classes," he said without looking up.

"I never thought you were a bad kid," he said, giving me a quick glance of disappointment.

A secretary sat next to the vice principal's desk with her legs crossed writing things down. She had really big boobs and the other kids called her, "Jugs." I never got the joke until now. When the vice principal finally did look up at me, I noticed his eyes were crossed and his glasses magnified this. He looked like a strange insect. There was a flush in his cheeks and I knew anger when I saw it on someone's face. His flush deepened and he grimaced as he spoke.

"There is a mandatory three-day suspension for fighting," he said defiantly.

"You will also receive an "E" in all of your classes for each of the three days."

Obviously the vice principal was not very smart. He was looking at my file, which was pasted with "E's", and whether I spent the next three days in or out of school, I'd still end up with no better than "D's." I tried desperately not to shown him what I was thinking.

The adrenaline rush began to subside while being chastised by the vice principal. Looking around the room, I noticed the shop teacher had left, but did not remember when. The forlorn look on my face, the momentary drooping of my eyes, showed the vice principal he had me dead to rights and my heart was sinking quickly. I forgot about Lauren and Tim. Totally forgot about final exams and suddenly I was filled with a gripping fear that I would have to repeat the 7th grade.

I sat obediently listening to the vice principal's lecture while waiting for Lauren to come and pick me up. I would not be allowed to take my last exam for the day or any of the others. My first year of junior high would end with a whimper. All that hard work down the drain because I defended myself. The realization of the suspension left my mouth dry and difficult to swallow. The courage shown in the courtyard was completely gone and now the panic set in. I was again docile, filled with fear and dying of loneliness.

This is what happens when I stand up for myself, I thought. It seems like a lot of work and not worth the risk. This left me feeling more lonely and scared. My voice trembled and I apologized to the vice principal. My apologies turned to begging and I began to cry. Something in the harsh glow of my eyes must have urged the vice principal to reconsider. The suspension was reduced to one-hour a day study hall before and after school. This was my chance to at least end the year with "D's" instead of "E's". I felt like shouting that it still was not my fault. The mean boys brought it on themselves, but I held back. I wanted to survive and education was the key. I still did not feel I did anything wrong, but I had to pretend I did. I had pretended my whole life and was really good at it. Although, the fear of failing was real.

The vice principal stood up when Lauren walked into his office. Her look was a mixture of delight and condemnation. The fact that she was going to have fun with what I had done was written all over her face. This was going to be a lecture to beat all others. Finally! Something for her to actually bitch about with substance.

There was the customary explanation, shaking of hands, and Lauren and I were off. I'd still miss my final exam for the day and take an "E." Lauren was already there to pick me up anyway, and the vice principal I'm sure, felt this was some sort of compromise. Funny thing –my last exam of the day was in Wood Shop. Yeah. *Fuck it.*

We weren't in the car for more than a minute before Lauren was already telling me how I failed her and Tim.

"Worst of all, Gregg, is that you failed yourself." This was her favorite line. In the beginning, it worked like a charm, but lately it didn't hold as much power. It was the same lecture. The same rhetoric:

"Tim and I worked hard to help you kids."

"I was hoping you would come around and straighten up."

"I am so ashamed of you."

"We expected more."

Just the sound of these words was bad enough, but it was the way she would say them without looking right at me that hurt like hell. It was as if I wasn't worth looking at.

"You honestly don't want to make it, Gregg."

Another one of Lauren's favorites. This one hurt the most because I wanted to make it more than anything. The sight and sound of her during the lecture was bringing back those feelings I had when I kicked the shit out of the bully. We reached the house and Lauren informed me that I was to wait in my bedroom for Tim to come home. When she turned the car off, I noticed her hand was trembling.

Tim came home and received a briefing from Lauren. Soon afterwards he was pushing through my bedroom door.

"I heard you got into a fight today," he said.

"Yes."

"Did you win or did you get your ass kicked?"

"I won."

"You're grounded."

"I catch you fighting again, I'll kick your ass." He ended all he had to say with those words. Confused and feeling a bit triumphant, I went back to studying.

The next day at school, after my mandatory hour of study hall in the morning, I was met with a mixture of congratulations from fellow students and ridicule from my teachers. More of the same, how I let them down. How they expected more from me. I constantly wondered where they got the idea I had amounted to anything in which to base their expectations. Hell, I'd been a failure at everything from the beginning.

Keeping to myself, I managed to finish the week without any more altercations. The day of the fight broke me. All I wanted was to pass 7th grade. I couldn't repeat this shit all over again. New hope presented itself in the nearing summer because I would use the time to study and catch up even more. Stay focused. That's all I had to do. Get my chores done. Keep my mouth shut. Stay out of trouble. Study. Read. It wasn't the air I breathed or the stars in the sky that mattered. It was survival and survival was only possible through education. I had no idea how I knew this. I just did. Maybe it was because the information, once learned, could not be taken from me, beaten or raped out of me.

My last class. The final exam over. The teacher's voice was clear and gentle. To me it rose like sweet music above the murmuring of the chattering and anxious children. He was my English teacher and had been suffering from kidney failure. Three times a week he would need dialysis, but never missed any school. The many enlarged lumps up and down both his arms from the illness was proof he was really sick.

He pushed me to read and was so kind when I failed to understand the lesson. It was his patience that lit a light inside me. He would always look at me when he spoke. When you don't see a kind face for years and you finally do, it brings up all those things wished for pretty much as if you wished for all of them only moments ago.

He left us with pleasant things to dream about before beginning our summer. His eyes were shining and when he spoke, I forgot about the loneliness. When he taught, he would lean a bit toward the class, as if he was really hoping to press the words into our hearts. For me, he was faith. He was beautiful.

The bell rang and we all lined up and shook his hand one by one as we hurried out the door of the class room. However, before leaving, he stopped me. Reached inside his pocket and drew out a thin folded piece of paper. When doing so, his face was like that of a young boy even though he was sick. Giving the folded paper to me, I unwrapped it. Written down in neat penmanship were several titles of books.

"Some ideas for reading over the summer," was all he said and smiled wanly.

I thanked him and left without really understanding the compassion that went into that gesture until after finding out he died later that summer. Moving through the hallway toward my locker, I was careful to shove the piece of paper deep into my pocket. The jostling and shoving of kids frightened me and I was afraid also that I would lose my English teacher's recommended reading list. It was an amazing gift, and up to that point, one of the most thoughtful I had received.

There was joyous laughter in the halls and kids were already planning their summers. When someone out of the blue told me to have a good summer, I replied with a little quiver in my throat. It was still both strange and wonderful when people were kind and their kindness was never lost on me.

A torn poster once promoting the JV football team hung askew from one of the brick walls. On it was a badly painted face of an American Indian. It was a joyous day for the other children, but not for me. I did not know if I would advance to the next grade and was still far behind academically. Emotionally for me, it was a wild and gloomy place. Stunted by years of abuse in every way, there was much work ahead. Haunted by nightmares and panic that made my blood run cold at night in my bed. And, everyone around me spoke in a language I did not understand.

Summer would begin with all these feelings and fears. Sometimes the days before me seemed inviting and other times if I stood still too long I could feel the horrors crashing down. I was shut in between the effects of the abuse –mostly the molestations and rapes – and finding the strength to push past these emotions to move forward. Like a shark, if I stopped swimming I would die.

As the hallways slowly emptied and we found our way to the circle of buses that would take us to our homes one last time, I found some relief in knowing I could study at my own pace. No longer under the pressure of prescriptive academic performance. It was a new day and growing closer within reach were more opportunities spawned by my continued quest for learning. What drove me still was the fear of becoming like Mother and Father and the hope I would find the long-awaited euphoria of acceptance through academic achievement.

As high as my hopes during the day, the nights brought with them the nightmares. Riddled with sweat when I woke, my face wet with tears, I would be shivering while cupping my genitals protectively. My thin body wrapped in a ball tangled in the blankets all around me. Sometimes the nightmares were so terrible I cried aloud and upon waking feared Lauren or Tim had heard me. This is why I wanted my own room the most. So that after the worst of the nightmares I could lay still listening to my breathing in order to calm down. And also, the solitude, in order to pray to an empty room.

During the school year, loneliness made me foolish and open to all manner of being taken advantage. I easily fell into the trap other children set for me by pretending to be my friend and then laughing about it when discovering they tricked me. I was still a child mentally and emotionally at twelve.

Tired, terribly lonely, and gullible; however, I always seemed to find my footing and roll forward.

At last, I was on the bus seated safely in the back. I liked it there. No one sat near me because that was where the losers found their place. The isolation was appealing. There, I would slip into another fantasy and sometimes the reality of Mother. Sometimes also, I would wonder how I was well enough to leave her when the feelings of despair and crushing fear overwhelmed me. Gaining some distance from the schoolhouse, I turned and looked back. I felt like crying.

Many things I had learned swam around in my head and I tried to hold on to them. I was weak and truly believed that the smarter I got the stronger I would become. Learning made me think and thinking was good. It was like a pool of sunlight I could draw from. Being aware of my surroundings. Only a few months had passed since being away from Mother and she was calling me back. I felt it and I could also still see her waving while Jessica drove us away. And this longing had been with me ever since. Never far from my mind and I would keep it with me always.

Soon, the school bus was at my drop and I had no idea what I would do on this first day of summer vacation. There were many changes happening. My voice sounded strange when I spoke. My body was developing physically and that felt strange too, and every now and then, I would find myself clenching my fists and trembling for no apparent reason.

Something was forcing me to feel this way. Some sort of struggle. I had come out of a wasteland into another place, but in many respects within the short time since Mother not much had changed. The food, shelter, and clothing were much improved that was for sure, but I had loved Mother and still loved her. Even when I remembered how her eyes would glare through me while grasping a clump of my hair and jerking my head back –I loved her. She still owned my heart and hovered always and incessantly above my every thought.

Approaching the home I shared with Lauren and Tim, I saw the thing that for a moment I had forgotten. The home was in need of painting and a small black patch against the gray wood stood out. The material needing application was creosote. Basically, a thick tar that would seal the exterior of the home. My first summer chore. With a gasping breath I walked toward the house. My fingers dug deeper into my palms and I shifted the backpack of books from one shoulder to the next. The fire of anger glowed inside me like a crimson flower. I just wanted to be left alone and read. I didn't want to paint the goddamn house.

I wasn't inside for more than a minute.

"Change your clothes and get to work!" Tim bellowed.

"No laying around this summer!"

"Lynn, help me in the kitchen!" Lauren commanded.

"Gregg, you and Carter get to work painting!" said Tim followed by a heckling laughter. He and Lauren were running out for a quick errand and they wanted to make sure we were working before they left.

This was our second home in less than a few months in which we moved. Lauren was a realtor and we would move five times while I was between the age of eleven and sixteen. We would purchase a home, fix it up, live in it for awhile, sell it, and start over. I hated moving. However, I would soon learn not nearly as much as I hated slinging tar.

Carter and me were slapping the creosote in thick globs and within minutes of doing so I had already forgotten it had been the last day of school. Bored stiff, Carter climbed up a ladder and now stood on the roof surveying the subdivision.

"I can see Caroline's house from here!" he said gleefully.

Caroline was our babysitter. It wasn't so much that Lauren and Tim felt Carter, Lynn, and I could not take care of ourselves, but rather it gave the two of them peace of mind we did not torch the house while they were out. Even if it was for only a couple hours. I was most assuredly infatuated with Caroline. She had this mysterious look about her with dark brown curly hair and matching eyes. Tall and slender and always tanned. Smooth skin that smelled of perfume soap. Though her best feature was full, red, soft lips. And on the few occasions she would allow me to kiss her goodbye, I would linger a bit and spend the rest of the evening tasting the sweet moisture of her mouth.

Afraid Tim would come home and find me not working, I continued to paint vigorously. I also wanted to finish the job and be done with it. Therefore, reaching a point of utter frustration, I picked up a half-full bucket of creosote and pumped the open container toward the side of the house. As fate would have it, the rubber-like tar substance literally bounced off the house and directly into my face and hair.

"Carter! Carter, it's burning!"

"It's burning!" I yelled frantically.

Carter half-jumped half-climbed down the ladder, grabbing my whole body and pushing me into the house. I could not open my eyelids and the creosote burned deep into my face and scalp. My eyes were quickly beginning to feel as though they were on fire as well. Carter dragged me through the house, leading me as one would lead a blind man, because I was blind. Once in the bathroom, he shoved me against the sink and hurriedly began breaking vials of the solvent that came with each purchased can of creosote. One after another, Carter poured the contents into my eyes. The solvent began working immediately, breaking down the thick film of tar sealing off my eyelids. I could now see Carter's hands reaching out to me and then he shoved my head under the running water of the faucet.

"Open your eyes, Gregg!" he yelled.

"Open your goddamn eyes and let the water wash them!"

It was working, and eventually the sting in my eyes began to subside, but my face and scalp still burned. I now saw that Carter's own eyes shone like stars and he kept advancing toward me with a look of absolute dread on his face. My God, he looked so worried.

"Are you okay?" Carter kept asking me.

"Gregg, are you okay?"

"No!" was all I muttered and began crying.

In the excitement, neither Carter nor I heard Tim calling our names from inside the house. Apparently, he and Lauren had returned home and saw the aftermath of spilled creosote, which looked like a large oil slick in the yard. Tim then burst into the bathroom.

"What the fuck happened?" he asked accusingly.

"Gregg got creosote on him," Carter responded.

"How in the fuck did you do that?" Tim said followed by the usual, "Are you stupid?"

There was no use in answering Tim. What I did was stupid, that's for sure. I was trying to hurry and get the damn job done. However, Tim wasn't my main concern. It was the fear of going blind. In addition, the burning creosote felt as if it was cracking my skull apart and peeling the skin off my face.

Watching Carter and Tim assess the situation wasn't helping matters. They both looked stunned and without a plan of action. Finally, Tim indicated we needed to get me to the doctor's. Then he laughed cheerfully which sent a shiver down my spine. What gave him pleasure always scared me.

"Lauren!" Tim called out. "We need to get your dumbass brother to the doctor's!"

During the drive, I felt my hair, which was like cement. The several stalks of hair fused together and poking from my skull were so hard they looked like dark razor-sharp knives. This combined with black tar smattering my face and forehead made me look like a demented punk rocker. I was reminded of a book I had read not too long ago about a tar baby being thrown into a briar patch. It was one of the many children's books I read during my first summer with Lauren and Tim. I tried concentrating on the meaning of the book as we drove to the doctor's office. Anything to distract me. Because in the deeper recesses of my mind I still waited for the blindness to come and steal my sight.

After a quick examination, one that left a puzzled look on the doctor's face, he finally prescribed a solution to wash the tar from my hair and a salve for my skin. The doctor also gave my eyes another rinse, and whatever he used, stung almost as bad as the creosote. The solution bleached my auburn hair blonde, making me look like a completely different person.

Upon returning home, I quickly went inside the bathroom to assess the damage. My face was pale, haggard, and I looked both freakish and ugly. The feeling of being ugly was always prevalent and now piled fresh agony on top of an already shattered self-esteem. The loneliness came back in a rush of emotion and I cried silently in front of the bathroom mirror. I could not look at my face without feeling disgust. At least I did not go blind and it was because of Carter. His hands had been shaking so badly while he dumped the liquid into my eyes. *Thank you for this, Carter.*

For the next several weeks, I stayed to myself. I was too embarrassed to play with the other kids in the subdivision or ask my friend Greg over until my normal hair color returned. The feelings of survival broke fresh and I studied harder, spending more and more time reading and working through rudimentary math problems. The more I learned, the more my confidence grew. It swept over me like a new kind of music, making my heart throb and my soul warm with joy.

It was during this summer before my 8th grade year, I would meet another boy, who quickly became one of my best friends. His name was Bruce and he was two years younger. Bruce was quiet and unassuming. Docile and reluctant to boast. He barely spoke, but when he did, his voice came out in a soft rasp. Bruce's eyes possessed a blue softness and it was with him I felt an innocent love between two boys. I now had two best friends; Greg and Bruce, and we were inseparable.

Together, the three of us also joined a Judo club at the local YMCA. Carter and Lynn, along with Bruce's older brother and younger sister also joined. All of us took to the fighting competitions with a great excitement. However, Judo gave to me more than something sporting. It brought with it a reason to fight back without ramifications like I had faced after beating the boy on the schoolyard. It fueled a burning violence inside me where there was far too much gloom. I went about each Judo match wailing and twisting more fiercely than the one before. I wanted the medals. I wanted to win. But most of all there was the desire to hurt someone. During the competitions, I'd be filled with a moaning sound that would turn into a scream with each movement. Flipping another boy and sending him slamming into the mat left me with a feeling of power. It stoked a growing anger and awakened a rage inside of me. The rage felt good, and to my astonishment, I realized fighting was something that came naturally. Like Carter, I was a death bomb.

Hanging on to my accomplishments, both academic and athletic, I continued to strive for even more. With every accomplishment came the desire to surpass it. In the form of a great burden, I crudely struggled to pull myself from where I once came while choking on the ashes of my past. I sprang toward every possibility while trying desperately to prove my self-worth.

Dragging myself from one day to the next, I looked for a sign of life. In the midst of all my effort, there was always the lingering and terrible picture of anguish that could not be shaken. Within my mind's ear I heard my Mother telling me in a sleeper's breath I was worthless. Most days, I saw no sign of movement in any forward direction. Perhaps it was the lectures from Lauren and Tim. Or the bored looking social worker Lauren asked to come and speak with me and my siblings because she felt we were troubled. Of which, there were only a few visits and then she never returned. But mostly, it was Mother, not far from my thoughts even now, and also the strangers lurking about, waiting their turn to do their ugly things while bartering over my worth.

What held life for me was something caught in the deep recesses of my heart. It was a folded bit of paper with several books written upon by the careful hand of a dying English teacher. This told me someone cared. Someone who wanted more from me than sex and who was in command of their mental and emotional faculties. Someone who did not slur their words or stagger when they walked. A good person in my stormy life.

I began to realize I had not died years before, but had been killed by the evil of others. They used many weapons and did well to cover their trail by using my shame as the perfect alibi. I would not be like them. I could not allow this. I knew at a much younger age than twelve what it meant to love someone, and so I knew what life meant.

As I spent the summer in preparation of yet another hurdle in the form of the 8th grade, I also realized what life was supposed to be. It came down to a folded piece of paper. Not so much what a good man had written upon it, but the time he took to write down the words, and with all his love, putting his hope into me.

CHAPTER FOUR

The Difference Between Sorrow
and Barely Breathing

*"My sole preoccupation is to just wake up,
only to begin the hunt for freedom all over again."*

LIKE SOMEONE DAZED BY A traffic accident I stood watching Tim jerk Matilda, his German Shorthair hunting dog, off Bruce. Mattie for short, she was a gray-black slender dog with a bobbed tail and had a spot on her back that resembled a tiny black saddle. She was Tim's hunting dog, but I soon adopted her as my own. I loved animals and they seemed to love me in return. Mattie would check on me while I slept by sniffing the bed and sometimes after her appointed rounds, she would climb in with me. I'd fall asleep spooning her from behind, feeling her warm soft coat as her small ribcage rose and fell.

Bruce and I had only been wrestling, but Mattie thought he was hurting me when hearing my shouts of laughter. We stopped fooling around immediately when we noticed Mattie standing motionless and glaring at Bruce. There came a low growl from her throat and then, without warning Mattie lunged, snapping at Bruce's face. Her sharp white teeth flashing. Tim had been standing nearby, acting as a referee of sorts. He grabbed Mattie, snatching her up by the neck. She let out a yelp, followed by gurgling sounds, and I screamed for him to stop. Ignoring me, Tim carried Mattie by the throat to the garage and threw her in a dog cage. From inside the house, I could hear her coughing and making choking sounds.

"Stay away from her!" Bill said, coming back into the living room.

I could no longer hear any sounds coming from Mattie since she was bodily whisked off to the garage and was afraid she had choked to death in her cage. That night, after Tim and Lauren had gone to sleep, I crept into the garage, which was right off my bedroom to check on Mattie. She was laying down in the cage, and upon seeing me, quickly raised her head. Her bobbed tail doing its best to wiggle. Quietly opening the cage door, I took her into my arms, while gently raking my fingers through her soft fur. It was time to say goodbye, because I knew Mattie would be gone the next day.

The loss of Mattie would awaken in me the memories of losing Sambirdio. The kind of memory that pursues a child into adulthood. Covering my pain, I concealed it as best I could from Tim. He would be angry with me for feeling sorry for Mattie, but it was difficult not to do. She had only been protecting me, but that was criminal enough to send her away.

The sudden burst of fear in the pit of my stomach when looking at the calendar told me school would begin soon. I spent that summer reading and picking over simple math problems. In addition, I kept to myself, always mindful of the instructions handed down by Lauren and Tim. Never talking back, I was both dutiful and obedient. Fear does that to a person. Blind tolerance to whoever you are in fear of.

I still had my best friends Greg and Bruce, but only Greg would be attending school with me due to the fact Bruce was two years our junior. I made a vow that I would no longer get into any more trouble at school. This meant no more fighting, even if the bullies picked on me. I did not fear them as much as before anyway. Not since I fought back. But I did fear the disgrace that came with having to struggle with the school work. The embarrassment was overpowering.

The conscious feeling of what it was like to be humiliated had always stayed with me. It was the first emotion I remember as a child and brought with it the sound of crackling needles in my head. Pin-pricks of shame when I stared up at the face looking down on me and it was usually the face of Mother. Sometimes behind her was a man whose face was covered with a scrubby beard. The beard was old, and his eyes and his voice I would have recognized anywhere. He was a regular.

I drew my small body upward and before completely standing, he had grasped my thin shoulders. There was excitement in his voice and face. His eyes shone a squint as he looked me over. Mother had let him into the house minutes before and then she disappeared. The man stared at my forehead, where there was a stain of blood. A scratch Mother had left when pulling me by my hair and out of the bed I shared with Carter when she heard the knock at the door.

"You hurt?" the man asked, not really interested.

I did not speak. He didn't care anyway and I was too afraid. The man opened his pants and was gripping my hands now and using them on his privates. Over near the door was a round chair Carter, Lynn and I used to turn upside-down, sitting in between the legs, while taking turns spinning one another. Afterwards, I'd nearly puke from dizziness. I felt that way touching the man. He pushed my hands away absently and knelt in front of me. The face of the man was now staring at my belly while he touched himself. With his other hand he reached around and squeezed my buttocks, gripping them painfully, while pulling me toward his waiting mouth. I didn't remember the man taking down my underwear that now lay in a crumpled bunch around my ankles.

His mouth was cold with saliva that felt like acid on my genitals. I moaned in despair while he moaned in ecstasy. The house was quiet except for a sick sucking noise while the man continued groping me and touching himself. His pace quickened and I fought back the tears, but they came anyway. He did not know because the man never looked up. Never looked at my face. At one point, the man seemed to chuckle a little, but I couldn't tell because it was muffled. His pace quickened still and the sucking became violent and more painful. The horrible fear my penis would be torn off never left me during these times with the strangers or with Mother. In spite of the fear, sometimes it was difficult for me to feel anything except numb all over.

The man gripped my buttocks hard and jerked me forward. I felt sticky warmness splash against my legs and almost threw up. The man thrust, again and again, quivering all over. A low cry now broke from his lips and he grunted. I saw the moon shining through the dirty living room window and there were a few stars near its glow. Neither the moon nor the stars did anything to help me.

The man now finished, told me to go in my room and shut the door. It was always the same. After the strangers were done, they never wanted me nearby. Before I was halfway down the short hallway leading to my bedroom, I heard the front door open and then the sound of the man quietly closing it behind him. My heart beating wildly, I climbed into the bed I shared with Carter, careful not to wake him up. I was also careful not to touch his skin with my own –it felt dirty.

There was the sound of movement on Mother's bed and I was startled by the suddenness of the noise. Her door had been shut, but now I saw her open it. Mother now stood in her doorway with the light of the moon shining through her window from behind, casting a silhouette. For a moment she seemed to stare right at me as I lay in bed. A wild flush filled my cheeks and I held my breath, releasing it slowly so as to not make a sound. Carter was still asleep. The horror of Mother beckoning me with her finger sent a chill through me, striking me dumb. I saw her feverish madness standing there in the darkness. She muttered to herself then staggered back to her own bed, whispering something over and over again. Not until Mother closed her door did I move. My blood was cold as I rolled to one side, facing away from Carter and moving as close to the edge of the bed as possible. Tomorrow, Mother would beat me for letting the man do those terrible things, while screaming I was queer and perverted, and I would believe her. She was Mother. She was the law and the only law I knew. I would be punished for what I did with the strangers. That was Mother's law. Outside, the moon and the stars shone, and did nothing to save me. I knew humiliation and it knew me well, too.

A few weeks before the school year began Tim made me and my brother attend a funeral of his friend's teenage son. The boy died in a motorcycle accident and Tim wanted to teach us a lesson. The lesson was to make us wary to the dangers of riding a motorcycle. I felt there were better ways of passing this wisdom along.

The dead boy could not have been more than seventeen, but because of the pancake makeup plastered all over his face in order to cover the deep scars, he looked much older. As a matter of fact he looked ancient. His face was not that of a young boy. For several minutes, I stared at him while he lay in his coffin. A sickness came over me and laid a heavy hand upon my heart. He was gone and would never know again what it felt like to ride with the wind in his face, laugh with his friends, or simply be cool. The darkened room of the funeral parlor was lit with only lamps and in this light the boy's face was white and drawn. His skin was pulled far too tightly down around his facial bones and skull. There were tense lines at the corners of his mouth and something strange and swollen above his right eye. At that, I stared the longest.

I overheard his father tell Tim that the gash above his son's right eye was the one that killed him and then something about a brain injury. The boy's father went on to say the paramedics could not suck the blood from his son's lungs fast enough and this comment stayed with me for some reason. I was also never going to forget the look of the boy. What I saw would haunt me in my sleep later that night.

At one point, while standing at the coffin, the boy's mother came and stood next to me. She then leaned over the coffin putting one of her hands on her son's arm and wept while rubbing the sleeve of his suit coat, which looked much too large. Watching this, I wondered if Mother would cry for me if I were dead. The boy's mother then began working her hands gently over her son's face. Over his powder white skin. I would have expected her to be afraid, but she was not frightened, and her eyes followed the contours of her son's face wonderingly. The boy's mother began to weep harder. Her lips quivered, but she made no sound while the tears welled up in her eyes, holding a clutched fist against her breast. The other, still tenderly caressing her son's face. Standing just behind his wife, I heard her husband whispering things, and then his arms crept tightly around her shoulders. He held her there and the brave smile once held on his lips throughout the funeral was now gone. Seeing this, what remained of me being too ashamed to let anyone see me cry, was now gone as well.

I watched as the boy's parents held one another and wept. Their bodies shaking and they kissed each other's cheeks. Her husband tried to keep a thickness out of his voice when trying to console his wife. His son's mother. I continued to watch them as they disappeared into the next room, leaving me standing at the edge of where their son lay inside his coffin. A groan of anguish broke from my lips realizing the dead boy's parents would never see their son again, never hold him again in their arms, smother him with embarrassing kisses, or feel the warmth of his face ever again.

Long before the boy's funeral, a menacing dread enveloped my heart. I knew before seeing the dead boy how life was slipping away, and at times, snatched from us. For me it did not go quickly or quietly, but my life was a slow grinding down where I was being swallowed up by the darkness. The boy's life now expired and his parents left to search and find him in every corner of their day-to-day lives. It was an accident that killed him. A mistake that could not be taken back. In the dark room of the funeral parlor, I wondered if Mother had been there, would she have exclaimed drunkenly that it should have been me.

I could hear her accusing voice while standing next to the coffin. In the stillness of the room, where people wept quietly and talked in whispers, I could hear Mother's low soughing voice. Her words hung heavy and close about me, chasing each other through my brain until they seemed to leave behind them a picture of me laying in the coffin instead. Mother often said I should have died and never been born. Adding credence to her claims was the fact she had tried to kill me many times. Staring at the boy, I saw myself as Mother must have seen me. Useless. Unmoving. And, like the boy –dead.

Tim said it was time to go and I was glad. There'd be a lecture to follow while we drove home and I dreaded it. In the car, Tim was pleasantly quiet for a short while, then he started to finally speak, and nothing but noise came out of his mouth. In his crude and heartless way, Tim began discussing the merits of safety and his words were like needles piercing the temples of my head. My throat felt as if it was clogged with something making breathing difficult and hard to swallow. I caught Tim's reflection in the car's rearview mirror and held his eyes for a few seconds before looking at the road again. His speech was the usual undone and scattered mess of nonsensical words. The lump in my throat was growing bigger and it choked me. The death of the boy brought with it a loneliness I could not shake. My hands trembled and twitched as I hid them behind the seat where Tim sat driving and lecturing tediously.

In spite of the feelings of sadness and fear, I also felt the shame that crept over me at the funeral. In those minutes we drove home, I could not get Mother's voice out of my head telling me that it should have been me in the coffin instead. My thoughts went to when she once lamented on about Jesus coming to her in a dream, proclaiming I was evil, and that I should be killed. In the dream Mother described, Jesus stood on a hillside in a blood red robe and spoke to her while weeping. He told Mother that her suffering was recognized by all of Heaven and that she was both noble and brave. According to Mother, the dream ended abruptly after Jesus informed her that I was evil. A bad seed. But Mother did not need a make-believe dream about Jesus to make me feel as though I were evil. All she had to do was remind me of the things I did with the strangers. In doing so, I could not deny that perhaps the dream was real.

When we finally arrived home, I felt a sudden thrill of not having to listen to Tim's sermon any longer. While getting out of the car he told me to mow the lawn. Gladly, it was something to get my mind off the day's events. After beginning to mow the lawn, I thought of the dead boy who would end up among the many names of the marked headstones in some cemetery. His face flashed before me, white pasty and swollen above his right eye. The thick makeup barely concealing the long red scar.

My blood grew hot as I thought of why Tim had taken Carter and me to the funeral. When largely it had been to teach us a difficult lesson, where we had already been taught so many already. It was a thoughtless and cruel thing to do. For a few moments I stood before a steep hill with the handle of the mower humming under my palms. Then, quickly caught myself and began moving again, pushing the mower up the incline. Tim might be watching and I did not want another lecture.

On the way to the funeral, it held a curious sort of fascination for me, but not any longer. A boy was dead and now funerals held a much different meaning. Several times while I mowed, I nearly cried, but kept moving so as not to. Subdued by the noise of the mower, I let out a breathless whimper from time to time and moaned. Under the summer sun I felt like fainting. When the sweat broke from my body it was not hot, but cold and the feelings of anger and sorrow rushed over me. By means of the funeral, Tim did succeed in teaching me a lesson. His work was complete. In a nightmare that evening I saw the dead boy's arms reaching for me from out of the coffin. He spoke incoherently and his voice was terrifying. The gash over his right eye started to bleed through the thick black stitching. It was not the lesson Tim had hoped I learned, but I had seen enough to learn one indisputable truth: I did not want to attend anymore goddamn funerals.

I began 8th grade, barely passing 7th, and already dying of humiliation before the first bell of the first class. Greg pushed me to take more advanced classes, but I would not because I could not. He was kind to offer, but I knew my limitations. I took the basic courses and still fought to keep up. It was a little easier than 7th grade, which gave me a bit more self-confidence. My grades also began to improve and my continuing participation in Judo helped bolster my self-esteem even more. Winning does that. And, I won quite a bit.

At one particular Judo competition there was a lottery. The name you drew was the person you fought. In this particular event, there were no age or weight divisions. Just gender. I drew one of the masters. A Shodan or senior ranking black belt who was also a club (Dojo) Sensei (teacher) and at least fifteen years my senior. He also outweighed me by at least forty pounds and was about three feet taller. Stepping onto the mat and bowing to him, I let out a short mirthless laugh. The kind of laugh that is supposed to cover up the fear. He returned the bow and the referee commenced the match by yelling, "Hajime!"

I was flung back and forth, up and down. Point after point the monstrous black belt scored and had no mercy. The crowd grew bored with the match and some even chided and laughed. After one of many foot-sweeps (Deashi-Barai) knocking me down with ease, my opponent became bored as well, and turning his back, began slowly walking toward his respective side of the mat.

I rushed him in a springing action (Hane-Goshi) and executed what is referred to as a Kata-Ashi-Dori, or kicking of the leg, and grabbing the collar of his Gi, rendered a perfectly executed Okuri-Ashi-Harai. The move was basically pulling the master backward with all my might and kicking the rear of his kneecaps as hard as I possibly could. I succeeded splendidly in carrying out a well performed Tsuri-Komi-Goshi. In order to complete the move, I threw myself toward the mat utilizing our combined weight. The Shodan flew backward and instinctively slapped the mat with his hands and forearms in order to break the fall. I was stunned upon hearing the referee yell, "Ippon!" Winner! The match was over. I was the victor. We faced one another and bowed (Ritsurei). The smile never left my face when leaving the mat, not even when walking past Tim who told me it was "a pussy move." When I was out of earshot and safely inside the locker room, I replied to Tim's comment:

"Suck my dick."

The victory was short lived. They all were. With every academic or athletic advancement, came ridicule from Lauren and Tim. The better I did, the worse it became. My grades continued to improve, but I was far from where I needed to be in comparison to the other students. I returned to my studies each and every day after school and would spend hours poring over a math problem or reading text books in an attempt to keep rhythm with the other students. Developing a solid study habit of one hour before school and at least five afterwards, I began to learn exponentially.

Oftentimes now, I did not have to refer to a dictionary or thesaurus and was also keeping the promise to myself that I would stay out of trouble. The closest I came to mischievous behavior was getting into an occasional rock throwing contest during the school lunch period. This involved the practice of students heaving stones at one another while finding hiding places in a park just off school property. It was like playing "Army," but instead, we used rocks instead of pretend guns. What ended this foolishness rather abruptly was when I saw a kid get clouted in the forehead with one of the flying rocks. It sent the poor sap reeling and knocked him out cold. Of course we all ran like hell afterwards. I don't know who found him or if anyone actually had the guts to tell a teacher, but the next time I saw the boy he had a lump above his eye as big as an acorn. That ended it for me.

I was still bullied by many of the same boys the year before. Apparently they had forgotten the beating I let loose the previous school year. Then again, my manner of appearance was far from menacing which told the schoolyard bullies my actions of returning an ass-kicking was remote.

Because of the bullying, I dreaded lunchtime. Something thick and uncomfortable would rise in my throat and my vision became blurry. This was panic and a feeling I knew well. I had delivered a magnificent fight that fateful day a year prior, but when I cracked the boy underneath his eye and felt something snap, I thought of Father crushing the side of Mother's face causing her own eye to pop out of its socket. The thought scared me because of how similar the two events were. Later that same evening pondering the near suspension and complete dismantling of all my efforts with regard to academics, I wondered what came over me. The fear of turning into my parents extinguished the elation of payback. It was the first time I began to realize I did not fully escape Mother and Father. Violence was their weapon, and I not only fell into the trap of using it, but also that unmistakable feeling of pleasure it brought. And then there was the lie I told myself that it would be the last time I would use this weapon.

Not willing to subject myself to the embarrassment of failing yet another sport, I focused only on my studies that year. My friend Greg however, talked me into going to school dances. It occurred to me while at these dances I was changing physically and becoming more interested in girls. I was taking a big chance on asking each one to dance because often I was turned down. But I kept asking. My confidence wasn't entirely obliterated by their refusals. It was probably due to the occasional reward of feeling the warm smoothness of a girl's skin next to mine, along with her budding breasts pressed against me during the few slow dances in which she had said yes. Rather swiftly, the reaction worked over my body and I had to be careful to keep my pelvis away from hers. For me it was obvious as to why, and had I pushed closer, it would have been quite noticeable to the girl as well. The feeling was quite distinct because it had been the first time I felt good about anything sensual. Before, with Mother and the strangers, it was always forced. Always ugly. And never consensual. Deeper into these feelings was another emotion. It was love. Puppy love they call it, but still a form of adoration that felt as if the girl loved me in return.

Outside of a few setbacks academically and the occasional slapping and pushing I'd have to withstand from a bully, 8th grade passed without much fanfare. Deeper into my studies I threw myself and continued to do exactly what Lauren and Tim commanded.

But then there came something that would cause me a great deal of stress due to the terrible similarities related to my past. Lauren and Tim took on two foster boys ages 7 and 9. The younger was Mike and his older brother was named Steve. Neither looked to be related biologically. Mike had dark features. Straight jet black hair with onyx deep-set eyes. The eyes of a caged animal with a mixture of both fear and danger within them. Making Mike even more menacing was the fact he never spoke. Almost mute unless the words were painfully dragged from him. In complete contrast was Steve who had blonde curly hair, pale skin, a bit portly and very talkative.

Both boys had been sexually molested by their mother and were forced to have sex with their twelve-year-old sister while their parents watched. All three children became wards of the state and entered the foster care program. How Lauren and Tim heard about them or why they were brought into our home was not shared with me or my siblings. I knew only through Lauren that they were products of sexual abuse. Adding a severe truth to this was the fact Steve had once shown me his penis, which was a mangled mess of skin and scar tissue from repeated lashings by his father's belt. Something fluttered in my gut when I looked with horror at his small and distorted penis. Something familiar and revolting.

Unlike Steve, who seemed somewhat jovial regardless of the physical and sexual abuse, Mike was forbidding. I would often find him masturbating while hiding somewhere in the house. The act repulsed me and I would often yell at him to stop. Both boys were threatening my way of life as it was. They were additional mouths to feed and underfoot. Trespassers in a world I was not entirely welcomed. Mike especially was a constant reminder of from where I came, and worst of all, who I was. An ugly remembrance of my own private hell that brought back the memories of guilt and shame.

Eventually, both boys were returned to the foster care program. Their stay had not lasted more than a few months. Perhaps it was too much for Lauren and Tim to handle. It was a great relief for me when they were gone and I made sure not to be around on the day the social worker came to pick them up.

The final stretch before summer passed quickly. The survival instinct rose in me and was stronger than ever. It warmed my blood with a strange feeling of a new destiny and one of escape. I was more than just another student now, I was quickly becoming recognized as "being smart." Instead of feeling like a hunted rat being chased from one place to another, I felt like one of the popular kids. Beginning to realize I must be more than those things Mother once beat into me, for the first time, I began to feel as though I were not wholly bad or worthless. Every now and then a twinge of pain would find my heart and squeeze when remembering my past. But then this new lease on life would bring with it a thrill of pleasure.

My loyalty was to perseverance and every opportunity that presented itself was another chance at triumph. Before me was a living, breathing reality in the form of education which had taken the place of the nightmare vision in my heart. And it was as real as the flesh and blood in which I was made. It was not enough yet to make me love myself, but the feeling of self-worth grew stronger and the thought of having faith in myself filled me with a strange elation.

To my surprise and delight, I ended my 8ᵗʰ grade year with "B's" and "C's". A vast improvement compared to the year before and even more so when considering I could barely read, tell time, or tie my own shoes only a year ago. In a few short months, I would enter high school and I felt closer to becoming normal. The fire was growing inside of me and I studied even harder to add fresh fuel.

My heart caught sight of the difference a year could make and it made me wonder what I could accomplish in only a few years. It wasn't that I was forgetting my past, but that old life was slipping away and may very well have been on the other side of the world. I started to really believe that I was built for better things. Lauren and Tim's ridicule would not stop me. The boys beating me up at school would not slow me down. The loss of one thing I loved after another would not cease the love I had for learning. My place was among the worthy and education drew it out.

Of course I still loved Mother, but I began to see it was a strong and ugly love. As the months passed, I stopped missing her as much too. More so, she became a subtle thought in the recesses of my mind, where she was no longer a part of me, nor I her. It was as if with a sudden breathless cry I thrust what was left of Mother's stranglehold on me and threw it onto a great fire.

Tim did his best from time to time and one of these attempts was introducing my brother and I to the world of riding motorcycles. We both worked odd jobs over the summer to earn enough money in which to purchase two used dirt bikes. In a nearby gravel pit we rode for endless hours. Learning motorcycle repair was also something Tim tried to teach us. I never quite got the hang of it, but Carter did much better. He was always more mechanically inclined. Not that strong academically, but he took to machinery easily.

It was in the garage about a week before school started I was changing the rear tire of my motorcycle. Unknowingly, I had put it on backwards and was in the process of trying to figure out what was wrong when Tim walked over. With only one look at what I was doing, he became incredibly agitated.

"You got the goddamn wheel on backwards, Gregg!" he said.

"I taught you better than that!"

As a matter of fact, he never did teach me how to change a motorcycle tire. I stood frozen while Tim worked himself into a frenzy. Until now I had only observed the storm growing steadily worse inside of him. But suddenly, I was caught in the middle of it. Tim broke loose with a right-hook that came crashing into my face. I heard myself let out a soft whimper and stumbled to the side, bouncing off his truck parked nearby. The hot piss filled my pants and formed a visible plume over the crotch. Tim took one look and went inside the house.

Alone in the garage I emptied what was left of my bladder. It couldn't be helped. Once the piss started, it had to run its course. Following the punch, I felt both stupid and guilty. By the time I reached the mudroom inside the house, fine white volleys of dots floated in front of my eyes. Anxiously making my way to the bathroom, I knelt and vomited in the toilet. A few feet away from the door I could hear Tim mumbling to Lauren. With my hands over my ears, I continued to puke in silence. Behind a gnarled and stunted emotional well-being, any aspirations of pleasing Tim were now gone. In a sweeping motion of Tim's fist for nothing more than not knowing how to replace a motorcycle tire, I was reduced to no more than a shadow. A shadow already desperately trying to fight my way out of the twisting blur of the storm that Mother beat into me for the first eleven years of my life. A storm that just would not end.

The summer before high school I began to separate myself into definitive parts. A frightened boy, which was the face I showed Lauren and Tim. A confident young man, which was the face I showed others. Showing Lauren and Tim confidence was like a pistol leveled at my chest. Sooner or later it was going to go off. The confidence made them nervous. Even when Tim would pretend he was only playing a game when touching Lynn's breasts, I kept quiet. I only watched, doing nothing, and felt sick to my stomach. The boy who had forced Lynn to hide while taking the advances of the strangers instead of her was now gone. The knowledge of what would be at stake if I protested was apparent. Losing all opportunities in which there was still hope in becoming something better. It wasn't a fair fight from the beginning, so I was learning how to play the game, but at Lynn's expense. I ignored her pleading looks even though the hatred burned inside of me for what Tim did and at how Lauren just looked away. I convinced myself that at least this was shelter, and with each passing year, there was the steady threat of losing it all. In the midst of what I had never been given, a chance at survival, I gave up the only thing that mattered –my soul. And with this sacrifice, this time, I did not protect Lynn. *I am so sorry.*

There developed a steely hardness inside of me. Surrounded by the evil of what people do, in a flash, I would be transported back to remembering the worst of their actions. Figuring it had been good fortune we ended up at Lauren and Tim's was now replaced with just trying to make it through each day without accusation or harm. It was difficult. Anything could set them off. A word from their only child I had played too rough would result in a smack across my face with a rolled magazine by Lauren. It was as if she didn't care enough to touch me even when rendering a slap.

Even the most honest mistakes escalated into tornados of violence. Tim once backed his truck from the garage, forgetting to close the driver side door. The door was ripped forward smashing the window, mirror, and nearly snapping it from its hinges. My brother and I had been standing in the garage when it happened and were blamed instantly for not warning Tim of the impending doom. After the accident, he leapt from the car pushing past us and went into the house. Moments later when Carter and I walked inside, there was broken glass and splintered wood everywhere from what appeared to be formerly his gun cabinet. I remembering asking Lauren what happened and she only glared at us. I could have cut my own tongue for even uttering the question, but the words were already out before I could stop from speaking. It was our fault. You could see it in her eyes. It was always our fault.

"Go outside!" Lauren said, clenching her teeth.

"What an asshole," Carter said when we left the house.

"What a stupid fucking asshole." I said.

And then we both laughed nervously.

My hands clenched fiercely and I made no reply after my last comment back to Carter. My mind was working over the incident and it scared me, because Tim was dangerous and he was also in charge.

The house was Lauren's domain. That's where she ruled, but the garage belonged to Tim. He would sweep the cement floor for hours, spreading that dust powder janitors always used in school that smelled like vomit, and then, sweep the garage floor again. For hours, Tim would bury himself blindly futzing around his tools and workbench. He'd wipe the tools with a red oil cloth and sweep the tops of the workbenches with a tiny dust broom. Tim would scarcely know anyone was nearby while going about his business, whispering to himself and usually bitching about something over and over again.

"Fuck. Fuck. Fuck," he'd moan.

To whom he was speaking, I do not know and did not ask. The only reason I was hanging around in the first place was because Tim had me doing some insignificant bullshit in the garage as well. Maybe he thought it was quality time. However, to me it was:

"Boring. Boring. Boring."

Once, when Lauren and Tim were gone, I jockeyed the keys to Lauren's new Camaro from a key hook just inside the mudroom door. Lynn was messing around with something on top of Tim's workbench when I climbed into the car and fired it up. She must have jumped a mile. I threw the Camaro into gear accidently and hit the accelerator, which was followed by a high-pitched squealing of tires. The sound was deafening as it echoed off the walls of the garage. By dumb luck, I managed to mash the brake with my left-foot just before the car crushed Lynn against the workbench. A hot rush of fear came over me at the thought of almost killing Lynn. I sat there motionless and staring blankly at her through the windshield. Lynn stared back with these huge saucer-like tearful eyes. A few seconds later, she bolted inside the house crying out loud as she ran away. Realizing I could have paralyzed or killed Lynn struck me with a deadly fear. She'd be gone and Lynn was all I had. My reaction was delayed and the full impact came when after hanging the keys back on their rightful hook, I staggered into the bathroom and threw up in the sink.

A couple hours later, Lauren and Tim came back and neither I or Lynn said a word. For the remainder of the day, I kept out of sight in fear of them seeing the guilt on my face that something had gone terribly wrong while they were away. Each hour that passed was met with the sight of almost crushing Lynn with Lauren's Camaro and the horror swept over me. By the time I went to bed that evening I was half-dead with a strange sickness because of the anxiety which built up since the near accident. It became so intense that I vomited again in a metal waste can near the desk I used for studying. When I was sure Lauren and Tim were asleep I crept outside and emptied its contents past the dog kennel then rinsed the metal can with the hose. The thought of hurting Lynn kept coming back to me leaving little chance of sleep that evening. In all the awful moments I had leading up to this one, it proved to be one of my most terrible days. A most terrible day having nearly killed the only person who loved me.

Exhausted all the time. That's how I felt. My face pinched in worry constantly. I spent the rest of the summer with my head down and mind alert. I gave Lauren and Tim no more than a glance as I went about my chores that Lauren always neatly penned on a large piece of paper tacked to a hanging corkboard in the kitchen. During that summer we would move into another house yet again. Another real-estate steal when you have cheap labor. In the desperate struggle against budding panic and anxiety there was neither rancor nor threat in my voice when I spoke. Only blind obedience and every attempt at disappearing when in public and hiding in my books when in private.

I was still half dead to the world and empty, save for the few academic and athletic triumphs. Everything was gone inside except survival. I was on automatic. As just a sort of reminder was the fact I still possessed a few of the remaining tics. Spitting, touching and retouching things. They had me pretty beat most times, but I hid them as best I could from everyone. I stopped pissing the bed, but the nightmares never left me. As shrewd as I may have thought I was being, I knew Lauren and Tim could see right through me. I left an easy trail of feebleness to follow. I'd have to put up with the occasional name calling like "faggot" or "sissy boy" from Tim, but I'd gotten used to it. There was no time for self-reflections and examination. What the fuck did a twelve-year-old know about that shit anyway?

As I got through what was left of the summer and prepared for another school year, I placed all the strength I had left into study and athletics. At first I ran only a few blocks but then blocks turned into a mile and a mile turned into a few miles. There was no betrayal in education or running. You got out of it what you put in and best of all, you got to keep what you earned. Sometimes the pain of not understanding what I was reading or a difficult math problem was like running. It left a stitch in my side and put a sneer on my lips; however, if I did not give up, I would eventually improve.

Although, there was a terrible thing happening at home. No longer was I comfortable with having the basics met; food, water, shelter. The warning signs were all around and I could easily see that Lauren and Tim were growing more exasperated with me and my siblings. Carter talked back more and it was only customary for a young teenager like him to begin rebelling. His eyes would blaze blue when speaking with Lauren or Tim and the harder they pushed him the more his eyes would splinter the light. What gave way to reason was the fact Carter began to hang out with the kids who did drugs. He also grew his hair long, which bothered both Lauren and Tim considerably. Carter scared them too. The older he got, the more he looked the part of a skull knocker and spinal cracker.

Two years my senior, Carter began dating sooner than me. Much sooner. I once walked downstairs and found a young girl about fifteen sitting naked squarely on top of his face. Carter seemed to have been struggling to push her off with his mouth, but not trying too terribly hard to do so. When she saw me, there was a loud clatter while both of them scrambled to their feet and dressed. I left hurriedly and went outside, still wondering why anyone would attempt such a position. I knew it had something to do with sex, but that was all.

It was different for me. Even approaching thirteen I was not interested in sex the way Carter was. What got me excited was the touch of Caroline's lips when she let me kiss her while babysitting. It would fill me with tender gratitude. Then there was the touch of her hands and the thrill of her presence just being near me. Perhaps these emotions were sex in some way and might be seen as such by the stiffness they made in my penis.

By the look on Caroline's face when we kissed, I could tell she felt something too. It may have been wrong in the sense our ages were so far apart; four years. Still, I was a fool for thinking it was anything other than a young boy's infatuation for her. No matter, from afar I would keep the fire burning inside for her and wait.

The first day of school. 9th grade. Rising sullenly, I was still suspicious of everything and everyone. Within my suspicion I found strength and approached each day with a burning desire to conquer it. No time for silly emotions, I threw out everything that did not serve my purpose of advancement. My actions had began to change from docile to dominant. I quickly slipped into something built not born. A boy becoming a young man made for battle where I could feel my blood grow colder with each passing day. No foolishness for me. Just a hard-pressed resistance to failing. Education was the key. It provided clear direction and surrounded me with a protective solid shining ring of gold.

While stepping off the bus enroute to the high school, my breath came more quickly. Careful not to make eye-contact, I moved toward the doors. I saw one of the boys who had picked on me for the last two years and for a moment the temptation to reach out and snap his neck was strong. I pulled myself away and kept moving. It would not serve me well to get expelled the first day of school. However, a thought crossed my mind when our eyes met in a glance. Maybe it was the way he quickly looked away that told me I'd win the fight. I adjusted the book bag on my shoulder and followed the stream of other kids into the brick building. My face was grim and set.

CHAPTER FIVE

The Power of Knowledge

"I am perfection in progress, a better angel in the making, a brighter star every day. If you can remember this – teach me how."

"THAT'S THE TRICK, GREGG!" THE wrestling coach bellowed gleefully.

"He hasn't got a chance!" the coach said to me while I worked on pinning the boy's shoulders to the mat.

It was only junior varsity wrestling, but I had finally made a sports team.

"It's up to you, Gregg!"

"Let's go!"

"All the way, now!"

The coach was whipped into a frenzy of excitement with his belly pressed against the mat, one arm raised in hysterical anticipation, and then he shouted, "Pinned!" The coach jumped to his feet grabbed my wrist and held it triumphantly into the air.

"Welcome to JV!" the coach said.

"You just earned your spot on the team!"

Yep, that's the trick, I thought. Like Carter and me used to say, "That's the way you fucking do things downtown." At making the team, I had a right to be angry and happy at the same time. When I told Tim both Carter and I were going out for junior varsity wrestling, his response was, "It still ain't varsity."

From the start of 9th grade, I could see the difficulty I'd have making my way through the AP courses as well as going out for sports, but I didn't care if I was good enough for varsity or not.

"You can't handle AP courses, Gregg," Lauren scolded.

"You can barely handle your regular courses."

Tim was a bit more tactical in his response. He'd just say, "You're too dumb."

Maybe they were both right, but I wouldn't know unless I tried.

As I made my way through the blizzard of high-level courses, the academic work requirements piled up quickly. So, I got up earlier before school and studied longer at night. In place of teaming up with Bruce or Greg, I chose to study.

Making it through the JV wrestling season with a pretty good record, 11-2 as a matter of fact, my interest in playing intramural basketball returned. However, the season was short-lived when I once asked Tim to drive me to a game. I never would have asked him in the first place, but Lauren told me to wake him up when it was time to go, while she was off selling a house. I knocked on the bedroom door and from inside I heard Tim's muffled and agitated response. Then suddenly, there was the familiar sound of things breaking. He begrudgingly got dressed and drove me to the game. On the way there, he bitched the whole time about how he works for a living, and then on the way home, he bitched about how badly I played. That ended intramural basketball once and for all.

Forging ahead in my studies, I was keeping up pretty well. I chose now to go out for the varsity track team. I never thought I'd make the cut, it was just that I loved to run. It felt good to put my whole body into something. The simple act of running appealed to me and I'd run until my lungs burned. Well, I did make the varsity track team as a sprinter and the coach said I would make a great miler too if I built up my wind. But I wanted to be a sprinter – I was thin and built for speed. Also, that was where all the glory was for me. I instinctively knew how to run and, in some fashion, had been doing just that as long as I could remember.

Lauren and Tim disapproved, but didn't give up much of a fight as long as I got my chores done and my grades did not suffer. Those goddamn chores. Weeding the garden, mowing the lawn, painting, shoveling, pushing a broom or pulling a brush. It was all the same to me. Nothing but free labor and it was daunting work as well. When Carter and I missed a spot mowing the lawn for example, Tim would drag us by the back of our necks to show us the spot we missed while pointing at it with his finger like a man discovering something awful. Most times, the patch of missed cut grass couldn't have been more than a few feet wide in length and width, but you'd think it was the size of Africa by how Tim carried on.

That's how he was. Always on edge. Gave me the creeps and scared the living shit out of both Carter and me. It wasn't just in the way he demanded things get done around the house, it was how we couldn't cut up or joke about anything either. Both Lauren and Tim were always wound pretty tight which made Carter, Lynn, and me pretty nervous. On the only occasion Lauren came to one of my wrestling matches, she lectured me afterwards about how I was laughing with my teammates while we waited to wrestle. She said I embarrassed myself by screwing off. And if Carter and I happened to be giggling about something at the dinner table, Tim would walk over and pound his fists on top of our heads. It would send a jolt of light through my brain and wrench the hell out of my neck. No fooling around. Just do what you're told and even then it was a crapshoot.

It seemed as though Carter didn't have the same outlet through school and sports like me. Lynn didn't do as well in school, but she was a great athlete and excelled in track. However, even though Carter did really well in Judo and wasn't too bad at JV wrestling, sports overall did not catch his interest enough to stay with them. I wasn't ever really sure what motivated Carter. All I knew is that he was downright climbing the walls living with Lauren and Tim; worse than Lynn and me. And with nothing to offset the weight of disapproval, he was on a downward spin with nothing to help him pull up. Carter did seem more comfortable hanging out with the bad boys. It was a comforting crowd for me too and I could see myself falling into that particular clique fairly easily. The biggest draw for me was that what you got in return was total acceptance without much effort.

As time went on, the arguments between Carter and Lauren worsened. He never talked back to Tim because, like me, he was afraid of the physical consequences. Carter and I were never really close and our differing paths drove a deeper wedge between us. One day I came home from school and found out Carter had run away to live with Father. I knew it was only a matter of time, but still I was surprised that Father allowed Carter to come and live with him. Tim told me all this and also that Carter had called the house from a pay phone dropping the news. I had no idea how Carter even got a hold of Father. It was all a mystery to me.

The last time I had seen Father was shortly after the court hearing when he and Mother actually drove together to see Carter, Lynn, and me. Lauren told us that day they would be coming, so I hid the whole day not knowing when. I stayed close to the house watching for Father and Mother and was ducking behind a nearby group of trees when they finally did show up. I held my breath and watched in secret while Father went to the front door and knocked. Mother sat in the car the whole time just staring straight ahead and my heart stopped when I thought she actually spotted me. I saw there was a brief exchange between Father and Tim, then Father returned to the car, said something to Mother, and they drove off. I was stunned to actually see them together and not trying to kill each other. Traces of courage may have been budding inside me at the time, but not enough to see Mother and Father again.

Tim told me that Carter couldn't hack it, which is why he went to live with Father.

"He's gonna amount to nothing," Tim went on lamenting.

Always one for the dramatic, Lauren would tell me later that Carter was a failure from the start and both Lauren and Tim were sure to use his leaving as a reminder that Lynn and me were not out of the woods yet. Failure was still an option.

"You could still end up like your mother," Lauren said. Hearing this just made me angry. Made me try harder. It made me strong.

The fact it was just Lynn and me wasn't far from my mind. The two foster boys were gone and now Carter. From the beginning this fact was a compelling reminder that our days were numbered. I had never felt comfortable or welcomed. Then again, I had never known these feelings. There were many nights I lay awake anticipating Lauren and Tim deciding it was time for me to go. Until the days I spent planning my flight from Mother, I had felt the same way.

I took a job as a busboy at a local restaurant. It had been my friend Greg's idea. He was already employed at the Beef Buffet, which specialized in roast beef, au gratin potatoes, and blueberry pie. It wasn't for the money because anything I earned went to Lauren and Tim. It was good to spend time with Greg and get out of the house. With already a full load of academics, track, chores, and now working at the Buffet, I kept busy and keeping busy helped me forget my past.

If I had been able to articulate it at the time, my emotions would have come out that I wanted to leave Mother far behind. Not think of her anymore. Not smell her pungent odor of alcohol and sex right before the panic attacks. The day she and Father drove to see us was a surprise visit. Well, at least it was a surprise to me. Lauren had never mentioned it until the day they were coming. Mother had brought gifts. They were old paintings in oil and water color she had done years before and she wanted me to have them. I remember Lauren throwing them out saying that they were probably riddled with cockroach eggs and she did not want them hatching in the house. I didn't want the goddamn things anyway. They were ugly renditions of my Mother's attempt at art under the influence of alcohol. Having them around meant another reminder of my history with her. I was running as fast as I could from that life and the only way I knew how was to simply keep moving.

Of course I cherished the time spent with Greg and Bruce. Sometimes, Lauren and Tim took us camping, along with Bruce's parents. We would load up two cars and travel north. The three-musketeers would find ourselves exploring on foot or riding our motorcycles through the woods. Even better was when Bruce would ride on back of my motorcycle with me as we rushed past the thick trees. Leaving Carter and Bruce's brother Doug far behind, we'd be so deep in the woods the roar of the cycle could not be heard. It was something about Bruce not caring if it looked queer when wrapping his arms around my waist. I still did not fully understand what it meant to be a homosexual regardless of how often Mother beat it into me that I was. What I did know was that it felt good to have Bruce that close and it didn't matter if I was gay or not. What mattered was that I loved him and while he held onto me, sometimes laying his head against my back while we rode –I felt safe.

Once when Bruce and I were riding through the woods, I saw a clearing and sped toward it. Stopping just short of the edge, we climbed off the bike and looked over. It had to have been a hundred foot drop straight down to a smattering of jagged rocks. Had I kept going we would have been obliterated against the stone floor.

"Holy Shit!" Bruce said.

"We would have been smashed for sure!"

Peering over what might have been our tomb, all we could do was laugh. It felt good not to care. Just me and my friend whom I loved unconditionally, and laughing. As it was, I knew at that moment I could never lose him.

Managing to make it through the outdoor track season with a paltry record, but still making it, fall was approaching. I used to love fall, but not then. It meant hunting season. If Bruce went along it was so much better. But most times, it was just Tim, Carter, and me. Now that Carter was gone, it was just Tim and me. The year before Carter ran away, the three of us had been hunting snowshoe rabbit up north. Carter and I got separated from Tim and in the deep thicket of woods we just kept yelling for him. Scared out of our wits. When Tim made his way to where we were standing, and half-holding onto one another, he was pissed.

"Goddamn sissies!" he said.

Then he trundled off again. We did not venture far from the spot in which he found us after that. We didn't yell out any more either.

It was on another hunting excursion I would bag my first kill. Snowshoe rabbit again. Tim said me and Carter weren't ready for the big game like deer, so it was squirrels, birds, and rabbits for us. I knew the rabbit was close because the beagles were going crazy. I loved the beagles. They were so playful, cute and when Tim wasn't home I'd leash them all up and have them pull me around the neighborhood on a skateboard.

I knew I had no time to lose once that rabbit popped over a snow-covered crest in the direction of where the dogs were howling, so I pulled back the hammer of my single-shot Ithaca 4/10 and waited. Quick as hell, this rabbit came bounding up, over and down the hill right toward me. I panicked and fired too soon.

At first, sure I had missed it, until it literally came to rest directly in front of me. It just stopped there like it wanted me to help it. The rabbit's foot had been blown to bits and it trailed by a thin furry piece of skin behind it. So close to me I could see its small belly move in and out. So, I ejected the spent shell, reloaded and aimed. The blast hit home and blew the rabbit apart. Before Tim came running upon hearing the two shots, I tried desperately to wipe away my tears. The thought of that rabbit just stopping in front of me stuck in my head for a long time. The one big beautiful eye I could see was blinking slowly. The suffering from blowing its leg almost clean off was unmistakable. The rabbit would not suffer long. I couldn't bear to let that happen. Pieces of the hare were tangled and splintered in the foliage around where it had sat and waited for death. As if to say, "You started this…now finish me." Red blood against the white snow was everywhere. Snow as white as the snowshoe's fur.

By mid-semester of my freshman year in high school I was pulling all A's and B's and not by taking the easy courses either. Convinced track was my sport, I decided to stay with it, and quit both Judo and wrestling. Still working at the Buffet I kept busy. The positive attention I was getting from teachers and coaches alike was too big a prize to lose, so I worked rapidly more determined than ever in my pursuit for higher learning and athletic achievement. I knew there were only two things I could do; succeed or fail. The fight for a life worth living depended upon success. Those in my life who first put the manacles around my wrists were quickly slipping into oblivion. I worked, studied, ran track, and when time permitted, hung out with my only two companions, Greg and Bruce.

However, I was still very much alone. The thought was not a pleasant one knowing the secrets that were harbored deep inside my mind and heart. I was still sorry for cheating Mother in order to escape. But it remained clear it had been for only one purpose –survival.

I lost contact with Carter altogether. It wasn't like he'd call the house to say hello. We were also forbidden to say his name. Tim and Lauren would break their own rules and mention Carter every now and then. Mostly it would be to emphasize a point they were trying to make with me or Lynn about how he didn't measure up. I often wondered what the outcome would have been if Carter had squared off with Tim. Carter didn't have the size advantage, but he sure had the guts. If Tim was getting the best of him, Carter also would not have hesitated by putting a bullet into him at the first opportunity. Maybe Tim saw this flash across Carter's eyes once or twice, because no one was more relieved than Tim when Carter left. There were also a lot of hunting guns in the house in which to choose from. Nothing would cover up the foul work Carter might have carried out, but Carter wasn't afraid of prison. His reward was vengeance and it played well into his mindset. You just don't fuck with someone who has nothing to lose.

The thought of Carter killing Tim made me afraid sometimes. I knew he was capable and I knew Carter had taken the situation fully into consideration. He would mention it from time to time when we were alone. It would dawn on me while Carter went into great detail describing how he would go about blasting Tim's head off with one of this shotguns. There was a bit of humor as well as tragedy in the way Carter told the story. Well armed, Carter would tell this elaborate story of how he would shoot up the house first, and then Tim. I was cautious not to interrupt while he spoke, mostly because he looked sometimes like he really he meant it. It was during these moments the idea filled me with fear rather than satisfaction.

I was no match for Tim or Lauren. They'd beat me mentally and emotionally every time. Perhaps this is why I avoided them at all costs. Tim's lips would be set grimly and there would be this hard light in his eyes when he'd glance at me every now and then. It was like he was capturing my soul. If it came down to a game of fox against fox, Tim would always win. I was easily outwitted. No one would ever mistake me for being able to hold my own. Not like Carter. The game of street smarts wasn't the path I chose. It was all academic to me. Yet deep down in my heart I hoped and believed that Tim and Lauren feared me a little. Not like they feared Carter, but just enough so that they wouldn't belittle me. Also, enough to protect Lynn from Tim's unwelcomed touching.

It was a terrible ordeal going about the business of trying not to be seen, but enough so that I commanded some respect. Lynn and I were still prisoners even away from Mother. It was a new jailhouse, but our faith was still broken. Our small innocent faces drawing nothing but grief under those not willing or able to love unconditionally. There Lynn and I stood waiting for that flash of Tim or Lauren's eyes that would bring despair and in the back of these looks I knew harbored a deep hatred. As time went on, I waited for that one moment –the fatal moment, when Tim and Lauren would understand what remained of Lynn and me was no more than suffering. It would be in that moment they would hold us while we wept and repay what had been taken away so long ago. The moment never came. Lynn and me, like Carter, were trained from the start to take the blame. We did our job and we did it well.

A picture of Mother rose before me. While she paused and got her wind back, her hand was partly covered in blood. She would beat the sin out of me. That's what Mother said.

"I'll beat the ever-living sin out of you!" she screamed.

"As Christ is my witness, Gregg!"

My head dipped in a frozen position while gleaming trails of light twinkled before my eyes as the pain settled. Fighting the urge to reach up and touch the places on my face, which were now wet and swelling. I could feel the imprint of her hand still stinging on my cheek. It was afternoon, but dark because a storm was coming. I loved a good storm and Mother was ruining it by beating me. The air was thick with electricity and the smell of rain. The burned out matches were on the dirty carpet next to me. Marks on my arms where the skin was melted stung painfully. At the farther end of the room Lynn sat in the corner crying. The worst of the beating had not even started. Mother was just warming up. The wind was slowly shifting and a fine mist of rain now gave way to a thicker downfall. The front door was hanging open, and naked, I shuddered from the chill in the living room. Crossing over into the blackness of my bedroom at Lauren's house I finally woke up. Shoving the covers in my mouth the fear swept over me like a hurricane and I wept until falling asleep once more. At fourteen-years-old they were still with me. Those dreams. Those goddamn dreams.

It was a half-mile up the road from the house and back but I knew I could run it with ease. Nearing the end of my freshman year indoor and outdoor track had done that. It began turning my body into something like a lung with feet. About fifty yards from the house I'd kick into an all out sprint. Moments later I'd be flying. Up against the other competitors I wasn't much of a threat, but I was getting faster. A year before and two years younger, Lynn was still faster than me. Not anymore. Not enough for bragging rights just yet, but I was getting better, and getting better at anything was good enough for me.

Nailing my freshman year felt both odd and wonderful. I had polished off the reading list given to me by my 8th grade English teacher and actually understood what I was reading. As a matter of fact, I was reading at the required level –finally. The fear of catching up slowly dissipated, allowing me to enjoy reading even more –so, I read even more. I now looked forward to my report card with excitement instead of dread. Finals were a breeze and my Biology report on Sexually Transmitted Diseases was a huge hit with the students and my teacher as well. He said he couldn't believe I had the guts to actually pick the subject matter. Still a virgin, it wasn't obvious to me how STDs were transmitted. Had I known, I would not have picked the subject matter. Too late. I still got an "A."

A few weeks after the school year ended, my report card showed up at the house. Lauren ripped it out of the envelope, took one look and handed it to Tim.

"All A's and one B," he grunted.

Followed by, "You can do better." And then he tossed me the report card.

It didn't bother me at all because growing thick all around his remark was complete bullshit. Shutting out what was left of Lauren and Tim's snide comments was the fact that I was proving them wrong with every accolade.

That summer before my 10th grade year I had it all planned out. I was going to run like crazy and be ready for track season. Not only was I going to make the team again, but I was going to take home a few medals. I sure liked the medals. The weight felt good in my hand. They also looked pretty sweet hanging off the varsity jackets. What the guys called, a "pussy coat." Whatever that meant. And, of course, I was going to read everything could.

We moved, yet again, and this time it was into a 'fixer-upper.' We would only live there for a couple months as we prepared it for reselling, but it was already my favorite house. Spruce and balsam grew thick about it creating a dark enchanted look to the home. I would hide in the mass of trees and rest. Isolated from the world. Sometimes the dogs would follow me and fall asleep near my feet making smooth, round pits in the green grass. My heart sometimes was filled with a sickening pain whenever I looked at the pups and I'd think of Sambirdio and Mattie.

I had not given Mother much thought lately, and realizing this did not send waves of terror through me any longer. The love I once had for her turned to revulsion and now the revulsion was falling away too. Although, more than once in the past three years I had thought that the nightmares were punishment for leaving Mother. And, the punishment was much greater than the crime. I was still suffering from panic attacks and tics, but kept these a secret from even Lynn, and all that suffering still made me cry when I was alone.

There were often moments even with the quick advancements I made in school and sport that life and freedom and happiness were just words and nothing I could actually feel. I had been willing to surrender everything for Mother, even my dignity, and had done so many times. It was easy then. This was the first woman I had ever loved.

I thought I was in love with Caroline, but when we moved she didn't come to mind that often. The same feelings came over me with some of the neighborhood girls, but still nothing short of a twinge here and there told me I was only somewhat interested. I was never in pursuit of any girl except maybe one or two, but the chase didn't last very long. My blood would leap a little when I saw them or they'd come over to the house and ask to take a walk with me. We would hold hands from time to time and I'd blush. Proof that it wasn't anything special was when we let go of each other's hands it was as if we had never been holding onto one another. Kissing was a little bit more exciting. My heart would beat faster than when we held hands, but even kissing didn't compare to the feeling of when I broke into a long, swinging run during a track competition. The girls were fresh and seemed to have many suitors. Perhaps that's why track was better. Owning the lane and setting my own pace had a safe quality about it. Fast or slow, it was still the same lane at the end in which I started.

Before moving from the enchanted house I liked to call it, I went for a run through the woods. I followed a thin trail that climbed a bit of a rough ridge. The trail then opened up a little and I took off in a full sprint. It was never long before my walks always turned into runs. The last twenty yards of wood-lined trees opened into a field. Nearing exhaustion, I lost my footing and fell forward, with my face crashing through the ribcage of a dead decomposing deer. Quickly pushing upward I got back on my feet, stumbled to a tree and vomited uncontrollably. Dropping to my knees I heaved until nothing came up, my stomach now empty but I could still taste the rotting dusty flesh in my mouth. The deer had died where it fell and I took one last look at it before leaving. A few moments later, I was heaving again. The enchanted woods now ruined. It was good we'd be moving soon.

The next house was my fourth in three years and would be my last with Lauren and Tim. It was a ranch style and what Lauren referred to as a "steal," and rightly so. It was a foreclosure and I had been with her the day she went to be sure the tenants were abiding by the eviction notice. Occupying the house were two women, both of whom looked to be in their thirties. When Lauren and I entered the house they were hurriedly packing and I instinctively looked down at my feet. It was too difficult to look at them. Their eyes were filled with tears and the women seemed just short of breaking off into cries of horror. Lauren stood sentry while the women packed up their belongings, and they were now throwing them into boxes haphazardly. Lauren's presence seemed to descend upon them and the women shrunk as if giving in under the weight of Lauren's disapproving and impatient stare. I knew that look very well. It plunged through me on many occasions, rocking me to the core. The last of the boxes now loaded into an old car parked in the driveway, the women left without saying a word. Watching this all play out in front of me made me realize what I was up against with Lauren and I didn't stand a chance.

The next few weeks Lynn and I worked on getting the house in shape to move in. Painting, weeding, mowing, scraping, pulling, pushing, general do this and do that type stuff and all under the surveillance of Lauren and Tim. I would have my own room again and that was good. The best part of having my own room was finding it the way I left it. It wasn't the privacy that was for sure, because Lauren and Tim reserved the right to rifle through our belongings any time they felt the urge.

That was how Lauren found the dirty cassette tapes Carter, Lynn, and me had made. It was just of us singing and cursing. Mostly cursing. We paid dearly for that transgression. Grounded, made to do chores, and no TV. I, for one, was never sure what additional retribution grounding brought down around our heads compared to any other day of the week. We always had chores and TV was already limited to only one-hour per day. Like Carter would say, "Big diff…what the fuck." He had the best lines.

The house had a finished basement. That was where my room was and it was a perfect location. Quiet and far from everyone. Still, it was like a trap. Lauren was always snooping around looking for incriminating evidence. I wasn't having sex or using drugs. I wasn't even masturbating. There wasn't anything wrong with the plumbing, but it just hadn't come naturally to me. Part of me resisted even trying to figure it out because the feelings of the strangers and Mother were too real whenever I touched myself. In addition, I was afraid I'd plunge my cock right through my crotch or something awful like that. Worse than that, the thought of injuring myself and having to tell Tim and Lauren sent a shrill of fear throughout my whole body.

Not until I started meeting Lynn's girlfriends did I really start getting interested in girls. My room had the perfect vantage point. An accordion door made of wood slats allowed me to peep in on them during sleepovers. At first, I was bothered by the fact the door wasn't solid, but catching a glimpse of a young girl donning nothing but panties and a bra soon put an end to that apprehension.

Her name was Barb and on one particular sleepover I managed to talk her into sneaking into my room when all the other girls were asleep. She had on only her panties and swung quickly into my bed. Wearing only underwear myself, it was as close to naked as I had ever been with a real girl. Innocent playfulness for the first time in my life. Nothing forced or ugly. We kissed and I remember wiping the hair from her forehead, which made her smile. Anxious joy overtook both of us as we embraced, dragging the breath from our mouths and gently pushing it into the other's. I could feel her bare breasts full and large for a girl only fourteen pressed against my chest. Nervous sweat beaded off our bodies and she smelled like perfume. The print of her panties were flowered and that seemed to make it even more sensual. Reaching underneath the waistband of my underwear she found I was erect and gently squeezed, then giggled. Suddenly, we stopped. Perhaps Barb felt as if it had gone further than she expected. Cautiously, she moved from my bed kissing me sweetly on the mouth before leaving. That was the best part. The kissing. Her perfume lingered and I could smell it on my sheets. It gave off an odor of inexperience that made it more caring. This is what love is supposed to feel like. Soft-hearted, agreeable, sweet-tempered. No expectations. I could get used to this kind of love. It was also adorable and easy. Within minutes of Barb leaving my room, I was fast asleep.

I became more cautious now around Lauren and Tim, feeling something was just not right. They did not speak much to me any longer and kept their distance. The shelter I had was filled with anxiety, but it was still a good place to build my life. Mother was certain death and as I grew older, I also became more convinced she would have killed me. Force of habit caused me to stay with my study routine over the summer and do my chores without question. Spending the night over at Greg's house when I could was a pleasant break. However, in trying to stifle the past, there was still far too much free time on my hands. Needing to keep myself busy, I also took part-time jobs de-tasseling corn and babysitting. De-tasseling corn ranked up there as the worst job I ever had. The blades of the corn stalks cut into my skin like razors. By the end of the day, my arms would be covered with swollen red lacerations. I also picked up a bad case of head lice from one of the other kids. The hair on my head, arms, and legs was loaded with ugly little mites that itched like crazy. Babysitting wasn't much better, but at least I didn't end up with a rash or a bad case of head lice.

I babysat the neighbor kids; two boys who were both rambunctious as hell and they had a massive Doberman named Morgan that ruled the house. While the dog lay sleeping, the younger of the two boys would lay his head on the dog's side while watching TV. So, one day when I was babysitting, I figured the dog looked big enough for the both of us and did the same. My head resting on the dog's ribcage watching TV was pretty neat. That is until the younger boy seemingly bored with the whole ordeal found the dog's testicles hanging loose against the floor and bit down hard. The dog let out an awful yelp, scrambled to his feet, and sunk his teeth into my arm. Four punctured holes reminded me that I should never trust a four-year-old around a dog's balls.

Lauren and Tim's caution around me seemed odd and empty. I wasn't a threat to them and gave them no reason to be uneasy. More of a machine than a young boy of fifteen, I went about my busy day without complaint. I didn't date. There was no arguing between me and Lauren. I did not run with a bad crowd or drink, smoke, nor get into any mischief. I worked swiftly to complete my chores and actually took pride in doing them right. There were the occasional mistakes made of not weeding the garden properly, or missing a section of the garage when sweeping, but nothing too terrible. If I took advantage of any situation, it was spending more time reading and working through textbooks checked out of the local library.

Whatever I had done to change their behavior toward me was unknown. The only significant change outside of me growing a little taller and a little bigger was the fact I was an honor roll student and budding athlete. I edged toward a discussion every now and then, but both Lauren and Tim would only make small talk. The stillness of their actions oppressed me even more whereas before I thought being left alone would have been better. Now, it was simply unnerving and I could feel something awful stirring in the air.

That feeling of something wasn't right was gladly interrupted by a break I desperately needed. Taking me away from Lauren and Tim was a plus for sure. The feeling was mutual, but I didn't care. Lauren and Tim sent me off to a two-week summer Judo camp. It was the International Shotokan Judo Training Facility. The camp was situated on a huge expanse of land surrounded by trees and located in a rural area of Ohio. I was easily ready for the rigors of the physical exercise. The camp was coeducational as well, of which, I was also easily ready. During this time my confidence grew and I even had the courage to kiss a couple girls. However, the real prize for me was winning the grand championship within my age and weight division. Winning was survival. To hell with glory – I wanted to live.

My sophomore year began with a bang: Ohio State Camp Shotokan Judo champion in addition to earning my place on the varsity track team. The academics were still AP Courses which meant I got to see my dear friend Greg in most of my classes. The academics came to me more effortlessly and I felt for the first time in my life that I was bound for college.

I fell into a healthy routine of school, track, working at The Buffet restaurant along with Greg and occasionally hanging out with both Greg and Bruce. Life was getting better. Lauren and Tim continued to have this strange sense about them. However, I maintained my chores and the three of us stayed out of each other's way. The feeling of uneasiness that came on initially when I felt like Lauren and Tim saw me as a leper was now replaced with just being happy they kept their distance.

The school year ended with straight "A's" in AP Courses in math, literature, geography, and all the sciences. A few weeks after my sophomore year ended, my report card finally arrived. Upon tearing it open, Tim and Lauren did not say a word. They just threw it on the kitchen writing desk where it came to end up on a pile of never-to-open junk mail. Again, I did not care. I nailed all of my classes and even made it through the track season with a few more wins than my freshman year. Like Carter would always say when things were really bad or abundantly wonderful: *Fuck it.*

Making the honor roll all four semesters was strangely astonishing. Seeing myself as more than just a lost and confused boy became a viable option. It would be my third year on the track team and I was sure to bring home more hardware. Having secured my position on the team the year before earned me my rightful spot. I even volunteered for a summer track clinic and was excited at the prospect of one day being able to purchase a varsity jacket. The prospect of me being considered a jock was exhilarating.

Because of my busy schedule, I was rarely home. When I was, it was to take care of my assigned chores, eat, sleep, and study. What little free time I had, I spent reading or hanging out with Bruce and Greg. Greg and I would occasionally play night tennis at the local community center. Greg was becoming a rather accomplished tennis player and a college scholarship looked promising. Greg could also depend upon his SAT and ACT scores to help him along. The feelings of hope launched me forward; however, I soon learned by putting my faith into something unbelievably out of reach is both a curse and a blessing.

During one summer evening, Greg and I decided to catch a game of night tennis after working at the restaurant. I had asked Lauren's permission that morning. She agreed to let me go, but had been acting very strange, and after returning home that evening I finally understood why.

Lauren was waiting up for me. Seeing her, I held my breath tensely at what I saw. There was no sign of emotion in her face. My heart thumped as she rose to her feet. Lynn was sleeping and Tim cowardly hid in their bedroom. Her voice was mechanical and she moved through the words uttered swiftly and quietly. It was then she told me that I had to move out the next morning. The cold and heartless expression never left her face. At that moment, she looked exactly like Mother.

I was terrified and could scarcely move. Astonished as to what possible reason Lauren and Tim could have to throw me from their home, all I could do was stare stupidly. My mind refused to believe she could be so callous and cavalier about what was to become of me. It was also astonishing to me as to how Lauren twisted her words in order to fit the reason. A reason never explained. By then, I had seen evil in many forms and disguises, most of which had been blood relatives, and though we were brethren cut from the same cloth, it made no difference to them.

Lauren made it sound as if this had been my fault. I searched my own mind for a reason I was being condemned, but found none. I had done nothing to deserve this. I fought back the tears of pain and anger. Every now and then, a smile stole across her lips and I wanted to rip out her fucking throat. Instead, I only sat in respectful silence, praying for a reprieve.

My thoughts continued to weave and melt into shape, ensuing within a slow process of recognition. As her words dug deeper into my consciousness, the painful realization that her decision was final began rising into my awareness. Once again, the visible reminders of my past surfaced, caught in the form of repeated doom.

I fought to suppress my hatred and tried desperately not to let it show. Although I kept telling myself I didn't deserve this, my heart called me a liar and the self-loathing returned. Lauren kept repeating this was best for everyone. Yet she could not tell me why.

Up to that point, I had embraced the long path of learning and discovery. I now feared all that would abruptly end. I pleaded with Lauren to change her mind, but she refused. Her decision was final and she carried it out with swift and horrible conviction. Lauren looked at me with dulled eyes and as I slowly realized what was actually happening a groan broke from my lips. The work no sooner complete, Lauren simply turned away from me and disappeared down the hallway and into her bedroom. I was no more than a rag doll slumped over a chair by then. My arms and body limp.

I went to my bedroom and in an instant was on my knees laying over the bed and weeping. Looking closely into Lauren's face only moments before told me there was no changing her mind. It was a face worn by a hardship and mental torture she brought upon herself. Her cheeks were thinned, and her steel-gray eyes looking back at me were vacant. Lauren was fighting her own storm. Her face showed a woman filled with fear and lacking the strength to fight. It also showed there was no association with fairness in a world where children need justice more than anything. She'd hardly drawn a breath when seeing the pain on my face and Lauren must have realized what she was doing would surely kill me. She struck me down from behind. Like I had known the day the women were forced from the very home where I was now being evicted as well: With Lauren, I never stood a chance.

The next morning I packed my things and went upstairs. Tim was sitting at the kitchen table and would not look at me. A coward to the bitter end. There was still a small ray of hope inside of me that thought during the night Lauren and Tim had changed their minds. Perhaps at least Tim believed bringing this terrible situation down upon me was a mistake, but that hope was quickly dashed, when still not making eye contact, he reached out as to shake my hand.

"Good luck, Gregg," was all he said. He spoke like a used-car salesman, but without as much heartfelt sympathy. I shook his hand in return, and afterwards, Tim quickly left the kitchen.

Lauren told me we had to get going immediately. Her display of ruthless efficiency showed she was in usual form. I thought to myself that she probably couldn't wait to get back and rearrange my old bedroom or vacuum the goddamn floor. She spoke rapidly and her voice was quivering with the emotion that inspired her words and never allowed our eyes to meet. Lauren would look at her watch and then the floor, stop and look at her watch again.

"Let's go!" she said.

Judging the situation as best I could I took Lauren's hand in mine. Grabbing it and tightening mine around hers for an instant.

"I'm sorry for whatever I did," I said tearfully. It was just the two of us in the kitchen now. "I'll do better. I promise."

Lauren promptly withdrew her hand from mine and absently wiped it on her slacks. Seeing this, there leapt a sudden flash of fire in my eyes and I glared at her. "You did this to yourself, Gregg." That bare excuse again. Yet another I did not understand.

"What did I do? Please tell me."

Lauren did look at me this time and I saw she had regained her composure. Her look cut me to the bone.

Through her teeth, Lauren hissed, "Get in the car."

However, before leaving the house my luggage was scrutinized by Lauren to make sure I hadn't packed anything that did not belong to me. I was stripped of everything I owned, except for a few clothes. After four years, all I was allowed to take with me fit easily inside a single grocery bag.

A sound from the other room made both Lauren and me jump. Tim yelled that we had to get moving. Lauren's face now flush and her voice trembling again, she pushed me toward the door. She looked a little embarrassed. Before walking out of the house, I asked if I could say goodbye to Lynn and was told I could not. I knew then she was told to stay in her room until I was gone.

"Lynn has been through enough, don't you think?" Lauren said to me.

I did agree. More than Lauren would ever know.

"I'm real sorry it has to be this way, Gregg," Lauren offered after I asked to see Lynn. It was deflection and it worked. Also obvious was that she refused to take the slightest bit of responsibility. Tim bellowed another command to get moving and laughed grimly from the other room.

The arrangement of where I would live was probably made weeks beforehand. The backroom deal ironed out was that I would live with Jessica. I wouldn't be surprised if money exchanged hands. On the drive over to Jessica's, Lauren lectured me the whole way. I was sick of her righteous speeches. They felt like a thousand needles piercing my brain. She preached about how I should continue striving for excellence and not give up. Because of the situation at hand, it was pretty goddamn difficult to accept her words of encouragement. It was as if the executioner were to give the condemned one last piece of advice.

Of course, Lauren made sure to interject the fact that she had done her very best all along, but somehow I failed her. I suppose instead of excelling academically and athletically, I should have been hooked on drugs and stealing to support my habit. I couldn't stand it anymore, so I blurted out, "What did I do to deserve this?"

There it was out in the open. Lauren sat in silence and drove. It was odd to see her speechless. I had spent the last four years listening to her rambling on about nothing at all. At first, I thought she was only going to ignore me, which was something else she did quite well; Lauren would get a bug up her ass and refuse to speak to me for days at a time. I allowed her to believe this was punishment.

Right about the time I gave up on an answer, she spoke. After hearing what she had to say, I wish she had kept her mouth shut. Her reply was short and to the point.

"You know what you did."

I could have screamed. Instead, I sat quietly the remainder of the trip. I could tell by the way her cheeks flushed she knew quite well she was full of shit. It didn't make me feel any better and suddenly I wanted to cry. Instead, I quickly looked out the window and stared at the passing cars.

When we arrived, Jessica and Lauren spoke in private. I wondered if Jessica knew Lauren called her a tramp behind her back. Lauren wanted to get out of there as quickly as possible now that the deed, carried out without mercy or remorse, was finally done.

If I had known what my life would soon become, I would have killed Lauren while she stood speaking with Jessica, but it wouldn't have made any difference. Because to me she was already dead. I waited in the yard while Lauren climbed into her car and backed out of the driveway. To my absolute astonishment, as she drove off, Lauren yelled from the window, "Keep up the good work, Gregg!"

I waited while the car disappeared around the corner. Jessica had gone inside the house. I was alone. To the left of me only a few houses down the street was a cemetery. It was then the thought occurred to me this is what it feels like to start over.

CHAPTER SIX

Fighting

"My war rages like a distant storm within a twisted soul.
I called your name for mercy, but all I heard was thunder."

THERE MIGHT HAVE BEEN EITHER a smile or grimace on my lips while standing in Jessica's front yard and I struggled to comprehend why I was, yet again, abandoned. Deep down I knew Lauren and Tim both feared and envied me. Perhaps this is why they kicked me out of their home.

Tugging at my heart was the fact I had done nothing wrong. Nothing to deserve this. Had I been in trouble, addicted to drugs or alcohol, I would have understood. I did not even talk back to Lauren and Tim and my chores were carried out with military precision. Obedient, trustworthy, and always diligent in my efforts to excel. This was what did me in. I was a living breathing example of something they never saw surviving the storm of abuse.

Then in a moment, I was frozen in horror. Not twenty feet from Jessica's home, I heard her scream with a rattling cry in her throat.

"Get in here, Gregg!"

"I want to go over the ground rules!"

Turning, I raised my hands to my chest and tried to slow my heart, pressing the panic backward. Half walking, half running toward the front door, my pale, thin face in a painful scowl. The voice I heard wasn't Jessica's. It was Mother's.

Walking into the kitchen, which was in utter disarray with dirty dishes in the sink along with all sorts of pots and pans scattered about, I tried to show Jessica an encouraging smile. With a wild cry, she rushed me and flung herself at my side, her hands gripping fiercely at my wrists. In a low guttural voice, Jessica let me know this was not her idea. A groan of anguish rose to my own lips, and I clenched my hands into hard fists, dreading the terrible moment when I would have to face Jessica and see the loathing in her eyes.

It was what she said next that brought me from fear to rage in an instant.

"Lauren couldn't handle you, but you won't get away with any goddamn shit with me," she harshly whispered.

I had no idea what she was talking about and I was unmoved by her blame. I swayed a little on my feet, Jessica still gripping my wrists. She now stood directly in front of me, much shorter and panting like a hunted animal. Years of smoking added to the excitement, I suppose.

I saw in her face the thing which I had feared more than the sting of death. No longer were her eyes filled with the earnest of passing on crucial information to me. They were hard and terrible and filled with that madness which made me think she was about to leap upon me. In Jessica's eyes, in the quivering of her bare throat, in the rise and fall of her breast as she fought for air was the rage, the grief, and the fear of someone whose life had turned suddenly into the deadliest of all responsibilities; raising an adolescent. I stood before her without a word on my lips, my own face as cold as the dirty white kitchen linoleum under my feet.

"You will not get into any trouble with me, mister!" Jessica insisted.

Still confused, I was wondering what Lauren had told her. What lies had Lauren spilled before driving off. The picture of what Lauren saw in me was becoming more vivid while Jessica rambled on. All I had to offer Lauren and Tim was affection, along with the successes one cannot buy or sell, but only earn through toil and perseverance. Perhaps Lauren saw herself as a failure every time she looked at me. I was making strides in areas of life where she had long since given up. Maybe what Lauren and Tim saw in me was a nemesis in the face of a child becoming a man. It was obvious I was rejected. Standing now before Jessica told me so. I still was not completely sure. Perhaps it was because of my triumphs. A punishment that is generally meted out by the pitiful and stupid.

The decision that I would live with Jessica must have been discussed weeks before the day I was promptly delivered and abandoned. It bothered me greatly that there had been clandestine meetings regarding my life. Details worked out that directly affected my welfare and the deceit that had taken place was now apparent. There was no thought given to the fact I would be forced to change schools, leave my friends, and start all over again. It was only a primitive reaction to immediate gratification. I felt as though they took what they could get and damn the consequences. I would have to claw and scratch all over again for a chance at survival and it had already begun only moments after Lauren left me. It was how Jessica spoke to me in that tone of displeasure and anger. In her voice was the significance of her choking words and they hurt me even more than if she had beat me.

While Jessica reviewed the ground rules of the house in that ugly kitchen where we now stood alone, there was none of the passion I had hoped for. Quietly, almost whisperingly uttered, her words stung me to my soul. I had built up yet another useless fantasy on the drive over. How Jessica would take me in and love me. Care for me. Welcome me with open arms. Instead, there was nothing but condemnation.

I had meant to tell Jessica how grateful I was she took me into her home. Prepared for it. However, the crude manner of how she saw my being there made me slow to speak, and even though my heart cried out for the words I practiced in my head, I could only stare, clenching my fists and fighting back the rage. And then there came the thing I had been expecting. Racing through me in a flurry and always at the ready was the anger building inside. Before me now was the face of my new enemy. Torn between rage and disappointment, all of the loathing I had worked so hard to overcome returned to me.

Taking a step forward, I looked down at Jessica who quickly let go of my wrist and now clasped her own. My quickness of movement even in that small step toward her was alarming.

"You and Lauren are goddamn liars," I spoke in a slow and emotionless tone.

"I have done nothing wrong and you know it." My words were nothing compared to the look in my eyes that shone bright with hatred.

This was all Jessica really had to see. She stepped away from me as if stung by a wasp. Her face whitened. Her hand shot out and sent me crashing against the sink. Once, twice and the blows that fell turned my face into fire. I could see her eyes were blazing red from pain and hatred.

Regaining my footing, I moved out of the way and toward the door. My one thought was that of survival. A foot taller and much stronger than Jessica; however, in an instant, I was reduced to a sobbing child. Jessica bellowed insults at me, but I did not hear them. I did not know how long it went on or how many times she struck me, but when at last I found the door and ran outside, the blood in my mouth had pooled enough to warrant a good glob of red spit. My nose felt wet inside and tender. I turned around in the yard and saw Jessica did not follow me, but I could still hear the shouting from her shrill voice.

The anger inside me was gone along with whatever power it brought. I could not protect myself even from Jessica. The old fear returned just as it had been when I was only a boy. My hands did not clench but lay slack against my sides. The last light of the day shone against my eyes and made me weep even harder. I made no effort not to cry standing in the open yard among the neighboring houses. The grief and despair in my heart grew and what came now was a burning glow of agony. Once more, I was left with nowhere to go and the yearning of faith seemed to be a distant memory.

Carter had raised the bong to his lips while sitting at Jessica's kitchen table. I watched in fascination as he plugged a small hole in the water-filled tube and pressed the top against his mouth making a tight seal. He sucked hard causing the water now to bubble and gurgle noisily. Releasing his finger over the tiny hole, he then forced the massive amount of smoke that had built up inside the colorful tube to escape into his lungs. Carter began choking immediately and cupped his free hand over his lips. Some of the smoke leaked through his fingers. More choking and then Carter opened his mouth wide blowing a colossal amount of smoke into my face.

"Ahhhhhhhh!" he gasped.

Followed by, "I'm so fucking high!"

The bong filled with marijuana was passed around the table and when it was handed it to me, I waved it off.

"Pussy Motherfucker!" Carter yelled.

"Get high with us, Gregg!"

"Even jocks get stoned!" Carter's words of wisdom were short-lived and I continued to refuse the weed.

"If I wasn't so fucking high, I'd kick your scrawny ass!" Carter warned.

I raised up from where I was to a sitting posture and was wiping the blood from my face when Carter rattled on. Less than an hour before I had been in another fist fight with a boy from town. I made a haphazard move to wipe the blood away once more and then gave up.

Carter motioned with his hand that he'd show me what a real ass-kicking felt like if I pussied out again. There was no doubt in my mind he would make good on the threat. One ass-kicking was enough for one night, so when the bong filled with weed was passed onto me again, I clumsily took a hit. Carter shouted with approval. His tone was no longer one of irritation but took on a gracious quality. It also took on a ring of authority as if he accomplished something grand and he gloated openly taking credit for getting me to submit. Even I was stunned by the sudden change in my behavior and how I obeyed without much of a fight.

It was summer. I did not have school to worry about and the track clinic wasn't an option any longer now that I lived in another town. It was too far away with no transportation and Jessica would never have driven me. It didn't matter anyway because being away from my only two friends, Greg and Bruce, brought with it a deep feeling of seclusion that drained the strength from my body physically.

Still, I ran every now and then in the nearby cemetery. Whisking by the headstones and underneath the thick trees interspersed throughout the graveyard was something of the old life that gave me some joy. But my confidence was badly injured and in exchange for what accounted for ambition was now self-hatred. I was in good company. All of my siblings were products of a dysfunctional environment – the diseased tree would bear disintegrating fruit and the fruit would not fall far from the tree. It began to chip away at my compassion and form the genesis of my own evils.

Within the first week of moving in with Jessica, it became evident I had returned to my roots. Her marriage was suffering. Drugs, alcohol, and promiscuity only added to the breakdown of the relationship. Jessica and her second husband argued constantly, and many times violently. The living space was already cramped before I came along. In addition to Jessica, her husband and her son and daughter, there were two foster girls. Both foster girls were older than me by about two years.

One of them was named Mary and she had dark hair, feathered bangs, big bright blue eyes and a beautiful smile. Her dark hair against lily-white skin made her look like Snow White from the Disney cartoon. I knew her eyes were on me from the moment we met. I could feel them wanting me and I wanted her too. The other foster girl was Deane. She was tall, thin and had platinum blonde hair. Unlike Mary, who was shy, which struck me as even more lovely, Deane was more outgoing. She had soft features that complimented her athletic build and ever so sweet. Mary was shorter and her frame was more voluptuous. Round and smooth in all the right places. The foster girls offered a more exciting prospect, but it wasn't exactly a model environment. Drugs and alcohol were readily available and frequently used. It was at Jessica's I had gotten drunk for the first time. It now seemed the opportunities that I had worked so hard to obtain were gone.

In an attempt to overcome my dysfunctional situation, I tried to keep with my joy of reading. While holed up in my bedroom at Jessica's, I read again: *To Kill A Mockingbird*, *A Tale of Two Cities*, and *The Pearl*. I found a different meaning of hope within these books. They helped me cope with a world that rarely made any sense. Before I was shunned by Lauren and Tim and made to live with Jessica, I started to believe that the very essence of my life must be for a reason beyond comprehension. These books were introduced to me by the same English Literature teacher who suffered and eventually died from kidney disease. He had often said, "All of life's mysteries are written in books – not one, but thousands." My English teacher forgot to mention the fact that life's mysteries were also written in blood.

Jessica and her husband's arguments always ended in violence. They would brutally attack one another in the heat of battle. Hiding in my bedroom, too afraid to intervene, these arguments brought back memories of my abusive past. Somewhere in the house, I could hear my niece and nephew crying and their small voices full of anxiety. Sometimes they would be pleading with their mother and stepfather to stop fighting, just as I had pleaded with my parents. Although ashamed, I did nothing to protect my niece and nephew. All I could do was listen in fear and want only to tuck myself away where I could not be found.

With nothing else to do, I began sneaking out at night and wandering the streets. Never through the noisy front door downstairs, my main escape was to climb out my upstairs bedroom window, onto the roof, and down the antennae. Once on the ground, I would run away from the house and toward town. Like Carter only a year before me, it was not long before I too fell in with the wrong crowd. It was comforting because, like me, they were bitter and lonely. Most of all, they too were angry and wanted revenge.

The anger grew inside of me with each passing day. My goal in life became to deaden all pain by any means possible. It took less than a month to destroy what I had worked so hard to attain in over four years. The sudden change in me was not surprising. It was there all along, but lay dormant. The rage inside of me was like a fire waiting to burst into a full inferno. The right moment with the wrong incentives, it would blossom until it burned everything to the ground. I still craved acceptance and now the only people who would accept me were the very people I had hurried from in order to choose a better life. These were my new friends and family. By returning to the cesspool I once escaped, I found a nauseating comfort. I felt an ugly sense of power by simply giving up and giving in. A peaceful death washed over me each time I engaged in a bitter fistfight or vandalized someone's property. Sometimes sober and other times after I consumed large amounts of alcohol. I was still paying for the sins of others. I was again home.

My days became a blur that summer living with Jessica. I felt discarded, like an uprooted weed tossed into the compost pile and left to rot. I woke each morning, only to leave the house and not return until I was sure everyone was asleep. It was during one of these evenings when I came home and found everyone had gone. The house empty, I crept into Jessica's bedroom, knowing exactly what I was looking for. It was a nickel-plated .357 magnum.

First going to my room and finding a pencil and piece of paper, a few minutes later I had finished writing a note in which I described in hateful words what was left of my life. What now held me prisoner and those responsible. Tucking the note inside my shirt pocket, I returned to Jessica's bedroom and pulled the gun from the dresser drawer where it was hidden under some clothes. Next to it was a box of the same caliber shells. I felt the weight of the gun in my hand, and with it, a deadly strength. I depressed the small push-lever and popped open the circular chamber. One by one, I slid the stubby, fat bullets inside each of the holes.

After I was through, I slapped the revolver with my left hand, listening to the clicking sound as it spun. Before the momentum had stopped, I slapped the spinning chamber again, smacking it home with one last, "click." The menacing handgun had now taken on more weight and felt awkward and off balance. I had once watched Jessica's ex-husband fire this very gun into a bale of hay behind Lauren and Tim's farmhouse. Flames shot from its barrel and the sound was deafening.

The house still empty, I now stood in front of Jessica's dresser and staring directly into a mirror bolted to the back of it. Clasping the gun with both hands, I pointed the barrel at the boy in the reflection. Compared to the gun, my hands looked so small. My face appeared sullen and worried at the same time. It was probably because my heart already knew what my mind was thinking. Still staring into the reflection, I slowly dropped one of my hands. The gun dipped as the hand holding on to it took on the entire weight. Before losing my nerve, I turned the gun away from the mirror and placed the barrel against my right temple. My eyes never left the lonely face staring back at me. I wondered if I had always looked so young and feeble. I also noticed that people had been right all along. I did look like a girl.

I couldn't bear to watch, but I hadn't the strength to turn away. So, I compensated by closing my eyes. *The noise will be deafening*, I thought to myself but then again I wouldn't hear it anyway. All I had to do was pull the trigger. Still holding the barrel against my temple, its once cold tip now warmed by my skin, I began to squeeze.

For the first time since the idea slammed into my brain after returning home, much like the bullet was about to, I began to consider my course of action. Many thoughts began to buzz like hungry bees around my head. I thought of all those people who took every ounce of love I had to give and returned nothing but misery. If I were to die, they would only clamor for sympathy for themselves —more martyrs in the making and becoming victims once more. My suicide would prove nothing.

I began to think that although the anger and despair I felt inside might kill me one day, I would not help it along. I removed the gun from my head, emptied its chamber by returning the bullets to their box, and placed both the gun and the shells back in the drawer. I wish it had been out of bravery alone that I chose to live. I would much rather proclaim I thwarted suicide because of a courageous desire for life. Of course, that would be a lie. In the end, I was simply too afraid.

Certain things I knew held me prisoner. Fighting was one of them. I grew to like it. Hell, I grew to love it. Assisting in this love was the fact that I took to it so easily and became very good at what we called *knuckling up*. Accompanying me were always a couple of town boys and we were always on the lookout for someone to fight. Preparing for each night on the prowl was the usual drinking. We were a determined hardnosed bunch of misfits. In all of our eyes was the distant look of sadness, and behind that, nothing but fury. The lack of faithfulness in what would become of our futures killed us. We all had our stories. Some of us had been beaten, molested, raped and neglected. For me, it had been all of these things and more.

Besides, I hated myself and this was one of the few things I was confident and could rely upon –the hatred. It was stronger than love and the results were immediate. I didn't have to work so hard and was rarely, if ever, disappointed. Hate was what I put in and got out. Whereas love was anyone's guess at the outcome. I pushed hard against so many hearts and their hearts were never full.

During one of my many night excursions, I again found myself in another battle of cuffs. The boy's name was Jake and not until I connected with his cheek did I feel the rush of exhilaration. Up to that point, I felt only a dull throb of emotion. I rendered him a terrific beating, but he kept getting up every time I knocked him to the ground. The drugs, probably a speed cocktail, were bringing Jake back to life with every crushing blow. Jumping to his feet, he just swayed and waited for me to hit him again. Jake wouldn't even put up his hands to block my punches. There was a vengeful leer on his bloody face and his eyes blazed almost white, but his voice was so low that I could barely hear the murmur of it.

"Come on pussy. Hit me again," Jake mumbled.

His words were meant for someone else, not me. The face Jake saw wasn't mine. Maybe his father's or mother's. I did not know or care. But what I did know was that I was going to kill him. What I saw in his eyes was also contempt and I could care less if it was meant for me or not. There was also a quality in Jake's low voice that gave off a familiar tone, which sent a curious shiver through me. It was Mother's and Jake was going to die for reminding me of her.

I made no reply with words, but sent another clear message I was all business by putting my weight into the next punch. Jake's head snapped backward and he finally stayed down. Motionless for far too long, we all just stared at his limp body.

"You fucking killed him, Milly!" cried one of the boys.

What followed next was someone yelling, "Run!"

We cut out of there as fast as our feet would carry us in all directions. I ended up back at Jessica's soaking wet with sweat. My knuckles were bloody with deep cuts. I knew immediately it was Jake's teeth that had sliced through my skin. Slowly catching my breath, I hid in the darkness of the backyard and waited for the sirens. Someone had to have seen, or at least heard the fight, and called the police. Soon, I did hear sirens and hurriedly shimmied up the antenna to the roof, through my bedroom window, and into bed. Still dressed, I laid there trying to hear if the sirens were getting closer to the house.

I struck Jake down with a death blow for sure. For a moment I dared not move, but when the sirens stopped I climbed from my bed and quietly snuck into the bathroom not far down the hall. Easing the faucet on, I passed my hands under the running water, stinging as the water rinsed away the blood. The pain was nothing compared to the rubbing alcohol that I poured over my knuckles.

I dared not look into the mirror over the sink, but couldn't help it and caught a glimpse of my face. I saw the change in me and my cheeks were flushed. My face burning with blood seemed like it was on fire when I caught my reflection. Green eyes like steel stared back at me. Through the dirty mirror, I saw what was to come and my grip on life slipping away. The pain in my

hands and the rush of adrenaline now subsiding made me sick to my stomach
and I puked into the sink. The nausea passed in only a few minutes. I had
been through worse.

What began to take over me was nothing new. Born into the sludge of
abuse I was loaded from the beginning and only needed a small trigger to set
me off. I wished that I had remained at Jessica's that night instead of finding
Jake and beating him. Had I remained in my room a little longer, I thought,
I would have never ran into the group of boys. Jake had it coming though.
Stumbling around town obviously stoned and talking out loud about how the
cars were melting. Before that, he sat on the monument in the park cutting
at his thumb with a knife. He was a waste of skin and needed to die. No
longer fearing anything it seemed made me even more angry with him. His
own face aflame combined with a dull pasty look reminded me of Father when
he beat Mother nearly to death. Too many memories. It was in that moment
when Jake held out his arms to me mockingly in a hugging fashion that caused
me to spring across the road and face him. It was as though he was sacrificing
himself before me.

"You know you're going to die, motherfucker," I whispered.

Then he started to cry and that did it. Like an angel of death in a shit
storm of vengeance, all the memories of Mother and Father came crashing
back. An eye for an eye and all that, and in Jake's case, a few teeth up for grabs
as well. There was something about how pathetic he was. Something that
made me want to do the worst to him. It was all I knew. The good and decent
boy doing his best was gone. All I had was rage in my heart and I gave it to
Jake. I gave it to him whether he really knew what was happening or not. I
wasn't ashamed either when it was all done and I was safe back in the bathroom of Jessica's nursing my wounds. Maybe it was because I had seen this all
before played out against me when I was so small and helpless. Maybe it was
because I was still so small and helpless. I wanted to hear Jake scream. Hear
his voice shriek and his bones break. The love I once had now gone, I felt this
is what I came into this world to do. I was built for violence and no matter
what road I took, it always came back to this. And, I wasn't going to give it
up for nothing and nobody. What was I to the world anyway, but another lost
youth, choking on my own voice.

A few weeks before my junior year, before I would turn sixteen, it would be one of the foster girls that showed me what it felt like to make love. It was Mary. Consensual sex for the first time and until then it had been nothing but rape committed by the strangers and Mother.

It had been her glorious eyes staring up at me, looking into my soul, and I looking straight back into hers that I saw my reward there. Mary turned her body ever so gently and guided me inside. As our hands gripped and released, our lips touched but did not kiss. We fell together and in our strong passion was that rarest of all things –love of one for one.

It was easy to be kind with her. The harshness I had developed would vanish leaving something soft and meaningful. Something innocent that offered me a safe place wrapped in her arms. I lied when I said we were never going to be apart, but it was a lie worth telling. Mary knew our relationship wouldn't last, but she too felt that it was something special. Sometimes, you know, the friend who lies is the only friend who you can trust –and Mary would lie a thousand times for me. She would tell me that everything was going to be okay and nothing bad was going to happen. These were good lies to hear and tell.

"There's something about you, Gregg," she would say smiling.

"And, for you," Mary would whisper, "I will wait forever."

Then we would make love and fall asleep while holding hands. And, before closing her bright blue eyes streaming with tears of happiness, for a moment, I believed her.

Once after making love, Mary's voice broke and she started to cry. It wasn't out of joy, but rather fear that I would be leaving soon. There were too many arguments between Jessica and me and they were escalating. Her husband began threatening me physically during many of these altercations. Mary would just sob, begging us to stop fighting. She was sweet, pure, and loyal and I felt like a thief when we were together. I was none of these things –not any longer. She would break down, sobbing like a child, and with her face buried in her hands, she would continue to plead for the fighting to stop. No matter how angry I was at the time, when I saw her eyes during the heated arguments, it caught my breath almost making me smile. But then I was back into the thick of it with Jessica or her husband, and even with Mary's love, I still felt so alone.

It was during one of those arguments that Jessica's husband rushed me and grabbed my throat. He was strong and before I could fight back, the blackness was already closing in. I could not draw a breath and when my body dropped to the floor, he must have let go. Not losing a second of an opportunity to escape, I half-crawled, half-stood, moving toward the door. Thrusting the door open, I could feel my eyes wet and bulging. I held something in my hand, a knife that I dropped before crashing into the fresh night air. I heard the neighbor scream something but I was coughing too loudly to make out what it was. Thrusting forward, I was soon running down the sidewalk. My throat felt torn apart and the imprint of the knife handle was in the palm of my hand. I don't remember picking up the knife. Dragging the air inside my lungs, I continued to run nowhere.

Where I was going was first to the woods near the factory. It was there I had carved *Mary + Gregg* into an oak tree. On the way, I found an old iron rod and picked it up for protection. At the base of the woods, even in the darkness, I could see the old trail leading to where the oak stood. When I reached the tree, I lay at its base and caught my breath. My lips seemed thick and there was something in my throat that choked me. Sitting with my back against the tree, with the carved initials somewhere above my head, I looked down at my feet. No shoes. No socks. My feet were getting cold and a thin fall mist was rising off a pond nearby. School would be starting soon and I had no place to live. My eyes blurred from panic and the tears now welled up and then began to spill down my checks. The sobbing broke the silence of the woods and in a low cry I muttered to myself. Then turning once to look down the trail making sure no one was following me, I laid my head against my knees.

A cold wind was beginning to moan in the oak once christened in the name of love and it made me feel even worse, because with the wind came the promise of more suffering, and like my bare feet, nothing to cover the misery.

CHAPTER SEVEN

Falling Down

*"Falling all over again comes back to me in memory and soul.
I am unmoved by blame or praise either."*

ISLEPT FOR ONLY A COUPLE hours before the cold woke me. It was near-ing dawn. With nowhere else to go, I headed back to Jessica's. Amid the storm that was probably brewing in the household, it was still the only refuge I had. Through the gloom of despair, I fought the urge to find a pay phone and call Father. I was desperate and Carter had gone to live with him, so per-haps I too would be welcomed. I hadn't any of the problems Carter did, so it seemed reasonable Father would accept me. At first, the thought filled me with hope, but then it all came crashing down into bitter realism. This was still the father who had abandoned me. Beat our mother nearly to death. And, throughout all of these years had not even tried to contact me or my sib-lings. Rumor had it also that Carter didn't stay long with Father and eventu-ally ran away again to live with Ashley.

When I returned, the first glimpse of Jessica's house filled me with dread and whatever reason kept me from turning away rang loudly in my head to keep going. It was basic survival I suppose: food, water, shelter. Of course Jes-sica laid into me with a violent lecture, followed by the usual guilt trip. For the next few weeks, I kept my head down and waited for school. I also kept out of Jessica and her husband's way. Throughout this time, I spent reading again and staying in at night. No more sneaking out. Also, time passed eas-ily when making love to Mary. She was delighted I came back and gave me another glimpse of something better. But the storm through which I had struggled for so many years gathered over my head. Behind me was desola-tion. Before me, day after day, was the rolling, twisting and moaning of the cracking hateful voices in my head.

The nightmares and panic roared inside me as well and I often thought of the gun in Jessica's bureau. It called to me and brought back once more the thick death-gloom of freedom. It drove me insane to think about the precious peace it could bring. Keeping busy was the key; therefore, I took up running again until my lungs burned and spent hours at the local library reading.

At last, the first day of school, and with it came some hope, but an ugly thought stuck in my head that there was the possibility I could end my life if things did not work out. It gave me some comfort. Now, sixteen-years-old and another birthday passing without notice, I entered a new high school. If all went well, I could again find the acceptance I had earned at my previous school. After all, I had ended my sophomore year with honors. This particular high school was one division lower and my assumption was that it would be much easier academically and athletically. As with assumptions, I would be wrong on both accounts.

My thin, fever-flushed face relaxed into a wan smile as I sat listening to the school counselor assigned to me. Trying desperately to hide the fact I felt like a child, expected to succeed with nothing but the tools for failure. Based on my former academic transcripts, I was automatically placed in college preparatory courses. However, long before the first semester ended I was already failing most of my classes. Figuring I'd be dead soon enough anyway, there wasn't much use in trying. I tried to revert back to my old study habits initially, but the weight of a terrible home life, fighting, depression, and alcohol soon got the best of me. Help would come too late if it came at all. Mary had taken a boyfriend, telling me that I was too young to be in a serious relationship. I drew a long line of girlfriends, but none of them amounted to anything. It was only sex and it all felt so dirty now. It felt ugly. Nothing but piled up masses of faces and grinding hips without regard of each other's hearts. There would be the somber discussion from time to time when there was talk of love and forever, but they were just words in the end. Words that young boys and girls tell each other in order to convince themselves that it was more than anything physical.

I tried out for track and made the final cut. I would be joining the sprint A-team as one of the top runners. However, every valiant effort I made at improving myself in the areas of academics or athletics was met with defeat. I reached for some glimmer of hope, only to pull back emptiness. I was too goddamn hungry and tired all the time to pay attention in school or play sports.

Failing school and now hardly holding my own on the track team, there came to me a low, never-ceasing thunder of the catastrophe my life had become. Broken now and by then a gigantic force that ripped me into shreds like a great knife. I heard no other voices except those bent on crushing the hope out of me. The anger and hatred that boiled inside of me flourished.

Violence was easy to find, and I was now fighting nearly every day. It didn't matter where I was when my temper flashed. At times, I leapt from my desk during classroom instruction and beat another boy into submission and the act brought with it more suspensions.

Many were caught off guard by my outward appearances. I was quiet, almost shy. I rarely looked up unless I was spoken to, and then it would be a dead stare. My hair hung in my face, long and curly at the ends. I was incredibly thin and looked girlish. However, my reflexes were quick and I continuously practiced speed drills. Whatever I learned from watching Mother and Father, on the streets, or in formal Judo lessons, I used to my advantage. The contempt I held for all humanity completed the package. All I had to do was think of my abusers and turn that anger toward another person. I always went too far and was often dragged from some unfortunate boy who lay unconscious and bleeding. I wanted to kill everyone, but mostly the monster that had been unleashed inside of me.

To those around me, including myself, I had become a shell. What was on the inside was built, not born. The legacy of my parents lived within me. I would be the new machine assembled through abuse and fueled by hatred. Although it was becoming more difficult to remember what I had once hoped for, it was still there. Dormant, but close. As my life enclosed me with its limitless possibilities for failure, I had yet to give up on salvation. It was like a candle burning through a small window. The whole of my future rested upon whether this candle stayed lit.

The violence soon left me, yet again, suspended from school. This was the last straw for Jessica and her husband. After telling them, they launched into a tirade. At first, it was bitter yelling, but then both of them grew steadily more aggravated. Jessica's husband left the room, slamming doors, and exclaiming how he was done with me. Without warning, he came back into the kitchen where I had been sitting at the kitchen table and hit me from behind. The chair I had been sitting on, along with me in it, went crashing to the floor. He then pulled me up from the floor and threw me over the fallen chair. I hit the refrigerator, knocking the door open.

"Get up!" he shouted.

There was no one to protect me. Jessica just stood there while her husband yanked me outside and on to the porch. I was weeping by now. I didn't have the strength to fight back. The tough man image I portrayed with my peers completely left me when it came to adults. As before, his hands were now wrapped around my throat as we stood on the porch. He pushed me against the side of the house and choked me. There was no point in resisting anyway. Seemingly tired of what physical activity he already spent, Jessica's husband suddenly let go of my neck and went back into the house. Jessica never came outside.

When I walked back inside Jessica and her husband were in their bedroom. I was alone and made my way upstairs and into bed. I could smell the piss, now drying. The odor of my urine once again brought tears to my eyes. It was obvious to me that I was running out of dreams and possessed a terrible longing for someone to listen to me, a touch of their hand, a glimpse of a caring set of eyes before I died at the hands of a madman.

Beyond the door of these soul assassins was an opportunity I knew awaited me, but I could not find the key. It seemed as though my attempts at patching the gaping tear in my soul left by the desolation of my past and present caused me more harm than good. So many doors in my life were nailed shut. I was supposed to be on my way to a better life. It was close at hand only a few short months before. There were the problems Lauren and Tim brought to the table, but I could bear them.

While lying in my bed stinking of my own piss and fear, it was evident that I would have to rely upon myself and trust no one. In the morning, Jessica would be waiting for me and perhaps her husband. No words would reach their hearts. I cried myself to sleep and the next morning promptly ran away. This time for good and my only regret was that I would be leaving my niece and nephew.

Before anyone awoke in the house and with a dry sob, I turned from Jessica's and walked a few feet to the rough broken sidewalk, while drawing a paper bag close to me and tucked under my arm. In it were all my worldly possessions. For the thousandth time, I held before my red and feverish eyes a photograph. It was a picture of me and Mary taken at one of those bowling alley picture booths. There used to be six all connected together, but now only one remained. Cut from the others given to Mary, I kept my favorite. She was marvelously beautiful and although the photograph was in black and white, I could imagine her blue eyes. And for the thousandth time I turned the picture over and read the word she had written on the back: *"Forever."*

The only place I knew to go was to the home of a girl I met at school. She was one of three sisters who lived with their mother. One daughter was my age, one two years older and the other two years younger. At fourteen, and the youngest, was the most beautiful, and she would come to fall in love with me. I was sixteen, so it was not to be. I kept my distance, but on occasion would lay with her on the floor and take naps. Holding her was sweet.

Their last name was Marais and all three daughters were very pretty. When I showed up at the door, it did not take long before the conversation escalated into an argument between the mother and her daughters. Reluctantly, I was taken in but warned by Ms. Marais it would only be for a short time and I was also warned to be sure and keep my hands to myself. Ms. Marais then showed me to a spare room, and afterwards, I laid down. Before falling asleep from exhaustion, I felt the usual fire burning inside my head and grew dizzy from panic. My thoughts were nothing but babble and incoherent. My hair was shaggy and I stunk of urine. When meeting me, I remember Ms. Marais sniffed at the air suspiciously. I was positive she smelled urine, and even more sure, after she suggested I shower. Which I did; however the only pants I had left to put back on were the ones that smelled.

Ms. Marais reminded me often that my stay would be only temporary and the first order of business was to get a job, which I did so easily, through the recommendation of a classmate. His name was Mike and he was short but well-built. A varsity wrestler. The job was part-time labor at a local dairy farm. Most of the time I was shoveling cow shit, but it was work and the farmer's wife made Mike and I lunch. It was usually my only meal of the day so I gobbled whatever was prepared greedily until my stomach hurt. I felt guilty taking food from the Marais' because they were on a fixed income with only one parent at home and working.

While Mike and I toiled away on the farm, I would often be forced to listen to his deliriums of how he once fucked one of the cows. I would whine softly, nervously, and offer up a half-hearted acknowledgement. Mike's claims would stop whatever I was doing at the time, but then I'd settle back into scraping up the dung or heaving stray into the bins where the cows would graze while being milked. Every now and then Mike would start punching on the cows or bend their tails until the cartridge cracked loudly in the open barn. From the cow's throats would come a low wailing, mourning cry, long-drawn and terrible. I'd yell at him to stop. He'd just laugh and go about carelessly pushing the electronic suction milkers on the cow teats. I hated how Mike hurt the cows and during these times found once more the fire and pain had returned in my head.

"Stop it, Mike! Goddamnit!" I'd shout.

"Stop hurting the cows or I'll kick your cow-fucking ass!"

Mike would just laugh and dismiss what I said as empty threats. Maybe it was because my voice did not sound threatening, but more like pleading. While insistent that Mike stop hurting the cows weakly, he would remind me about how he had been responsible for getting me the job and to shut my mouth. There'd be a quiet exchange of glances and we both would go back to work. It was probably the fact even though Mike had size on me, he didn't want to fall victim to my ass-whipping skills, which by then had grown to be a bit of legend in the small school and surrounding community.

The farm itself sprawled across wheat and cornfields. In the center was the dairy section where I worked. I had grown into the habit of talking to myself while I moved about the cows, petting them, watching them chew with their lower jaws moving from side-to-side. My own voice was often the one thing that calmed me down and killed the monotony. When the farmer was in the house, I would stand at the edge of the wheat field and look into a stretch of limitless color. Beneath the overhung sky, the wheat field always made me think of a picture I once saw in a book. It was a beautiful picture of a low, thick sky, like purple and blue granite, always threatening to pitch itself down and swallow up all the wheat. Between the earth and the sky was the thin, smothered world in which I now lived. A world that felt more like a trap every day.

Through the gloom of what lay ahead for me and a feverish vision of despair, I could not see very far. Living with strangers and eating only what a farmer's wife made for lunch, I had only the cows and the dank of their shit. My athleticism suffered as well as my academics. Regardless of how many times the coach warned I'd be cut from the track team if I skipped another practice, he never did. The competitions came and went without much effort put into them as before. Like the textbooks I used to enjoy reading, but now struggled to comprehend. And then there were the girls. At first it was only something to keep me preoccupied, but I eventually always felt something more than they did. My feelings for them would loom larger, a straying misguided love, but then never allowing them to get too close. They would all reach a certain point where the bristles along my spine rose stiff and their affection became menacing. Harder and harder, I tried to let each one inside my heart a little more, but against the cold memory of rejection, there was also a gasping cry of desperation in the end and I wanted nothing more than escape.

Suddenly, Mike shrieked with excitement as he flew by executing a move we called "shit skating." Donned in rubber boots, we would hold onto the tails of the dairy cows and be pulled through the slippery crap. It was Mike who came up with the idea and I quickly caught on. The cows were easily startled, so anything got them running. I watched as Mike went sailing by, bent, almost doubled-over, and then he caught some dry cement, falling forward with a face-plant. He started gagging immediately after getting some cow shit in his mouth. But then Mike jumped up again, grabbing the tail of another cow, finding another nice patch of cow shit. In a zigzag fashion, he advanced forward behind the ass of a half-crazy dairy cow.

I made my way to an unsuspecting cow and joined in. Overcome by loss of balance and unexpected speed, I quickly dropped flat on my face too. Soon, I was sliding through a tundra of shit and gagging while trying like hell to laugh and not puke at the same time. Getting up, I made my way feebly to the barn and pushed the heavy door open just enough to slip inside. Overcome by weakness I fell back on a hayloft and rested.

It seemed forever before I heard Mike come inside the barn. He was laughing his ass off and stumbling a bit himself. An instant later, the farmer appeared at the door. It was a terrible face, overgrown with dark stubble, with wild and staring eyes.

"You bust up my cows, I'll bust you up!" he shouted.

I sprang to my feet with sudden strength as the farmer approached. The farmer stared at me with the look of an insane animal.

"I was wrong to hire you!" he said and then followed by what I expected.

"You're fired!"

The farmer could really only let one of us go and I figured it was going to be me. Mike had worked for him longer. I was the outsider, yet again.

My first move was to beat the farmer, but instead I sheepishly dragged myself toward the barn doors and sank in shame as I passed him, then began the five-mile trek back to the Marais' house.

Mike didn't even defend me. I figured I'd kick the living shit out of him later, but at that moment the thought of telling Ms. Marais I no longer had a job was taking up all my strength.

While working on the dairy farm, I had been dating a girl from school named Britney. As timing would have it, we had broken up the day before I was fired. It was right after she lost the second round of the Ms. Teen U.S.A. pageant. Apparently, the depression was too great for her to handle and having a boyfriend was only adding to her stress. It didn't matter anyway. We had enough sex to know that it wasn't that great to begin with, leaving much to be desired. It was awkward and she usually complained I took too long to orgasm anyway. Seemingly bored most of the time while in the midst of sex, I got used to just trying to wrap things up as fast as I could. It took longer because the motivation to actually enjoy what I was doing ended shortly after getting started. However, she did have a beautiful singing voice and nice breasts. I honestly enjoyed her singing more than her breasts even though they were huge and all natural too.

Stinking of cow shit and sweat, I knocked on the door of the Marais home. The youngest daughter was the only one there. Sue was her name. She stared at me and grinned. Between the matted down hair hanging over my face, she saw my eyes and they didn't lie. I could have easily loved her. Perhaps not letting her get any further than the others into my heart, but with Sue, I was willing to try. Her look cleared my head. For some reason that I could not explain, she was wearing only a robe and it was mid-afternoon. I ventured to wonder what was underneath, but quickly pushed the thought away and walked past her into the bathroom.

Locking the door behind me, I showered and put on the only clean pair of clothes I had. When I came out of the bathroom, Sue had already put my dirty clothes in the washer and was cooking me a late breakfast. Without warning she then walked up to me and gave me a gentle kiss on the mouth. I could have stopped her, but didn't. She then unsheathed the robe and it fell to the floor. Sue was wearing a small pair of underwear. The kind a fourteen-year-old girl would wear. Simple print, nothing special but worn and I could make out the hair underneath. She led me to the table where I sat down and ate the cooked food ravenously. Not until I was through and still seated at the table, did she come over and sit on my lap.

"Gregg, I love you."

It was the way she said it. Not lustful or wanting, but naïve, blameless and not guilty. An hour ago, I was skidding in cow shit, fired from the only source of income I had, and left to return to the only home in which to live. A home occupied by strangers, but then there was Sue. And the sweet smell of her skin rose to my nostrils and I was swept away by her cuteness. We kissed and this time it wasn't just a soft gentle peck. This time, we kissed like we were in love and would be forever.

Neither Sue or I heard her Mother walk in the house. By the time we saw her, she was already scowling with fury

"She's only fourteen!" Ms. Marais yelled, and I suddenly felt like a pervert. It felt ugly and wrong.

Sue jumped from my lap and quickly put her robe back on. We only kissed. I wouldn't have dared to touch her. Not in a sexual way, but admittedly my hand did find the smooth nape of her neck and rested there while our mouths worked together in tandem.

"Pack your things and get out!" demanded Ms. Marais.

I was already doing so before she commanded me to leave. Sue wept while I quickly loaded my wet clothes from the washer into a bag, gathering what little I had and left. Everything felt immoral and this angered me. It was my only bright spot to an already failure of an afternoon. It was too late to apologize and I had already confessed to more sins I had not committed let alone one in which I was a willing participant.

Weak with shame, I set off to Mike's house. I thought about going back and trying to work things out with Ms. Marais, but it wasn't because I wanted a place to live. It was because I wanted Sue and this made me change my mind. She was two years younger and regardless of how innocent it felt. How wonderful. It was still wrong.

Mike convinced his parents to allow me a place to stay for a couple days. Of course, when I told Mike what had happened he said I should have nailed Sue when I had the chance. "Someone's gonna bust that little slut sooner or later," he said. This led to a punch I had been dying to deliver. It came with a swiftness that took Mike by surprise and a startled cry broke from his busted lips. It knocked him down and to my astonishment, he just got up and shook it off.

"Fucking-A, Milligan," he whimpered. It wasn't that he was afraid of me. Mike could hold his own. It was the fact he saw I was beaten, alone and afraid. He looked at me in the gray light of the day now fading while we stood outside in his parent's backyard. He raised his eyes as if to say something and then let it go. Mike turned out to be an okay friend. Even if he was serious about fucking a cow, he was alright in my book.

"I'm not dating anyone," I told her, jokingly and she just giggled while doing her best to flirt with me. Mid-semester I met another girl and her name was Darla. She was very pretty and easily homecoming queen material; however, she was too hard-nosed and her reputation for a being a party-girl left her out of the running. The homecoming committee would never vote for a girl like Darla. Regardless, she had kicked more than half the girls' asses on the planning committee to even get an honorable mention for homecoming court.

"You have a girlfriend, I just know it!" Darla said, still teasing. She had half-risen, her small hands clutching a notebook sitting on the school desk in front of her when I walked into the classroom. It was an accident I walked in at all. It wasn't my class and when I went to leave, Darla half-stood and looked at me. What she said was perfect. In an inquisitive, playful tone, she said my first and last name. Her sweet face, like that of a china doll, pushed forward a little in anticipation, her whole body in an attitude that sent a tingling feeling all over mine.

"So you dating anyone or not?"

I again, replied "No."

And then laughed because she really didn't believe me. "Want to?" she said and the banter was playful.

In an oath to myself I was going to be with her, I sprang from the room. Before doing so, I asked her name. From her, came another perfect response. "Find out."

I did find out and that very night she drove me to her house in an old Lincoln once owned by her father. "This used to be my dad's car and it's now mine." she said with pride. "It's got a 454 and a bitch of a kick."

I had no idea what she was talking about, but her small frame behind that giant wheel looked to be both cute and somehow sexy. I immediately liked her and if I had any doubts she felt the same way about me, they were soon dashed when she put her free hand on my leg while we sped off down the dirt road going much too fast.

The feel of her hand was warm and perfect reach within how close I had been sitting to her. Darla lived deep in the woods and the brush at the sides of the road leading to her house crept all the way to the side. So close, the wide bumpers of the Lincoln smacked into it loudly and I could hear the sound of twigs cracking. "Where in the hell do you live?" I asked.

"Back in the woods," Darla said. Followed by saying, "Where no one will ever find you." And she giggled.

Laying my hand on top of hers still resting on my leg, something caught up in my throat and I swallowed hard. From my lips, there came a long sigh and I could feel my heart falling with a crash. "You still dating that skank, Britney?" Darla asked, speeding up just a little.

"No. She dumped me," I said.

"Oh. Really?" was all Darla replied. Her hand never leaving my leg and mine never leaving hers.

Darla didn't like Britney long before I dated her. Darla was right not to. Britney was stuck on herself and had good reason by high school standards. She had tits out to Texas and an ass the shape of a perfect peach. Small waist and shapely legs with piercing brown eyes and brown hair cut short. However, I always felt that even though she came from money, she was at least one hump away from pure white trash.

On her way to becoming the next Ms. Teen U.S.A., Britney was way past homecoming queen material. She was big time and she knew it. Her heart was ice and that was fine with me. She said I caught her eye which I'm sure was true, but what really got her panties wet was the fact that all Britney wanted was to get a good railing by a bad boy. Our relationship ended as quickly as it began.

I remember the day she told me it was over. Her grip of my hand relaxed and then let go, dropping to her side. With no more than a groan, I watched as Britney walked away. Working hard to bury my feelings, I stood there grinning like a fool. A coolness ran down my spine. I'd been left before and did my share of leaving as well. The way the anger flashed for a second when Britney broke up with me turned to nothing more than a twinge a couple seconds later. Maybe some sadness welled up in my heart, but it stopped midway of turning into something that could be considered longing. Britney didn't glitter any more for me. She had a beautiful singing voice, but that wouldn't be missed either. Her short black hair was perfect as usual and she probably spent an hour fixing it just for this occasion. For a second, I wanted to reach up and take a hold of that hair and yank it as hard as I could. Snatching a clump of it from her skull would be a reminder of the heartache. Not for me, but for her. It wouldn't be worth it in the end. She was gone now and whatever there was between us was gone too. But there still was something that Britney couldn't take with her when she broke off our relationship. It was the life I had come to expect. A low subtle reminder that everyone leaves in the end.

I looked over at Darla wildly. The Lincoln was still picking up speed. Winding our way through what looked like more of a path than a dirt road, we headed toward her house. In the light of the dashboard, Darla noticed the scars lacing my knuckles, but she didn't say anything. Nearing Darla's house I began to feel sick. At first, I just thought it to be nerves, but I would end up spending the night because by the next morning I would have a full-blown case of pneumonia.

Her parents were kind-hearted and as sick as I had become they clearly were not worried about me taking advantage of their only daughter. For the next ten days I laid in a spare bedroom, suffering from the sickness, and was in and out of consciousness. What medication I received was paid for by Darla's parents.

Sometimes when I awoke and was sure no one was in the room, I would weep. Turned to one side with my face cradled in my hands, I wept and wondered what would become of me now. I wept until the infection in my chest burned even more and my belly felt like it was made of stone.

CHAPTER EIGHT

Those Missing Things

"A child has died. In his place, there now sits a man – ruined.
You were supposed to have saved me."

Darla lingered close to me while I lay ill. I moved slowly, leading her with my eyes. I was awake, but barely. Just past the bedroom door was the living room, where I would spend the next ten days fighting a bronchial infection, along with pneumonia. In it was a large overstuffed chair. From that chair was a perfect vantage point. That is where Darla sat most days as soon as she came home from school. I would watch her watching me. When I opened my eyes, she would be sitting there. And, when I closed my eyes again she was the last thing I saw.

Every one of my muscles strained and ached just to turn over. At sixteen I felt as though I was a hundred. My chest burned and it hurt to breathe. For a time the excitement of having a place to live gave me some strength, which soon faded as I became sick. But the weakness did not entirely destroy the hope beginning to build inside of me.

Not only did I have a place to live, for now anyway, but I had someone who loved me. I found that the worst trouble at first was due to the fact I could not return the love. The fever had made me feeble and even my vision was hampered so that the world around me was blurred. But I knew Darla was there in the chair or somewhere nearby in the house while I rested and worked through the illness. I knew she was only a few feet away from me at any given time. Sometimes the sickness was so strong it made everything around me turn gray and black. It struck me that there was some humor as well as tragedy in the situation, and that was the fact Darla's parents had no choice but to take me in. They would not make me leave until I was better so perhaps the longer I was sick the more they would grow to love me too.

The fact was that this home where I now lived and convalesced was not mine. It belonged to a generous family who would have taken me in regardless of whether or not Darla was my girlfriend, but she was my girlfriend and this had become official the night she took me to her home. My fever skyrocketed and I could do nothing but lay on the couch. By the time her parents returned from a night out the sickness was in full swing and my body trembled and sweat uncontrollably. I remember Darla's mother and father helping me walk to the car and taking me to a clinic. After that, I just remember the comfort of the bed in which I would lay for the next two weeks.

There is a vast and empty place that is refuge to creatures such as me. Cast away and always tramping for a place to eat and lay our heads. It was known throughout my world as home. Being confined to a bed was not a terrible thing. The illness gave me a reprieve of sorts. A chance to collect myself. Under the weight of immeasurable heartache and unable to snap the chains of abuse, I remained a prisoner of hope and an eternal dreamer. And, during my illness I dreamt of a better day.

As the illness passed, I was able to take short walks with Darla. Her home was nestled deep in a wooded area where a lake shone brightly not far from the back entrance. We used to play a game of hide-and-seek. Darla would tie a handkerchief over my eyes and then lead me through an old orchard. I could smell the apples and it was there she would kiss me while I was still blindfolded. With the handkerchief still over my eyes, I would sometimes bump her lips and we would both laugh. At first I was afraid that my feet would catch a root and I would go tumbling face downward onto the ground. But Darla never let me trip or fall. She would see me through the full soft rain of the haunting memories. I just knew it.

We played for hours in the nearby woods and at night she would sneak into my room and make love to me. Near the bed was an old transistor radio and it was set to a rock-ballad station. Our favorite song was "Babe" by Styx and when the song came on the radio we would both giggle, picking up our love-making where we left off.

At seventeen, Darla was one year older and there was a lot of experience packed into that one year. We weren't each other's first lover, but it felt that way to the both of us. When she came to me at night, her hair would be in a big brown braid and it all came undone soon after we lay together. I'd hug her close and make promises that we were going to make a home together one day. Promises that no sixteen-year-old, especially one as broken and confused as I, could ever keep. There was within me a chronic capitulation to fear that at any time all I had would be taken from me and this was a feeling I certainly came by honestly. So, the promises were a way to drive a stake into the ground. A way in which I could lie to myself and the lies just might come true.

In the bedroom of Darla's home, I hugged her up closer and made my promises. I would gently stroke her long hair and say things which neither Darla or me really believed. But whatever promises found their way into my voice, the fear inside me remained in my heart. I grew to expect abandonment, which formed a living picture that could not for even a moment be forgotten. It never occurred to me that the difference between a lie and a promise wasn't that far apart. It was easy to pride myself in the shrewdness of telling Darla what she wanted to hear. It was survival after all and sometimes it actually felt like the truth. Especially, when we made love, because it caused my heart to grow stronger. It revived me somehow and told me that there was still a chance. If I had been a bit older perhaps I would have seen and recognized how foolish we both were. As it was, I went on lying to Darla and myself, filled with nothing but hope.

"We'll make it, Gregg," Darla whispered to me in the moonlit bedroom.

In her eyes I could see that she really wanted to believe this. There was a sharp pain in my chest every now and then, remnants of the sickness slowly passing. My legs no longer felt as they were wearily dragging along as I walked. Soon, I would be well enough and return to school.

There was not much change in the season, but it seemed as if the intervals between daylight and darkness were becoming shorter. I scarcely noticed this at first now that I had a home with food on the table and a young girl to love. The time passed with not much dark spaces and my craving for fighting slowly gave way to something more peaceful.

A rhythm returned and soon I was in the habit of attending classes, studying vigorously, and running track. The meets when Darla came to watch were always my best performances. Lined up with the other runners, my head dropped, a low groan would come from my lungs right before the starting gun.

The crack of the shot would snap through the air, propelling my legs to thrust from the blocks, and I would be leading the pack. My teammates would be tugging on each other excitedly while the coach's jaw hung limp. The first turn of the 400m, I would give a quick look over my shoulder; the crowd cheering sounded like muffled whining. For a time, I could see Darla in the stands, front row and straining to get a better look. A glance back at her and I was sucking in air and pumping my arms and legs. I pushed harder, pulling at the rubber track with my spikes. A strange thing happened when competing. Each time, I rose up a little bit more out of the depths of despair. It roused me.

Upon winning, I'd rub my eyes and wipe the sweat from my face, staggering at bit in my lane from fatigue, while settling my breathing. My chest ached because there was no pacing myself. I ran literally trying to force my heart to explode. It wasn't just the victory of winning. It was the fact that when I ran, it was at a doomed pace toward absolute bliss.

Rest and a place to call home had cleared my head again but I knew that it was due to end sometime, and I could see Darla's parents getting restless. Perhaps they heard us making love. It would catch up to us sooner or later. You can't hide things like that for long from parents. Not the good ones anyway. But I wasted no time worrying about these things. Born into abuse and bitter disappointment, I knew the end was always close at my heels.

So, I rose early for track practice and studied. No more drinking or fighting. The only risks taken were having unprotected sex with Darla. There were a couple close-calls, but never a pregnancy. Still, there was that looming uncomfortable feeling in her parents' house. There was no talk of me leaving. No actions taken on her mother and father's part to send me away that I was aware of; however, instinctively I knew something wasn't right. Stretched out behind me was proof nothing good ever lasts. I was alert to what came next but never really expected it. Not until I walked into Darla's house after school one day close to mid-semester and saw the social worker. My eyes burned fiercely from the tears and a low growl rumbled in my throat.

"Gregg, we're so sorry, but it would be best if you left," said Darla's mother and I saw she was crying too. Darla was right behind me and she looked at the people in the living room, moved slowly toward me, and held my hand. She pulled me away as if to somehow stop what was happening.

For a moment, I stared and said nothing. Then a low cry broke from my lips and I sat down hard on one of the chairs in the living room. Darla fell upon her knees next to the chair, hugging my legs and wept.

"You lied!" Darla kept saying over and over to her parents.

"You said you wouldn't send him away!"

I, in turn, sat quietly. There was nothing for me to say. I was dead. I had died long ago and this was yet another moment in my life reminding me it was true. I rose to my feet, pushing Darla's hands away. All that her parents had done for me amounted to nothing. It was hard for me to see it any other way. My weakened nerves shattered by a sound and a movement from the farthest and darkest part of my mind; it was Mother, Lauren, Jessica, all of them tugging at what was left of my hope. Leaving traces of broken possibilities were their voices, panting and whining, once barely held back by a young girl's love. Now, in the room where Darla wept and her parents looked ashamed, a social worker waited to take me away. And, the sound that came to me was unheard by anyone else but me; a wailing, sobbing cry of a wasted boy.

With my only belongings still fitting inside a large paper bag I darted toward the door. It took me but an instant to say goodbye. No use lingering. I kissed Darla sweetly and as I drew back from her face, my heart leaped up and choked me. The light fell full upon her thin pale face and smooth hair of a young girl in love. A pair of big frightened eyes were staring up at me; and as I stood there, powerless to move or speak in the face of this image, her eyes closed and spilling from them was a wash of pent-up tears. I turned and flung the door open angrily. The social worker followed. As we drove away from Darla's house, I too suddenly lost all strength and wept openly.

"Where are we going?" I asked, my breath coming in sobbing gasps.

"You'll be living with foster parents," the social worker responded mechanically.

"It's for the best."

My hands trembled and fidgeted as I kept blinking the wetness from my eyes and trying to focus them on the road. I pleaded while terrified at the thought of living with strangers. The social worker did not speak and the quiet frightened me.

Darla had promised many things as well. She promised there would never be anyone else. In my arms she had said this while I kissed her lips. During that moment, her eyes shot open looking into mine and life seemed to spring from her body.

"I will be with only you, Gregg," she said.

"I will be with only you, forever."

Her tiny hands were gripping mine by the wrist when she made these promises. The thought of Darla giving herself only to me was thrilling. I wrapped her in my arms warmly so her small face was hidden against my chest. Her tangled hair fell around her shoulders, and I looked down upon her wide-eyed and wondered if she was telling the truth.

My fear grew as we approached our destination. Reminding me that I was still a ward of the state, the social worker described my new family. I would have to change schools mid-semester, which would be my third high school in three years.

We turned down a narrow street and at the end of it was a modest ranch home amidst cornfields on three sides. The driveway was recently tarred and jet black against a deep blue sky. The home looked inviting and peaceful. A farmhouse with a big red barn at the end of the driveway. Where the corn did not grow there was a field, and in it, were two horses grazing.

A few minutes later, we were knocking at the door. I stood behind the social worker and stared at my feet. A larger woman answered and swung the door open inviting us both inside. She was stout and had rugged features. Unkind eyes and a square jaw. She was much taller and wider than her husband who seemed shy but dangerous. I hated them both on sight.

The man of the house, whose eyes were much too close together, offered me no welcome. The woman shook my hand and wouldn't stop talking. It was irritating and making it worse was no sooner had I arrived, she was already covering the house rules. Of which, every single one of them I planned on breaking.

However, to my delight, there was a boy about the same age living there. His name was Nate and I liked him immediately. His warm and sensitive nature reminded me of Bruce. He moved awkwardly and with great effort to lift one leg that was badly deformed. Not until I noticed his deformed leg, did I begin to take in all of his features. His face was a mass of grotesque mangled lumps of skin. One eye socket hung much lower than the other, which made his forehead look larger on one side. Nate did not have any lips and he was missing an ear, leaving only a distorted hole. Covering his head and hanging askew was a badly made wig. I would find out later that he was tricked into retrieving a football that had been kicked into an open electrical plant. Nate had bravely climbed the fence, too young to understand the danger signs, fell into a transformer and was burned.

Surviving the terrible accident left him disfigured and handicapped, and because of this, he told me that his parents gave him up for adoption. Nate entered the social services program as a foster child not because he was abused or came from a broken home. Not because his parents were drug addicts or alcoholics. Instead, Nate was handed over to the state by his parents simply because he was an embarrassment.

He shared with me one evening that the nickname given to him by the neighborhood kids was "Elephant Boy." Named after the badly deformed John Merrick, from the movie, "The Elephant Man." Like John Merrick, Nate was abandoned because of his ugly and bizarre facial features, deformed leg and arm with what used to be a hand twisted and crimped in a ball of useless fingers. This was his outward appearance. But on the inside, Nate was a saint. A young man to be reckoned with. A worthy and sweet boy. And like Bruce, he was easy to love.

In the basement of the foster home was a weight bench. Free weights. I marveled at the strength Nate possessed and how he learned to compensate for his injured arm and hand. From its stump of flesh, he balanced the bar of weights, lowering it slowly, and then thrusting it upward. The bar would bend slightly causing the lifting of weights to look even more impressive. Standing, Nate could also lift the bar of weights easily. Stretching his arms above his head and breathing deeply of the cool damp basement air. It seemed as though something had loosened inside of him, that a crushing pain of shame had given him superhuman strength. I would cheer him on and Nate's eyes would shine wet with joy.

Even with Nate as my new friend, I felt sick most of the time. Not just emotionally, but physically as well. Within the first week of living at the foster home, I had already written and mailed Darla three to four letters, but received no reply. When I called her home, she was never there and always out with friends I was told.

"She's gone for good," I thought to myself.

"She's gone and she lied."

Angry and feeling abandoned, I began to sneak out at night and soon found trouble. Trouble was something that could easily be found without looking very hard. I didn't want that sick feeling inside of me anymore. It followed me everywhere. What helped was no longer the wholesome work of academics or athletics, but violence. The more I engaged in physical violence, the easier and more enjoyable it became and the better I felt. In time, what was once revulsion became compulsion. It again was a way in which I could even the playing field.

Finding dejected peers like me was effortless and we roamed the streets looking for battle. It didn't make any difference to me if I beat the hell out of another boy or engaged in random acts of vandalism. All I wanted was revenge.

In order to escape the foster home one evening, I once kicked out a sheet of thick plastic covering my upstairs bedroom window, climbed onto the roof, and down a wooden trellis. The next day, a verbal berating by the old man of the house told me the window had been weatherized which explained the plastic. I thought it was just another way of keeping me prisoner. Turning my back on school and sports, I began skipping classes and spending the days wandering the city. Only recently enrolled in school, it was easy to slip through the cracks and my truancy went unnoticed.

In desperation one evening, I hitchhiked to where Darla attended school. It was Friday and I knew her old haunts. I fully expected to find her there, but to my terrible surprise, I did not intend on finding her having sex in the backseat of another boy's car. But she was, and also to my surprise, I did not feel sick or angry. Instead, a calm came over me. I stared through the window of the car then slowly knocked. They both scrambled and began dressing. Darla looked worried, but the boy she was with looked afraid. That was the look that gave me a cheerful glow inside, and it was growing warmer.

When Darla stepped from the car she was still dressing, straightening her skirt. The boy exited without his shirt which he held in one hand. He threw the first punch and it skipped off my shoulder bouncing against my face. The hit didn't have the seriousness behind it and it only moved my head a little to the side. Darla rushed me and wrapped her arms around my waist. Pushing her aside as if she was only paper, I drew down heavy with my fist and connected with the boy's jaw. The boy staggered backward, his body being stopped short from falling down altogether by the car. I turned briefly and stared down at Darla's little thin face, her long hair curled and messy just as it was when we made love. Seeing this, I became even more enraged.

Focusing my attention on the boy who was just having sex with the girl who promised me she would only be mine, I was starving for payback. A hot light burned inside my belly. My head bent lower and lower, while slowly and a little fearfully the boy pushed his back harder against the side of the car. Once again, I swung hard and connected with the boy's cheek. He made a rough grizzled sound. My anger was worsened by the intense feelings I had for Darla and the thought of her making love to another boy while nestled up against his body before and afterwards.

With my left hand, I held the boy's throat and pressed him hard against the car while pummeling his face with my right. The world swam in sparks of light and color while I listened to the wet thudding noise each and every time my fist struck his face. Squatting on the ground and weeping uncontrollably was Darla, begging me to stop.

"Gregg, please stop!" she cried.

"You're killing him!"

If there was any chance of stopping me, it had long since passed. I was in the zone. Like Carter used to refer to as, "skull cracking." Seeing Darla having sex with this boy I was now beating was the end of my world. Another well-aimed punch crashed into the side of his face and the impact made a grinding thump. A loud hiss escaped from his throat. The boy's eyes rolled back and it was then I let him drop. He slid down the car and fell, dead weight pulling him to the ground. Darla crawled over to his side and wept aloud rocking back and forth. She curled herself next to the boy's body, which fueled a hatred inside of me that grew deeper and stronger for the both of them. I could feel the beat of my heart in my head and chest, my cheeks red and the whole of my body numb. My hands clenching and unclenching, and every now and then I would grip the air and squeeze while holding my fist out before me.

A hundred questions ran through my mind now. Why would she betray me? Why would she abandon me? And I, so frail and alone, how could she? How could I have ever come to love Darla? The tragedy before me was the happenstance of trust. I should have known better. Somehow I was conscious of a sensation of defeat as I reasoned there was no answer to these questions. Darla did not belong to me. She never did. I had found her by accident. The whole relationship was an accident. While I watched her tenderly care for the injured boy, I had no doubt she had been a mistake. I thrust a cut and bloody hand into my pocket and pulled from it a cheap locket that was to be Darla's. It was going to be a surprise. It never occurred to me that I'd find her with another boy. The old fears and sickness put in me from years of abuse returned.

"I hate you," I breathed softly.

"I hope that fucker dies," I added and then, "You did this."

"You made me do this."

Tossing the locket on the ground next to Darla, she just gazed up at me still crying. Her eyes were so pretty, even then. She picked the locket from the dirt and looked at it then cried harder still. Now babbling incoherently, Darla seemed to be pleading with me. It was just nonsense to my ears and heart. When I had heard enough, I just turned and walked away, saying nothing.

The locket had been a foolish inspiration anyway. What little money I had was used to purchase it. *What a waste*, I thought now. To my astonishment, I was actually feeling worse as I walked back toward the foster home. Rendering the boy a satisfactory beating did not give me a sense of accomplishment. My right hand hurt and my eyes stung with fresh tears. Something rose in my throat and choked me. The goddamn lump, one of many tics, and a familiar fire leapt all at once through my body. The thought of losing Darla now blinded me with hot tears and I was once again reminded, while sobbing like a child, I am broken.

CHAPTER NINE

Secrets of the Dead

"So human am I, that I give myself neither compliments nor chances."

HE WAS WAITING FOR ME when I got back after my encounter with Darla and her new boy toy. "You busted out my goddamn window!" he shouted as I walked up the driveway lit by only a small bulb atop the large barn doors. Not much light, but enough to see the foster dad was pissed and meant business. "I just weather-proofed 'em and that's money, boy!"

It was that last word, "boy." There was something about how it found its way to the center of my heart and twisted there like a screw. I just walked past the old man and went upstairs. At the bottom, he kept bitching about the busted window, but it seemed harmless.

Nate was sitting on his bed looking worried. I'd only been in the foster home a few weeks up to that point. Long enough for me and Nate to get pretty close and I could tell he was afraid I'd be sent away. I didn't blame him. Not too many friends had come along before me that were willing to hang out with Nate in private, let alone go to the movies with him like I had. Slamming the door behind me, drowning out the old man, I told Nate not to worry about it.

I was exhausted and my feet felt like they weighed a thousand pounds. Crawling into bed I told myself I'd go see Lynn the next day. She was still living with Lauren and Tim and only four miles away. It was something I had just recently found out after running into someone at my new high school that knew her. The thought of having to face Lauren and Tim brought back old fears rising up in my throat, which left that lump again. It was hard to fall asleep because it felt like I couldn't take in enough air. I dreaded the thought of having to see them, but Lynn was worth it. After all, she was my baby sister. During the time we had been apart I thought of her often. The day Lauren kicked me out I hadn't the chance to say goodbye, but I knew in my heart she still loved me.

The next morning, the old man was sitting at the kitchen table waiting for me to come downstairs. I had half-hoped the frenzy he'd worked himself into the night before would have given him a heart attack. I sat and listened to the lecture and in all the right spots, nodded and said I was sorry. It was no secret I was still an outsider and no one, especially me, expected me to stay very long. When the old man threatened that if I kept up the bullshit I'd be gone, I again nodded and said I was sorry. Finished with the ass-chewing, I left the house and headed for Lynn's.

Mile after mile, as I hurried straight toward the unknown, my loneliness and heartbreak weighed more and more heavily upon me. I tried to force Darla out of my thoughts, but it was impossible. A thousand visions of her rose before me, and each mile that I drew closer to Lynn left me with a strange pain in my heart. I almost started crying a few times, but worked hard to stifle the near-sobbing breaths that teased at my lips. And yet, with my own grief and hopelessness, I felt a little joy deep from within when thinking I would see Lynn again. It was the joy of knowing that I had saved her, and in doing so, had given her a chance at life. Putting myself in the way of the strangers and taking the tricks instead of Lynn had given back life to me as well. Each day I wondered about Lynn's progress. Not for a moment had I regretted what I had done for her. *Lynn, not for a moment and I would do it all over again if only to save you.*

When approximately a half-mile away, I saw the farmhouse where Lynn now lived with Lauren and Tim. Of course, they had moved yet again. Wondering what I would say to gain entrance and actually speak to Lynn was playing itself out in my mind. Mentally I rehearsed the words, and was sure both Lauren and Tim would see the fear in my eyes.

There was a long gravel road leading to the house and it felt much too wide. I was too exposed and felt as though Lauren and Tim would see me coming, lock the doors and pretend no one was home. My visit came without warning. There was no way to call Lynn, because I had no number. No way to ask for permission and making it all the worse was the fact I knew for certain that I was not welcomed. Lauren had made that clear the day I was dropped off at Jessica's, which now seemed such a long time ago.

I knew what I would tell Lynn. I would tell her how I had missed her all this time and thought of her often. How I loved her. And then suddenly a terrible thought came to my mind, what if they weren't home? What if all I found was a deserted house and they did not live there at all? This was after all information gleaned from a girl at the high school where I had just recently enrolled. What if it was a trick? It seemed as though the girl had been telling the truth. She described Lynn's features and mannerisms. She knew her for sure. And it seemed believable because Lauren and Tim were always changing houses. I wondered if they knew when they moved it was only four miles from the foster home where I was now staying. It was like a terrible joke played out in real life. Perhaps the farmhouse sat empty. This revelation left me feeling desolate, but I was already upon the house and it was too late to turn back.

My pace quickened as I came closer to the open gate, where the gravel driveway began leading to the house. The sloping driveway winded in an "S" pattern. Staring at the front door of the house, closer still, a fear tugged harder at my heart. I could smell the animals, which reminded me of the dairy farm I worked while living with the Marais', and of course, Sue.

At last I came to the door, hesitated, then knocked. Lauren answered, but said nothing, only stared reluctantly at me. Folding her arms across her chest, she finally spoke in a mechanical voice and asked what I was doing there.

"What do you want, Gregg?" she asked coldly.

"I'd like to see Lynn if that's okay?" I replied apologetically.

I was certain Lauren saw my bloodshot eyes because she smiled a little. Careful to keep hidden my battered hand from beating Darla's new boyfriend, it stayed in my pocket. The last thing I needed was Lauren refusing my request based on the fact I had been fighting. It was enough of an excuse for her.

Just then, Lynn came into view behind Lauren, and running past her and out the door, she jumped into my arms hugging me. All debate with Lauren ended abruptly. Lauren then grimly instructed Lynn to stay near the porch, and with an audible bang, shut the front door.

"Bo Bo!" Lynn cried. "I missed you!"

"I missed you too, Pug!" I responded and choked a little on the words.

We ignored Lauren's instruction to stay near the porch and walked a few feet from the house to an old wooden fence that wrapped itself around the farm. Sitting on the fence, we talked about simple things. Nothing of the past that was painful, but mostly where I was staying and how things were going. I kept the conversation positive. There was no need to upset Lynn.

At one point in the conversation, Lynn stared off into the distance and spoke in a low voice telling me she felt like a prisoner. Lynn told me of an incident when Lauren went through her dresser drawers and found a note. The note had been written by a girl who professed her love for Lynn and from that point on Lynn was accused of being a lesbian by both Lauren and Tim. Lynn wiped away at her cheeks while telling me this. After she was through, I moved her face gently so that we were now looking directly at one another.

"Pug, it doesn't matter if you are a lesbian," I said. Followed by, "There is nothing wrong with being in love with another boy or girl."

A deep breath of relief fell from Lynn's lips and we held one another under a perfect sky sitting on an old wooden fence while she wept.

A few minutes later, straight up from an open field just past the barn, rose a thick column of smoke. "Tim's burning leaves." Lynn said. It reminded me of a time when Tim stood on a pile of old twigs and brush dumping kerosene all about the mound. There was a sudden popping noise and then a flame shot up near his foot. Bug-eyed and scared out of his wits, Tim let out a yelp and scrambled from the impending inferno. Carter and I were in the yard and could only watch this display of ignorance play out as if in slow motion. It was Carter who later described the whole ordeal succinctly by referring to Tim as a "Dumbass." Then Carter mockingly pretended to be Tim dashing from the woodpile when it caught fire. I laughed until my sides split. He had the eyes perfect and everything.

Tim walked from his fire and toward Lynn and me with his usual swagger of dominance. Apparently, Lauren had warned him I was at the house. It was evident he wasn't pleased with me being there and when he got within earshot his sharp tone made it even more clear.

"Whatcha doing here, boy?" he said in almost a drawl.

At that, my blood started to boil, but I held it together for Lynn's sake.

"Just wanted to see Lynn," I replied almost sheepishly. "I'm living at a foster home now only a few miles away."

"Last I heard you were in some boys' home and got yourself kicked out of school," Tim said both accusingly and smug.

All I could say to that was, "You must be thinking of Carter."

I didn't want to bust on Carter like that, but it was the only thing that came to mind. I just wanted to shut Tim up and get on with spending time with Lynn –just the two of us.

Tim hesitated, giving me a displeased look, then twisted on the gravel and looked toward the house. "You two can sit on the porch where we can keep an eye on ya," he commanded.

There was no use arguing, so Lynn and I just moved to the porch and sat down. Satisfied, Tim went back to his fire. Both Lynn and I were sure Lauren was lurking near the door listening to every word we said.

We hadn't started talking again before Tim returned, rounding the corner of the house, and stepped up onto the porch. His hand was on the door knob when he stopped. A smirk played across his lips. Startled wonderment filled Tim's face as he bent close to the door and for a moment my heart throbbed with a terrible fear I would be asked to leave immediately.

Tim said nothing and walked into the house. We could hear him raving inside about me being there. The sound of his voice sent a chill of horror through my veins and I tried to hide this from Lynn. A sob broke from her lips, and she turned her face toward mine. Before I could hold her, Tim opened the door, and this time, did tell me to leave. It was not the same look of wonderment he had in his eyes moments earlier. It was now rage mixed with joy.

I stared at Tim and thought about cutting loose with all the things pent up and needing to be said for so long. But again I thought of Lynn sitting next to me and said nothing. A quick hug, more sobbing from Lynn, and I left.

I had traveled a hard four miles on my way over, but it would be even more difficult on my way back to the foster home. Away from Lynn, and for an instant before passing through the gate of the farmhouse, I thought of running back and hugging her one more time. What flashed in my mind was Tim running outside with a shotgun and whether or not this was a real possibility didn't matter. I kept walking. Not more than a mile away, I couldn't stop wringing my hands and crying. There was no sign of hope in my heart now. Like in a terrible nightmare, everything felt surreal.

I continued walking along the edge of the road, head down hiding my face from the oncoming traffic. Suddenly a car came from behind and was so close that when it passed I was nearly knocked down. The car skidded to a stop making a loud screeching noise. What I saw could not be real, I thought. It was Tim, and swinging the driver's side door open, he jumped from the car. He had swung the door open so quickly that it bounced back into his gut, which seemed to enrage him even more. "You little bastard!" he shouted. "Don't you ever come near Lynn again!"

All I could do was stand in utter disbelief. *He's finally gone insane*, I thought. How could I not think this while staring into the face of a madman?

Half inside the car with one leg up on the runner and one on the road, Tim continued to berate me for upsetting Lynn. "We've been waiting and watching for you to show up and fuck with her head!" Tim cried out.

"You stay away!" he demanded, then fully climbed back into the car, slamming the door, and sped off. The spinning tires against the gravel road shot razor-like pebbles at me and I had to throw my arms up in order to protect my face. The rocks stung like a thousand angry bees. Only a little while ago I thought I was dying of heartbreak –I thought I was alone in the world. But now, I was absolutely sure of it.

Climbing the stairs of the porch leading into the foster home, I was tired, angry, and could still feel the sting of the rocks on my skin. They left little pock marks and sweating during the walk back made the pain worse. Had I noticed the social services emblem on the car parked in the driveway, I would have kept walking past the foster home and found refuge in the nearby cornfield.

Too late, I was already in the kitchen with accusing eyes upon me. The foster parents stood, while the social worker sat at the table drinking a cup of coffee. It was the same man who brought me to the foster home in the first place. The same man who took me from Darla. Nate was standing off to the side and almost in the other room. The look on his face, even through the disfigurement, was easy to read. Fear and sorrow. The social worker spoke up and told me that I would be leaving the next morning. First thing. The old man was gripping some paperwork in his hand, which turned out to be legal documents. The foster mother forced a smile and told me they wish it could have been different. Then there was mention of me being a bad influence.

"I'll pick you up in the morning," the social worker said.

"Where will I go?" I asked.

There was a brief pause and what came next nearly brought me to my knees.

"Your father's," the social worker replied.

He put his hands to his face as if deep in thought and explained that contact was made weeks ago with Father and he agreed to take me in. For a moment I was delighted and then felt crushed and frightened. I could not understand why after all this time Father had not looked for me. Had not wanted me until now. Nate's eyes shone bright with tears and he whispered huskily, asking if I had to go. There was no need to answer. We all knew what was done could not be undone.

The look of astonishment in my face changed to confusion. I accepted the fate handed down mechanically and slowly went upstairs. It would be my last night in the foster home. My last night with Nate. Not long after I was in my bedroom, there was a knock on the door and the foster mother walked in. She told me my sister, Lauren was waiting in her car just outside to speak with me.

Nothing could have surprised me more than Lauren's unexpected visit. I walked downstairs and out the kitchen door. Lauren sat motionless in her car. Climbing into the passenger seat, I asked where we were going. Lauren did not answer and continued to stare out the windshield. It never occurred to me how she knew where I was staying. Perhaps she knew the whole time. Slowly, Lauren began to speak; however, still not looking at me.

"Gregg, you will amount to nothing."

"You have wasted your life."

I continued to sit in silence while Lauren explained how I had failed her and that my future looked bleak and unpromising. Her words felt like the tiny stone razors I was peppered with by Tim's car, cutting into my flesh each time she spoke.

"That's why we needed to separate you from Lynn ... she still has a chance, you don't."

Lauren pressed onward telling me that she along with Tim had once thought I would make it, but now they felt I would join the ranks of my degenerate siblings.

"You had so much promise, Gregg . . . What happened to you?" she asked.

I sat for almost an hour listening to Lauren degrade me. The tears stood in my eyes. Gathering what was left of my strength I fought hard not to let them spill down my cheeks. It would have only given Lauren more satisfaction. I looked closely into her face. There was a strange pleasure that shone in her eyes. She sometimes laughed, but did not seem to notice it.

When Lauren had finished, I quickly stepped out of the car. During Lauren's maniacal speech, it had began to storm and I found relief in the fact the rain would mercifully hide the tears that now fell in torrents as I walked back into the house.

In the bedroom I shared with Nate, he sat on his bed and stared at me. There were little red splashes of color that appeared in the few places on his cheeks that were not burned by the electricity from the transformer. And his eyes looked more blue than ever before. I packed, which took only minutes. The two of us did not speak.

That night, as I lay in bed trying to fall asleep, the excitement of being with Father was fleeting. In its place was the ever-present feeling that he did not want me. He had rejected me when I was only a child, this was true. He had rejected all of his children. The next day I was going to live with a father who had abandoned me so many times before.

With this thought came a sense of horror dragged from the depths of my heart. It was a terrible thought that I would only end up abandoned yet again. I shivered under my blankets, and every moment added more disappointment.

There was no contact of any kind for years and now Father had suddenly agreed to allow me to live with him. There was nothing that helped solve this particular mystery and it left me wondering what I would find. Rolling with my back to Nate so he would not see me cry, I did so quietly. Covering my face with the pillow to silence my sobs I descended into a slumber filled with nightmares.

The foster parents were in their usual morning place at the breakfast table. The social worker was waiting at the door. On my way out, I said a farewell without looking at anyone. Nate was standing in the kitchen. He paused and then in a mad race across the room he ran up to me and extended his hand. We shook hands like men and the tears shone in our eyes. I let go of his hand and then opened my arms, we hugged each other and I could feel his damaged cheek against mine. The dead skin was chilly. When we pulled apart, I looked at my foster brother and whispered, "Look on your bed." Nate smiled and jumped a bit on his feet. Then his face grew serious as I walked past him and out the door. He had been my only friend. On his bed, I left two of my championship Judo medals. They were my most prized possessions and no one was more deserving than Nate.

Buried beneath his distorted features Nate held fast to so many dreams of being an athlete. He would talk for hours about achieving greatness in any competitive sport. I could see the dreams dance in his deep blue eyes. I hoped for Nate he would find the greatness buried deep within his heart, protected by a soul still willing to fight, that held true to so many dreams made possible by the love of soft gentle people.

We drove away from the foster home while the social worker made small talk. He was a crippled man who walked with a cane. His hair and beard were now almost completely gray. He spoke softly and his features reminded me of a picture I once saw in a book by Hemingway. He had a puzzled look in his eyes and asked me if I was sure I wanted to live with Father. The thought of another foster home was far too taxing on my heart, so I agreed to do so. The next stop was to be the parking lot of a restaurant where we would rendezvous with Father. We spoke very little as we drove toward our destination, while the fear was threatening to tear me apart.

When we finally arrived, I saw Father sitting in his car. Shivering with anticipation, I slowly walked from the social worker's car to where Father was parked. Father exited and there was a brief conversation between him and the social worker. I climbed into the backseat of Father's car while the two men spoke. There was nothing on either of their faces that gave me a clue as to what was being discussed. In the front passenger seat and smiling sympathetically was Father's new girlfriend, Marie. She spoke with a thick southern accent and gently told me not to be scared. "Nuttin ain't gonna get you." Marie said jokingly with kindly eyes. Followed by, "You're with your people now."

Father climbed inside the driver side and settled in his seat before starting the car.

"You hungry?" he asked.

"No, I'm okay. Thanks." I was hungry. As a matter of fact I was starving, but was too nervous to eat.

"Well, maybe later," he said and then started the car and we drove to my new home.

It was the first question I had asked since seeing Father and it was after we walked into the house. "Where's my room?"

"You'll sleep in our room until we move into a bigger house." Father said, sending a sudden shutter of revulsion through my body. For the next several weeks, that's where I slept. In the same bed Father and his girlfriend had made love.

Father's girlfriend was an angel. A tall thin woman with thick black curly hair and beautiful brown eyes. Her hands were slender like her features and moved gently through the air when she spoke. Marie was from the South and spoke with a charming accent. She was timid and kind. Soft spoken and easy to love. Compared to Marie, Father was a brute. A beast of a man and he would come to break her heart.

I wiped my face uneasily while unpacking what little clothes I had and placed them neatly inside the bureau next to Father's bed. Father stood in the doorway of the bedroom and stared at me for some time saying nothing. Then, he spoke.

"We need to get you registered for school," he said in his usual authoritative and gruff voice. Followed by, "You're not going to be a fuck-up like your brother."

As it turned out, my brother had not lived with Father for more than two weeks before he ran away to live with Madison. Father and I stared at each other for a few seconds, and having made his point, he then turned and walked away. This would be the fourth high school I would attend in only three years. Leaving my last high school mid-semester cut my junior year in half and put me even further behind. I leaned forward listening for Father's footsteps as he walked away and when sure he was out of earshot, I sighed and said, "Fuck."

The next day I would register for school, but that night I laid in bed feeling nauseous, anticipating what would come next. Father said we'd be moving soon to a new house and I'd have my own room. I thought, *Christ, how many times have I moved since leaving Mother?* I figured it had to be at least six or seven by now. As I lay there something unpleasant found its way into my mind. Something didn't feel right. But then again, it never had before.

Registering for classes was uneventful; however, the size of the new school gave me a fright. It was classified as AAA, and the largest school I had attended up to that point had only been a class B. The attraction to the athletic field, with an Olympic-sized track held some fascination for me, but I had not seriously considered trying out for the team. Father told me that if I put my mind to it, I just might graduate. This, coming from a man who ran away from his wife and children didn't quite have the impact on me he had hoped. We drove away from the school and there was idle conversation about the courses for which I had registered. It was then I told Father they had all been college preparatory. He quickly informed me that it was a waste of time due to the fact college was not in my future. "It's best you set your sights on the military," he said.

I did not respond and again we went back to staring silently at the road. Every now and then I'd see the dull shimmer of Father's eyes as he struggled for something to say, but never quite finding the words. I wondered when looking at him sometimes how he could have beared to leave his children or beat his wife. He once told me when I was much younger that a man sometimes has to beat his wife so she understands who is boss. I'd wonder too how he could take up with another woman. I bet he thought his children were too young to remember all this. I bet he thought we didn't even know. But I knew and I remembered. It ate away at me and made me feel a quick, tense stiffening all over my body when I thought about the things Father did. As a matter of fact, I did more than just remember all the terrible things. I still felt them as if they were happening, because they were.

A few weeks later, I was in the new house and attending my new school, but the feelings of anxiety and fear were not new. They crawled all over me inside and out. And, they spoke to my mind in a low, unnatural voice, telling me I was doomed. Telling me all this wasn't fair and that someday all this would make sense. And that, maybe someday, someone, would come along and save me.

While Father made a life for himself with Marie, I worked to rise above the mischief and violence that became so common in the months since being sent away by Lauren and Tim. The sacredness that was associated with the act of attending classes gave way to learning again. Still unsettled, but focusing again on my studies felt good and right. Although I was corrupted, my love of books was not. I was vulgar, crude, a skull-cracker, as Carter referred to it, but my spirit was still trying to break free. It did not take much time before learning again became an escape and a way in which to recover what was both lost inside of me or stolen.

Of course, I started out all wrong. My family life was torment. I was a product of the evils done unto me and, at times, I too became perverted and sluggish without regard for principles. But I still clamored for peace and found solace among the endless shelves of books within the school library. In the books, yet again, while my head bent reading, hope was coming back to me. However, I had my own demons to deal with. There was the violence, of course, and also a craving for promiscuity. These two vices were as much a part of me as breathing.

Education helped considerably and my love of learning was also a very large part of me. The healthy part and it was evident that the books brought out the best in what I had to offer. I was certainly capable of doing terrible things and well used was my ability to destroy. This was the worst of my traits. The fondness of bloodshed. The rage blinded me at times. Convincing me that it was an acceptable means to an end.

Soon after moving in with Father there was one other matter that needed addressing with regard to my new living arrangement. Father made an appointment with the Department of Social Services to make sure he was no longer responsible for paying child support. This, of course, made him very happy.

During Father's appointment with the social worker, I sat in a tiny diner located inside the municipal building. Just outside the diner were the Child Welfare Offices and the waiting room was in plain sight. It was filled with disgruntled parents and was the final battleground where the children were used as weapons. I sat on a stool watching these ugly battles through a pane of glass. Several arguments broke out between the mothers and fathers and on the faces of their children was the familiar look of despair. While the parents were busy hating one another, their children were dying. These innocent pawns forced to face a dragon they could never tame.

I was instructed by Father to attend school, come straight home, and not be seen nor heard and that is exactly what I did. Spending hours in my room studying, exerting all action into bringing my grades from failing back to A's and B's. Upon reviewing my transcripts with the school counselor during enrollment, I was astounded. The pattern of decline was extremely apparent.

Father began working third-shift and whether it was intentional or not did not matter. What mattered was that it gave us both peace. Being late in the season, participation in track was not an option. So I went to school, and for a time, kept to myself. However, the baffling draw to promiscuity was strong. Even more mysterious was the fact I avoided, at all costs, those girls that offered both kindness and fidelity. The loyalty that may have rested in somebody would have been missed altogether anyway. I had suffered under the promise of trust and had been fooled so many times that I soon reached the conclusion allegiance of any sort was not possible.

Her name was Kim and she was the homecoming queen. She was a gamble from the beginning. Standing, Kim was as tall as me and could work magic with her body. The way she moved through the hallways commanded gawking respect from both the boys and girls. It may have seemed to be my good fortune to have been chosen by her, but as the wheel rolls, I lost all that was put into our relationship. I stole, fought, and lied for her. If Kim fancied a necklace, I pilfered it from the shop. If a boy even looked at her, I busted him in the mouth. And I told myself she loved me, which was a lie.

Consumed by anything and everything Kim wanted, I allowed her to drag me down and with every impish whim was her victory over me. Easily manipulated, my abusers had prepared me well so that a tender kiss from a pretty girl could triumph over what little principles I had. My compulsions underscored the defects in my character and they were clearly not hidden. For all to see and take advantage. Perhaps that is why Kim wanted me. I was a plaything. By far, a used tool, but adequate for what needs a selfish sixteen-year-old girl may have. Every pleasure she gave to me, I paid for with a penalty of being owned. She could and would flirt, but I was not allowed to even smile at another girl. I gave and Kim took. It was the ebb and flow of our relationship. It was, indeed, a perfect representation of what I had with Mother. An inevitable dualism bisected my emotions between self-loathing and elation. What Kim paid out in affection paled by comparison to what I gave her in return, but it came natural to me. Convinced that any small act of kindness passed on to me was more than I deserved, my relationship with Kim accommodated the whole of what I was and echoed my destiny.

It was a boy who I once thought a friend that Kim slept with, and like Darla, she too begged me to stop while I pounded him with my fists. However, I could not stop even if I had wanted. Once the rage took over, I was under its power. In addition, fighting was the only act of defiance that remained within me. It fostered a chance at survival and was a way in which to prove to myself there was something inside of me still worth fighting for.

The time Father and I spent together was uncomfortable from the beginning, which is probably the reason he purchased my first car for me. In doing so, he was no longer required to drive me places. I'm sure for Father, the reduction of responsibility when it came to another human being was money well spent. Therefore, after passing driver's education, Father and I went and purchased what would become my first car, 1974 Pinto. A truly ugly car, but I fancied it. It didn't glide down the highway at abnormal speeds; however, it got me where I needed to go and most of all offered freedom. It was held together by hanger wire and rope, with a radio that only received AM frequency, but I didn't care. There was a certain power that came with having my own transportation. Knowing the Pinto sat waiting for me when it was needed gave me a sense of exaltation, a personal victory.

Facing my studies head on, I was able to finish the last semester of my junior year with a solid C average. All things considered, it would at least allow me to enter my senior year and possibly graduate. When the school year ended, I immediately found work at a local restaurant. This time, I would keep the money earned. Taking shape now was a young man with a vicious temperament, uncontrollable distrust for all people, but who was still drawn into the world of learning. If I was not working or out running, I was locked inside my room reading. So far, the love of books was the only love that had yet to betray me. Fountains of knowledge poured from the pages into my brain and I was moved to both laughter and tears by many of them. Knowledge was more than power, it was life. And these properties of life propelled my self-worth, solidified my existence, and incited me to believe in blessings not yet afforded.

It was summer and I was enjoying the pleasure of reading in my room when I heard the terrible thud followed by the sound of something crashing against the wall just outside my door. The unmistakable drunken slur of Father's voice rumbled. He was in the midst of serving up an awful beating in which Marie was on the receiving end and frantically begging him to stop. When I swung my bedroom door open, he was straddling Marie's thin frame, his full weight on her chest. Her mouth was contorted and desperately trying to breathe. The power of Father's strength was evident when I tried to push him off Marie. He was like an unmovable stone. His rage made him even more powerful.

Something strange and extravagant had broken loose from me and at first I tried pulling Father from Marie, but gave up quickly. What followed next was an act of curious heroism. I stood above Father and swung a hard and closed fist downward, which smashed into the side of his face sending him rolling off Marie. In a seizure of drawing as much air into her lungs as she possible could, Marie grabbed her throat and crawled away and into their bedroom. By the time she had slammed the door shut, locking it, Father was on his feet and lunging toward me. I did what I was afraid to do which was strike him. And for my actions, I would pay the price of unconsciousness. If I had seen Father's fist rocketing through the air it quickly became a memory soon forgotten. All that I recall was his ridiculously large figure and then my vision went black.

When the light came back into the hallway and the world stopped swimming, I was being helped to my feet by Marie and into the bathroom, where she placed a cold washcloth on the back of my neck. In the mirror over the sink I saw a look of grief that engulfed my whole face along with the swelling of my left cheek. The house was quiet. Marie said Father had broken through their bedroom door, crawled onto the bed, and promptly passed out. Marie looked exhausted and every now and then she would cough huskily. I was now certain Father would never change and that he hated Marie and me too. He hated himself as well. The face in the bathroom mirror, distorted from Father's cuff, told me this. It also told me that there was nothing left between Father and me, and there never was.

CHAPTER TEN

In Defiance of Refuge

"Ever since I stood as a boy, I have wished for a savior."

I SLEPT DURING WHAT REMAINED OF the day after Father hit me. After Marie had done her best to help me, I went inside my bedroom and closed the door. Falling onto my bed, night eventually came and nearly went. What awakened me was the sound of Marie crying. Her sorrowful muffled sounds aroused me from a deep sleep of exhaustion an hour or two before dawn of the following morning. Before getting out of bed, I went over all the things that had happened the day before. Listening to Marie cry, my first thought was that Father had again beat her, and that I had slept through it. I could hear her deep sobs coming from the living room and floating down the narrow hallway. I also wondered where Father was. Gathering up my courage, I got out of bed and went to the living room. Marie was sitting on a chair with her hands in her face and had not seen me at first.

"What's wrong?" I said. My voice startled her and she quickly began trying to hide the fact she was crying.

"Your father has moved out. He left me for another woman," Marie said, and then hurriedly retreated to what was once the bedroom she shared with Father.

We had not been in the house for more than three weeks. There was no indication Father had been seeing another woman, but he would never have revealed her identity. That was Father. There were no warnings. No conversations leading up to his decisions and never anything to explain whatever mystery lurked behind his eyes. Moments later, after Marie had apparently gathered herself, she walked back into the living room.

"You can stay here for a few days, but I'll need you to move out," her words were calculating and mechanical. I wasn't surprised and had suspected this was to be. After all, I must have reminded her of Father.

That evening I packed and prepared to call the Department of Social Services the next day. I had nowhere else to live. It was very early in the morning and still dark outside when I awoke, having felt someone staring at me. Standing in the doorway of my bedroom was Father and he was drunk. I could tell by how he swayed from side to side. The hallway light behind him cast his large frame in the figure of a dark menacing shadow.

"Get up and come with me," he said, and walked from the house and waited in his car. Marie never left her bedroom, but I knew she was aware Father was in the house. I quickly packed my few belongings, left the house, and climbed inside the passenger side of his car, which sat running in the driveway. Father said nothing as we drove away.

We had driven for approximately a half-hour in silence before turning into a trailer park. There was a large sign that stood at the entrance, "No Motorcycles Allowed." A few minutes later, he parked the car and got out. I followed Father into a trailer resembling so many others like it that were lined like boxes in long rows on both sides of a small asphalt road. No sooner had we walked inside, a woman appeared from the tiny kitchen, which was barely hidden by a short wall shared by the living room. Her eyes were blue and they had in them little spots of brown. They were unusual eyes, and I noticed the brown in them because it added to their menacing glare.

I couldn't believe this was Father's girlfriend. I thought to myself that his association with her was purely an act of desperation. Her name was Becky and she was a spiteful woman with an awful mean streak. That night we met, she was bold enough to tell me the decision to allow me to live with them was against her better judgment. There was small conversation and then Father and Becky retired to a small bedroom at the end of a very short hallway. Their bed was perfectly round and blood red. It was both hideous and creepy. My stomach turned when I first saw the bed. The room directly across from theirs was where I would sleep.

Becky was also tall, nearly six feet. Making her height even more pronounced was the fact she often wore large wigs. Generally, blonde with high swirls and buns on top, making her appear gigantic. Her voice was shrill and she spoke loudly. Even her conversational tone was earsplitting. It became obvious that before we met, Becky had formed an unfavorable opinion of me, determining a course of action that would eventually leave me homeless, yet again.

I was instructed by Father not to speak of Mother or what had happened to me and my siblings in front of Becky. He did not speak of those things either. I would not have said a word to anyone regardless. It was the way things were with Father. Nothing was to be discussed about the past. I would never be able to confide in him the secrets that were killing me. If I were to do so, Father would surely feel as though I were weak and somehow a traitor to the laws of being a man. To share my painful story with Father would have been treachery to him. Realizing this, I said nothing. However, I must have reminded Father of the past. Evidence of this was when he decided to accept a position in another state only a few weeks after he moved me in with him and Becky.

Father had been concealing his plans to move away for quite some time. Working to achieve his own end, which was total escape from any and all responsibility, Father made his plans in secrecy to be rid of the life he had constructed for himself. His motives were always selfish and he probably figured giving me a place to live evened score for smashing me in the face.

There was no fanfare before he set out. One morning before I woke up, he was just gone. He must have moved about the trailer softly so as not to wake me. When I did finally rise and walk to the living room, Becky was sitting on the couch smoking. Her look of ice on that morning was no different than any other.

"I don't want you here, Gregg," she said coldly. The summer sun was brilliantly shining through the trailer's larger window and I suddenly wanted to be outside running before it disappeared.

An hour later, after Becky telling me I was not wanted, a storm moved in, and the sun was blotted out by some gray murky clouds that would turn the horizon black. Crouched inside the tip of a makeshift rocket within a child's playground near the trailer park, I played Becky's words over in my mind. While the rain beat down on the thin metal roof of the rocket and I shivered soaking wet, I thought seriously of suicide for the first time since putting Jessica's revolver to my head.

After Becky informed me that my stay was to be short-lived, we argued bitterly. I had been living in fear of exile for years. Then there was the violence that existed between Father and every woman in his life, including Becky. Just a week before I now sat freezing in the tiny rocket ship thinking of suicide, I had come to her rescue. Father had her pinned to the floor of the trailer by straddling Becky's chest, just as he had Marie, strangling Becky as well, while she gurgled muffled screams. Like so many times when Father beat Mother, I struggled to pull his hands free from around her neck. Becky's blonde wig was dangling from her head like a flap of hairy skin. This time, I did not punch him. He simply let go and left the trailer, returning later that night drunk.

A week later, I would return from the library to find Father sitting in my bedroom with the barrel of a rifle in his mouth, the butt of it resting on the floor, and one of his fingers on the trigger. Speaking softly, I gently took the rifle from Father. He said nothing while never taking his eyes off the floor. Then, laying down as if nothing happened, he fell asleep. He had been drunk at that time as well. Upon examining the rifle afterwards, I found it was loaded with the safety off.

I defended Becky and saved Father's life. Now she wanted me out of her house and Father wanted nothing to do with me. Father even ended up marrying Becky and I stood next to the both of them at the wedding. I found out twelve years later that Father had never divorced Mother. Although, the bigotry was minor compared to the sins already committed by Father. Mother agreed to signing the divorce papers, and the day she signed the court documents, Ashley had told me she wept. My heart broke for her. And now, I was to be evicted for, yet again, doing nothing wrong. Sent away for what was none other than a shameless betrayal.

The next few days I spent trying to locate a place to live. I just could not bring myself to live in another foster home, so I called on Ashley who had been living with another man at the time. She cried joyously when I called and asked to stay with her. Her apartment was small, but it was a place to live. To bide my time and push hard to finish high school –graduation became an obsession.

It was just before the start of my senior year when I moved in with Ashley and I had traded in my Pinto for a motorcycle a month before. It was an impulsive decision and one in which I regretted when winter came. Having no mode of transportation left me even more trapped. However, it was still summer, and for now, it felt good to ride in the open air with the feel of the wind pressing against my body.

Calling Ashley from the trailer in order to arrange for my moving became impossible due to the fact Becky had promptly placed a small lock on the phone dialer. She had also installed bike wire with locks on all the cupboards containing food along with the refrigerator.

"Look! Now you can't go eatin' all the damn food and tying up the phone," she bellowed. "You're already costing me money taking those long showers!"

With the phone locked, I would have to call Ashley from a payphone, but eventually we settled on a date when I could move in with her. The day I left the trailer, Becky was at work and Father was still out of state. She came home that evening and found me gone. Something told me that life for her was just as miserable after I left. At least, I hoped so.

It wasn't Ashley's apartment. It belonged to her boyfriend and he was sure to remind me who paid the bills the day I came to live there. Of course I was agreeable to everything having no place else to go, aside from going back into the foster program. His name was Jerry and he was incredibly tall with a pear-shape. Big round deep-set eyes that were dark and with his perfectly trim haircut, I thought, they made him look like a rapist. From the beginning, I felt there was something not quite right with Jerry. Had I known what he was capable of, I would have taken my chances with another foster home.

Jerry and Ashley would argue all the time. Sometimes violently and I was again put in the awful position of being not only a witness, but worst of all, a participant. When I would break up the fights by forcing my body in between the two of theirs, Jerry would push me away easily. He was much taller and stronger. I just wanted to keep the peace long enough to get from one minute to the next while fighting my own inner battles of gloom and despair.

Reading still helped a little and I'd often bury myself in a book holed up somewhere within the small apartment. Always trying to stay hidden. It was safer that way. The more noticeable I became, the better the chances were at someone making me leave. That's how I saw it. But, that's also how it was, so it made sense. Summer edged along and the sun rose later each day and spent less time in the sky, and soon the warmth of the wind began to grow cooler. The approaching fall gave evidence of school about to begin and I was more and more filled with the thunderous echoes of uncertainty.

The fights between Ashley and Jerry became increasingly worse until one evening they escalated to the point where Jerry finally broke. He loaded a shotgun and chased another man he suspected was having an affair with Ashley through the halls of the apartment complex. Ashley and I ran as well and hid in another apartment, while her assailant boyfriend scoured the halls shouting for the man to come out from wherever he was hiding.

I left the safety of the apartment in which I was to get a look at what was going on; however, so did Ashley's alleged lover. Stupidly, he went looking for Jerry, perhaps to reason with him. The three of us met unexpectedly in one of the hallways. Jerry leveled the shotgun at the surprised man's face, giving him just enough time to grab hold of the barrel that he was now staring directly down. There was an audible click of the trigger but the shotgun did not fire. Gaining wisdom from his near-death experience, Ashley's pseudo-lover let go of the shotgun's barrel and broke the land speed record down the hallway and out the front doors of the apartment complex. I ran as well.

By the time the police arrived, Jerry had hidden the shotgun under the bed of his and Ashley's apartment. He was arrested and taken away. Great tears broke from Ashley when we were together again. I think it was because she thought Jerry could have killed me. I wept too, and weakened from fear, I laid next to Ashley and we slept.

The next morning, Jerry returned to our dismay having been released on his own recognizance. My days were numbered, but I had my last year of high school to contend with and running out of choices, I stuck it out with Ashley and Jerry, spending as much time away as possible. Down from the north the powerful winds began to move their grinding, roaring pushes toward fall. Riding my motorcycle became more difficult in the cold at night. It was only a week before school would start and maybe I had a good month or two where I could continue to ride. Afterwards, I had no transportation. The school bus did not stop at the apartment complex and Ashley had no car. I was not about to ask Jerry for a ride to school.

Something other than a violent streak bothered me about Jerry. It soon became evident a couple days before school started when I came back to the apartment and Ashley was out. As I walked to my bedroom, Jerry sat on top of my bed with his pants down and penis fully erect. He was stroking it and next to his leg was a twenty dollar bill. "There's more if you suck me off," he said in a whisper, still stroking his hardened cock.

"Fuck you," was my immediate reply and I quickly left the apartment.

Certain that I could never tell Ashley, more out of shame than anything else, that night I slept near the school library sequestered near an alcove leading to the front entrance. I had pushed my motorcycle as far as I could inside the recess shadow the alcove created and buried myself in the darkest corner upon a bench. There I slept on and off until daybreak. Gathering my wits, I rode back to Ashley's hoping she was home. She was, but there was no way I could look directly at her due to what happened with Jerry the night before. The weight of shame and rush of memories of Mother and all those strangers was too great. Ashley would have seen in my eyes something was wrong and it wasn't so much the terrible violence that would have ensued, it was the ugly disgrace my heart could not withstand.

There was no way I felt strong enough emotionally to endure another school year. There were several periods where my mind, ready to snap and barely holding onto reality pushed uneasily through these moments. Most times, I felt that I was barely skirting along the edge of madness. Therefore, I waited for what came next with trepidation, knowing sooner or later something or someone would end me and I would finally be free.

School began and with it the toil of academics and tussle to simply try and fit in. My features seemed to draw a fair amount of attention from both girls and boys and the charm, which seemed to come naturally, helped me move from one clique to the next.

Late one afternoon, just when school ended, I walked over to the track and stood on a hill watching the thunderous movement of the team practicing. A pang of jealously ran through me. Standing with arms folded and a whistle hanging from his neck was the coach only a few paces away. He was a short wiry black man who wore a cap over his head. Coach Sampson was his name. He stared intently at the runners in silence that was broken only by the occasional tweet of the whistle that seemed to be the only command the runners needed to quicken or slow their pace. I watched earnestly as a gray sky hovered overhead and in the distance what looked like the dark clouds of rain. My vision was drawn to the runners and I had thoughts of flying around the track and owning my lane.

On this afternoon, at the start of what would be my last year of school and my last chance, I thought, of ever participating in track – it felt as though I was at the rim of hell. My heart was leaden and under my feet I could feel the rumble of the runners, the earth shivering with their crashing spikes. My ears were filled with the steady roar of their harsh breathing, like the echoes of distant thunder, broken now and then by a quick blow of the coach's whistle. When I closed my eyes, I could hear the sharp report of a starter pistol. Followed by the wailings and strange muffled screeching sounds of a crowd cheering.

"You a runner?" the coach asked and startled me while daydreaming.

"I used to be," I answered quietly.

"Well, this is hell week and down there all those runners are trying out for the team," he went on to explain. "All you gotta do is run until I say stop."

"You come by here tomorrow and try out if ya like." With this, he smiled and walked down the hill leading to the runners. I noticed there had to be at least a hundred boys on that track and every one of them dying of exhaustion. There was no way I'd make this level of competition, but what did I have to lose. The next day, in a pair of old shorts and worn out track sneakers, I showed up for practice.

Two days later, I stood alongside several other boys jostling for a position to read the varsity track roster. I scarcely could hear the din of shouts while we all pushed and shoved our way to the bulletin board posted outside the locker room. I strained to read the names before having to get right up on the sheet of paper, but was afraid to look. Even more afraid of the other boys seeing the disappointment in my face when seeing I had not made the cut. I was now close enough to the roster and looking directly at the names, reading them one by one. There was only one name I was searching for and in a dead stare, unable to move, I found it. I had made the cut. On a list of forty boys, I was one of them. One of the chosen few and now all I had to do was what came so easily after all these years. Run. Run fast and hard. Run, until my heart exploded.

Suited up with a fresh set of track sweats, new sneakers, and meals provided during away meets, I did my best. I also worked hard to keep up with my studies while earning a solid position as a sprinter on the track team. A month had passed since school started and I was looking forward to walking the year down. I belonged to something again and it was more than a distraction. It was a chance at more opportunities. Those of which I did not understand, but it felt right. Perhaps it was the way in which the academics and athletics steered the decisions of my life in a purposeful and wholesome manner. They helped me during the dead gloom of anxiety and lowliness. They helped me deal with the gray monotony that weighted my heart. But the sounds still came to me, mostly at night, the sounds of Mother and the strangers pleading with me to do what they wanted or beating me because I did not. And sometimes, the sound of them laughing.

I had just returned from an overnight track invitational when I tried my key in the lock to Ashley's apartment and found it did not work. Jerry had changed the lock. He and Ashley broke off their relationship and soon would be moving. A few months more was all I needed. After that, I did not know what would come, but graduating was a milestone I set for myself. Ashley offered that I could stay with her and a new boyfriend. But I declined the offer, deciding it was not going to last, and soon I would be in need of another place to live. Leaving the apartment, Ashley and me hugged and said goodbye. Jerry continued to pack and would not look at me; obviously both of us were too ashamed, so we parted ways without speaking.

In desperation, I rode my motorcycle to Kim's house. Her father and stepmother were always kind, and on occasion, allowed me a place to sleep and always fed me. I knocked on the door and Kim's stepmother answered. A cry broke from my lips, and never looking up from the porch, I gripped my hands in despair. It did not matter I was no longer dating Kim. Her father and stepmother took me in as one of their own, and for the next couple weeks, calls were made to find me a more permanent residence. There happened to be a local minister willing to allow me a place to live, which afforded me the opportunity to continue attending the same high school until graduation. He presided over a Methodist church located directly across from his home. His name was Peter and preferred I called him by his first name and not 'father.' When Kim's father drove me to Peter's home he was there waiting for me. He smiled when we met and shook my hand. He did not ask me of my past and the world in which I had come. There was no discussion of what would come of me after graduation, but I didn't care. For now, I had refuge. Peter laughed a lot and I liked that. When he did, the joy on his face shone bright and it helped take away the sting of what was like a mocking ghost of my own past life. Peter must have realized the life in which I came, perhaps even what was done to me. He was a wise man. He must have seen the meekness in my face and heard me weep at night during the nightmares. But Peter did not speak of these things. Instead, there came only his gentle words of encouragement, sending a flood of warmth through my veins. And, in those moments came also the ability to turn my heart toward the sweet face of hope.

Through Peter's love and acceptance I blossomed once again, focusing on my studies and track. Although it did not take much convincing, I also agreed to act in two church theatrical events Peter directed himself; both were leading roles. One of which was the part of Joseph in the Christmas play and the other was the part of Christ during the Easter production.

Within walking distance of Peter, lived a girl who quickly became a close friend, Sherry. She was pretty by any standard, but she had the most amazing heart. Mature for her age of only sixteen, she had grown up fast by caring for an alcoholic father and her younger sister. Her mother was a sweet woman, and her father was sweet too, when he wasn't drinking.

Sherry had also befriended probably the only boy in school who was admittedly gay. His name was Craig and he was as kind as Sherry. Craig was a diver for the school's varsity swim team and good enough to earn a full-ride to a large university. The three of us were inseparable. A misfit crew in which I was perfectly comfortable. It made no difference to me if Craig was gay and openly infatuated with me. He was caring and that was all that mattered.

I pulled myself from bed after hearing the phone ring. Peter was out late again that evening which was common due to his ministry requirements generally at local hospitals and elderly communities. When I picked up the receiver it sound as if Sherry was laughing, but then I heard the distinct sound of her crying. She choked on the words and from what I was barely able to comprehend in both pronunciation and meaning was that her father had shot himself.

I don't remember hanging up or running to her home, but I do remember Sherry meeting me at the door and falling in my arms weeping uncontrollably. Her face was ashen gray and Sherry's younger sister stood behind her weeping as well while holding on to a blanket.

The sadness of the moment had drawn the night down even darker and it was difficult to see inside their home while standing at the door. My first impression was that Sherry's father lay dead somewhere in the house. As she calmed only a little, I was told he was at the hospital. It was winter and a thick blanket of snow covered the ground, roads, and sidewalks. I nearly fell on my ass several times while sprinting over to Sherry's. I, along with Sherry and her younger sister, all climbed into her father's old truck and headed for the hospital. Sherry's mother was already there having ridden in the ambulance with her husband. On the way over, Sherry described how her father became enraged while drunk, put a .22 revolver to his chin, and pulled the trigger. The gun had sent a bullet ripping through this mouth, nasal cavity, and lodged itself between his skull and brain.

"He didn't think it was loaded, Gregg!" Sherry said over and over while weeping.

"If he thought it was loaded, he never would have done that!" she cried as if pleading with me to tell her this was true.

The old truck rumbled and thundered over the snow-covered road as we drove toward the hospital leaving the violent chaos that was once made up of police and paramedics only moments before I arrived. As we drove I thought of Jessica's .357 and what it would have done to my skull. I also thought of the paramedics pushing the electricity into Mother as she lay dying on the dirty living room carpet of my childhood home. For several minutes, I thought of nothing else but these things growing blue-black in my mind, while I stared out the windshield of a dying or dead man's truck.

At the hospital Sherry and I stood looking through glass at her father now unrecognizable under all the bandages. What little of his face that was not tightly sealed in white bulging gauze was covered with thick plastic tubes. Clear tape held his eyes shut. We could not hear any sounds coming from the room, but could see the heart monitor. The beat, illustrated by a thin green line, was interrupted occasionally by a small upward blip on the screen. Sherry's father was alive, but barely. I held Sherry in my arms while I faced the window of her father's hospital room. She hid her face against my chest and sobbed. I stood looking into the room where her father lay, watching the heart monitor. Staring at it and waiting. Waiting for the tiny bouncing blip representing the only sign of life to those of us outside his window, after a life of bad choices that ultimately led him here, to finally and mercifully stop.

The breaking of Sherry's heart, and the moaning of her mother and younger sister's discontent, echoed through the hospital corridor. And, there I was, thrust back into a life in which I could not escape. The air seemed thick and difficult to breathe along with the growling monotone of the giant currents sucking me backward the harder I tried to get away.

I could not take what was happening any longer and I could feel the unseen hands strangling the life from me. Amidst so much pain and misery that seemed to hold some twisted fascination for my life, it became so that nothing was too perverse or strange. But now, as I stood holding Sherry and watching her father in a hospital bed only a few feet away, there rose above all the other sounds one that I had not heard since only eleven. My body became suddenly tense and alert as I faced my friend's dying father with his daughter wrapped tightly in my arms. For what seemed an eternity I listened, then gently pushed Sherry from me, kissing her sweetly on the mouth, turned and walked away.

The sound I heard was that of survival, which is the same sound of hope. I could no longer be surrounded by death and the destruction of one's life. It broke my heart to leave Sherry at the hospital, but I had to. Even the long walk home in the freezing cold would not dissuade me. If I did not begin to take control of my life, then I would lose it to nothingness for sure. I was gripped with this realization as if by a giant squeezing my shoulders. As I made my way back to Peter's the breaking moaning in the winter air through the trees sounded just like Sherry's weeping. By the time I reached Peter's home, it may have been the cold against my ears, but the sound became like roaring. I could not allow this to make me turn back and run to her. Maybe it was selfish of me not to, but there was already far too much drama and pain in my life. The pain was worsening, and bringing with it was an enormous blast of anguish. It already haunted my dreams with the most awful nightmares and awakened me to frightened cries.

It did not sound like Sherry's voice when I walked, almost ran, from her at the hospital. She clutched at my arm as a fresh burst of tears fell from her eyes. The sound she made came from a terrible place I knew too well. It was where I was expected to care for someone at all costs. Even if caring meant giving up my innocence, my entire soul.

Sherry was absent the following day at school, but Craig was there and he had heard the news, which travels at lightning speed in high school. "Were you with her, Gregg?" Craig asked.

"Afterwards ... when it was all done," I said. "Then at the hospital for awhile."

Too ashamed to talk anymore, I hurriedly went to class.

Only two weeks before, Craig had confessed his love to me while we sat in his car of the school parking lot waiting for the first bell signaling the official start of school. He had wept while telling me he loved me. I couldn't stop thinking to myself how incredibly brave he was to admit this. Especially due to the fact it was high school, with its collection of cruelty that permeates every high school, and he being so openly gay.

What was also amazing was the trust Craig had in me. I could have been mean-spirited and made fun of him, or punched him in the face like most of the other boys would have done. I could have told our classmates and the torrent of teasing would never cease. It would have been easy to do any or all of these things. Instead, I chose to gently refuse his love, telling him that I was not gay, and afterwards he cried harder still. With his head bent toward the steering wheel weeping, I pulled Craig to me, cradling him against my chest. I let him weep while still holding on to him until the first bell rang, then the second, and finally the third.

I never heard crying like that from a man. It seem to come from deep within Craig and was a wailing burst of savage grief. Whenever I wept, it was conditioned to remain quiet. If Mother heard me, she would strike fresh blood from my already battered body. But Craig sounded wounded, almost fearful. The sound nearly made me shriek in the small front seat of his car and threatened to tear my mind apart.

As I held him, there was the possibility someone would see us and I kept waiting for the jeering and pointing of fingers outside the passenger window. The students would appear out of nowhere as these things always happen. It caused me to feel a little guilty, but I pushed those fears aside and would not let go of Craig. There are many reasons why I did not. However, the one that kept coming back to me was remembering how often I wished for someone to hold me while I wept. While my weeping sounds were more like that of a slow tolling half whimper, I had wanted so badly for someone to cradle me in their arms and rock me until the agony was over.

Sherry's father survived the gunshot, but would have a permanent and obvious dent in the middle of his forehead where the bullet finally came to a rest. It's not that I didn't care for Sherry, I did very much. But it was that I couldn't be around her much after the incident. Whatever my reasons, they all came down to knowing that where there is all that dysfunction, nothing good ever followed. I could barely care for myself and here I was again taking on another responsibility, and regardless of how sweet Sherry was, she still came with far too much baggage. It was dragging me down while unleashing a gush of anxiety. There were too many reminders of what I was running from and never quite being able to get away.

Recently too, making all things worse, was now that I was living with the minister, I was only a few miles from Mother. The shorter distance between us never slipped my mind. Often I'd find myself at a point of indecision when contemplating seeing her again. While living with Ashley, she provided me updates on Mother. They were never good. She was still drinking and had recently taken in male borders. The thought of another man living with her made me cringe. Imagining the type of man that would share a residence with Mother left me feeling nauseous. A pang of dread would shoot through me when wondering if sex was involved. And I would see Mother taking the money from the man, her face white and set.

One evening, Ashley called the minister's house and left a message that Mother had been found laying on the living room floor unconscious. She was taken to the nearby hospital where Ashley informed me that Mother had suffered two broken ribs and punctured a lung. It had been a long time since I saw Mother. The hospital was within a few miles of Peter's and I could ride my motorcycle. It was late fall and it'd be cold, but worth it. This was the woman who beat me, raped me, and prostituted me out for what money she could get, but she was hurt and I still loved her.

In an instant after getting Ashley's message through Peter, I jumped on my motorcycle and rode to the hospital. When I walked into the room where Mother now rested, she looked up at me and smiled. There was a wicked blue-black bruise on the left side of her face and she winced every time she moved. She was actually excited to see me, but none of the same enthusiasm revealed itself in my face. I was guarded and wary of Mother. She was still the reason I suffered and would be for years to come. But now, laid up in that hospital bed all broken down and weak, she was vulnerable and the same love came rushing back to me. Regardless of what she did and who she was, the love I had was real. Best of all, she was sober and I had not seen this side of her in years.

Mother didn't fight me for being there. Instead, she seemed to welcome the visit. She also seemed normal somehow. Not insane or suffering from the usual sick madness that consumed her. I couldn't figure out if she was lonely or loved me too, but every now and then when we'd talk, she would cover my hand in her own and let it sit there for awhile. It was the only chance I'd ever have to try and reach her, maybe get Mother to open up. That's why I spent the next ten days, every day after school, going to see her. That, and each time we spent time together, I secretly prayed she'd hold my hand looking up at my face and tell me how sorry she was.

I pushed open her hospital door on the tenth day of my visit and stepped into the room. The bed was empty and my first thought was that she died. There was a low howling inside my belly while I stood there unable to move. A nurse walked up behind me and I jumped.

"Your mother left today," the nurse said. "She signed herself out."

Running out of the room down the hospital corridor and out into the cold night, I had only one thought in mind and that was to ride my motorcycle to

Mother's as fast as I could. I kicked the bike and it wouldn't turn over. There was this cracking noise followed by a strange grinding. The panic sucked my heart down into my gut and I kicked frantically at the bike again and again and then it finally burst to life with a soft roar. It must have been the cold. Whipping the bike in gear and onto the road made me feel better. Turning down Mother's street, I suddenly realized I had not been home in years and nearly dumped the motorcycle, lost in a haze of fear. Pulling into the driveway was surreal and filled me with dread at the same time.

I could see that the old house was still listing to one side. The living room curtains were closed as usual. There was a sound from inside that sounded like shouting and a dim form moved behind the dirty curtains. Off my bike and a few steps later, I was on the porch and without even thinking opened the battered screen door and pushed through the beaten inner door made of cheap wood.

Breaking the silence as I walked into the living room, Mother looked up at me. Still in the doorway, she shouted at me to get out. Lost in a mass of bad makeup and a wig that she wore askew, I could still make out that she was drunk. Mother raised her voice even louder to a holler and demanded I leave her house.

There was no one else in the house. Only Mother and she had been shouting at nothing. She'd gone mad again with the alcohol. A score of emotions broke from me and I wept, but still could not leave as commanded. Drawing up as much courage as possible, I pleaded with her to talk to me like we had for the last ten days. She flung something at me and it struck me hard in the leg. Then she rose up and moved in on me, her jaw cracking viciously.

When Mother had gotten close enough she grabbed my hair yanking my head down to her height. Then suddenly, as if she was going to kiss my cheek, Mother sank her dentures deep into the soft flesh of my neck. Biting down hard, Mother held me in place and I screamed with agony and sorrow. She unlocked her jaw and pushed me away. I stumbled, found my footing, and ran out the door crying. The blood ran from my neck and the cold air stung at the bite wound. As I labored to start my motorcycle, Mother stood in the door way laughing.

I rode back to Peter's, the cold night air freezing my tears and making it hard to see. Mother was still as quick as a rabid dog and just as mean. I was so terribly stupid for letting this happen to me. I saw Mother's white and black eyes staring at me out of her skeletal, malicious face, but I just stood there like a dumb child, like so many times before.

She was still stronger than me, and armed with a hatred that would kill an army of men. When I got back to Peter's I quickly ran into the bathroom to inspect the bite. There was two sets of teeth marks forming a strange eye-shape, which was hideously red and swollen. I washed it with soap and applied hydrogen peroxide that foamed up, causing a burning sting that was excruciating.

As I laid in my bed that night and wept quietly, I could still see Mother advancing on me while talking in a language that was like the rapid clack of knuckles against wood. Like the sound teeth would make grinding on bone.

"You up?" Peter asked from the bottom of the stairs.

"Yes," I said and walked out of my room already dressed and ready for school.

"What happened to your neck?" he asked.

Thankfully, I had covered the bite wound with gauze.

"I was working on my motorcycle and got too close to the hot muffler," I answered not looking at his face.

He didn't believe me, but he didn't press it either.

"Look, I've got something to tell you." Peter said, then paused.

"I'm being transferred to another church," he finished.

I did not respond. Only waited for what I knew would follow next.

"You're going to have to find another place to live." Peter told me and then maybe he apologized, I don't remember. All I do remember is trying like hell not to burst into tears.

A few weeks passed, and in that time, I did the only thing I could do. I called Becky and Father and begged to live with them just to finish out the school year. It was mid-semester and I was so goddamn close. Father had been transferred back home, and again, did not try and find out where I was or if I were even alive. When I called from Peter's, he answered the phone and upon saying hello, I could hear Father groan. He just kept saying it'd be best if I found another place, but I pleaded and eventually Father relented begrudgingly.

"No more bullshit between you and Becky!" he said over the phone.

"And, it's only until you graduate then you're outta the house," Father said gruffly.

The bullshit he referred to had not been my fault, but that didn't matter. I agreed to the terms and soon moved back with him and Becky.

Father would raise his voice every now and then telling me that he did not want me upsetting Becky after he left for work, and when telling me this, Becky just stood off to the side smiling. She'd stare at me in silence for a moment and then point her finger toward the door as further warning. "You understand me, boy?" Father would say and I'd nod.

I went back to keeping to myself and reading in my room. There were no more locks on the phone, cupboards, and refrigerator. However, Becky had strict rules about what I could eat and when. I'd catch hell if she caught me sneaking a snack and it reminded me of living with Lauren and Bill. Food was always used as a form of control and punishment. Becky would come sailing into the kitchen, grabbing my arm, and swatting the snack from my hand.

"Come on, goddamnit!" she'd yell. "You've been warned! Are you stupid?"

Having breached the security of the kitchen, I'd have to listen to Becky bitch for several minutes. She would break out in a few words of command, like a dozen quick, sharp yelps of a dog, and then drop the definitive warning that I'd be kicked out again if I didn't follow the rules. The black-hearted woman would raise hell over a frigging Twinkie and lament in a shrill voice like a whistle being blown inside a metallic canister.

A month away from graduating high school, I had not applied for any colleges or universities. I scarcely had the grades and certainly did not have the funds. Father was pushing me toward the military and during these conversations his voice would rise until it was almost a scream.

"Don't fuck your life up!" he would shriek. "The military is the best option for you!" Ironically, Father had never served in the military.

Finals were upon me and soon afterwards, I attended the compulsory graduation ceremony where I received a diploma, which was to me not worth the paper on which it was printed.

The evening of my graduation, Father again demanded that the very next day we find a military recruiter, and get me signed up. I openly refused, raising my own voice, just a little. At this, Father stepped toward me shoving his finger into my chest. His eyes were suddenly widened with both surprise and anger, and in another moment he had me pinned against the thin cheap trailer wall. It buckled from the pressure slightly giving way to popping noises every now and then. Father uttered his intent to drive me to a recruiter the next day and make it final.

A small cry fell from my lips when Becky sprang into the room, but she only watched in curious fascination. Father pushed me backward, harder against the wall, his massive hands covering all of my chest and shoulders. He then dragged me from the wall and pushed me against the couch causing me to catch my legs and fall down hard. There may have been a slight warning that came from Becky, but I could not tell if she was telling Father to stop or encouraging him to continue.

Father leapt toward me from where he stood, crashing his fist into the wall above my head. In another instant, his face was only inches from mine, where he breathed harshly, leveled his eyes into mine and glared. Father's voice rose again making that weird almost scream sound. He doubled himself back and raised his fist.

Simultaneously, I leapt from the couch and standing before him, I swung hard. My fist connected squarely against Father's chin and he dropped to the floor. Becky let out a shrill cry that sounded like half pain and half shock. Father staggered to his feet, a stream of blood running from his bottom lip. He sprang at me, and I ran for the door, bursting through it and into the summer night. When I had turned around a few feet from the trailer, Becky was closing the door, and then I heard the lock snap. That night I rode my motorcycle to a nearby park, hiding it behind the restrooms, I sat on the ground against my motorcycle and waited for morning. It was Father's Day.

The next morning, I rode to where Ashley was now living. When I saw Ashley, her face became flush with excitement. There was almost a triumph in her eyes and she met my gaze.

"Hey kiddo! You made it!" she exclaimed. "You finally graduated!"

We talked of the night before and wept some too. Ashley listened as I told her what had happened. My voice had a rumbling monotone quality to it as I drifted in and out conversation, ending with asking "What do I do now?"

"What do you want to do?" Ashley asked.

"I don't know," I answered.

"Listen, Tyler. I've been talking to Jessica and she says Lauren sold this college track coach a house," Ashley said and without waiting for a reply, she continued. "Why don't you give Lauren a call and ask her to introduce you to this coach?"

Ashley sat smiling confidently while I thought about what she said. At last, putting all things aside, including pride and fear, I agreed to give it a try and call Lauren. Ashley fed me and I slept afterwards nearly the whole day and into the next morning. Later that day, I called Lauren and she actually agreed to set up a meeting with this coach. Perhaps she heard how vulnerable I was and took pity on me. Or, she was just hoping I would fall flat on my face and fail miserably. Whatever her reasons, I kept the appointment and went.

The university was well out of my academic range, but there was nothing heavy enough to penetrate the fear inside of me except hope. So, I put on my cleanest clothes and went to the meeting, riding on a motorcycle badly in need of repair that had seen better days. The meeting was a long shot, but it felt safe because I had nothing to lose. I was early, and not knowing where to go, I found myself wandering the campus. The university was small, private, and situated between green sloping hills. It was both beautiful and stately.

Sitting on a wooden bench outside the coach's office, I waited and twisted my hands inside one another. I practiced smiling and trying to relax for when I greeted the coach.

Hello, my name is … nice to meet you. Shit. Everything in my head sounded lame.

I would very much like to attend your university. Christ, this didn't sound like something I'd say at all.

As I waited, the fear crept up and threatened to choke me. The panic was hovering just above me now and ready to come crashing down on my head any second.

They won't have me! I thought. *Look at this place!*

Even if I get in, I'll never make it!

My mind wouldn't stop telling me these things, but it wasn't my voice. It was Father's. It was Lauren, Tim, Jessica, Becky, it was all of their voices, but the loudest voice of all was Mother's.

Suddenly, the door to the coach's office opened and a young secretary broke the sound of the voices in my head by telling me it would be only a few minutes longer. Time enough to practice my greeting some more. Time enough to run away. I could hear my heart beat and felt as though it would crash right through my chest. The panic was now tearing away at me and I could hear laughter coming from somewhere in the building. It sounded young. Maybe students. The panic worsened and I knew what that meant. It meant death, but something more terrible than that. It meant failure.

My face felt flushed and I nearly darted from the building. What stopped me was the gentle voice of the young assistant beckoning me to come. When she spoke, I rose to my feet, and I walked through a thick wooden door leading to the coach's office. She smiled and closed the door behind me.

CHAPTER ELEVEN

Faith and Mercy

"I cannot help but understand the indisputable truth that my life should be used for other things, leaving traces of adoration falling short of nothing less than worship."

ON HIS SIDE OF THE desk, the coach began speaking, while tugging gently at his beard. He was a short man, but his body was fit and gave the illusion of being much taller. I don't remember our introductions, but his name was Pat, or Coach Palmer. The laughter outside in a distant hallway had ceased. Almost immediately, Pat began putting me at ease. Perhaps he saw the dull red flashes in my cheeks showing how afraid I was. He commanded without even noticing, but in a way that encouraged you where one would be compelled to follow. Not because he gave off the presence of a man who has seen darker days and survived, instead it felt more like someone would follow Pat into hell because it was the right and just thing to do.

I had drawn back early in the conversation and only listened. My contributions were limited and it was not necessary to review my high school transcripts. If they had been at the level required, I would not have had a special audience with Coach Palmer. I would have made application to the university, supplied my academic pedigrees, and waited like so many other students hoping to attend. But I was different. I had not the strong academic credentials, strong ACT or SAT scores. I did not posses letters written on my behalf by high school counselors and teachers. All I had was the fire in my belly, the desire in my heart, and Pat. And while sitting across from him, early into our first meeting, something good rose up and told me that he was all I needed.

We faced one another for quite some time. Pat sitting at his desk looking through me with piercing blue eyes that did not seem to be judging me, but more like trying to get inside my head so he could do his level best to get inside my heart. Outside the green sloping landscape winded around the university and it was already getting dark.

"Gregg, it would be a trial semester," Pat said, while leaning closer.

"You would have to work maintenance and housekeeping all this summer."

"Perhaps we could work out a partial track scholarship if you hold your own on the team," he said, then smiled.

It was a kind smile, but there was something behind it. Like mischievous in a wholesome way. Pat's voice never wavered while he spoke. In his tone there were no promises other than those he expected me to keep.

Pat finished with, "It'd all be up to you, Gregg."

I was agreeing to the terms at the first sound of possibility in Pat's tone. As part of the package, there was something I had not expected, a place to live. I'd live on campus while I worked at the university the summer before what would be my first year of college.

With his eyebrows raised inquisitively, Pat looked at me over two powerful looking hands holding up his bearded chin. I could see the fresh lines where he shaved his neck line above a crisp shirt and tie. It would be a lot of work, but it was safe. It had never been safe for me and my faith was as full of holes as old cheese. As if to verify my doubting thoughts, Pat leaned over his desk a little closer still and seemed to be drawing the agreement from me.

"You in, Gregg?" he asked.

"I'm in," I said and it came out sounding unsure.

I had no delusions of sky-rocketing through the academics. I was scared and had a half-million reasons to be. However, Pat wouldn't let me off easy. It was like now that he had hold of me, he wasn't letting go. His mind was already made up. I was going to attend the university and that was final. It was like he was telling me that I shouldn't wonder whether or not I'd make it. Instead, how I was going to succeed.

There was a pile of evidence against me proving I would fail. This just didn't seem to be an option when it came to Pat. Completely shaded by the fact I didn't have any of the confidence in myself that Pat seemed to have in me, was the burning truth that I was broken. How many of these fresh looking bright-eyed students had sex with their mother? How many were prostituted out with strangers? How many were beaten until unconscious and then beaten some more? I guessed none, but the one sitting in front of this man called Coach Palmer trying not to look like I had, in fact, suffered all these horrors.

Pat had faith. This was an unknown word to me in the service of my abusers. Yet, here was this man telling me to either fight or die. Telling me to not be afraid of the dark and he was going to be more than just my companion. My coach. My mentor. He was going to be my refuge. That was the only way he saw it and what shone in his eyes was already saving me. I had already given up before meeting Pat, but until then, I had not realized it. Now, as he spoke to me, it came like a train crashing into my head that I had to fight it out and that meant going back and starting over. If I didn't, I would be lost, never to be found again.

Stunned into silence by this strange thing happening, all I could do was sit and stare at Pat. I wanted to cry and run at Pat, hugging him. He was in the lead and I was going to follow. The fear of letting Pat down was overwhelming and I had just met him. It was evident he had made up his mind to save me, that was certain.

Fifteen minutes into our meeting, I had realized there was something about him that was bundled all up and thick with possibilities. It was as if he needed to push these into me and make them stay. I caught myself nearly weeping and held back the tears. There was no lying to this man, but I didn't feel ashamed of what he might have already been told about me by Lauren. With Pat, I was exposed, but not vulnerable. In the lining of his words, the way he looked at me, his smile, was something that drew me down close and toward something I had never felt before until then. The strange emotion fell down from somewhere special and all over me. It was like a child's upturned face into freshly falling snow. Cool and soft.

In this vision that now presented itself to me was what I had been searching for all my life up to that point and it was being offered unconditionally by this man. Pat may have referred to it as opportunity, or even a chance at something better. I knew the vision by another name. To me, it was always barely within reach until Pat gave it to me without question. I will forever remember it as – mercy.

"Dear God."

I wept, and caught myself, smothering my mouth so no one would hear me who might be passing just outside the old wooden door of my dorm room. Bringing myself to calm down while wondering about the strangeness of this situation, I tucked the nest made of blankets up under my chin, pressing my back against the wall. The tears were streaming down my face and I kept my eyes steadily upon the mirror in front of me across the room over the small dresser. I saw the face staring back at me and it looked both happy and afraid. Without dropping my head, I lifted the pillow and shoved it against my belly. A summer wind was nipping and whining at my only window.

It's all up to me, I thought.

I climbed from the bed and stood near my door then shut off the light. It was dark, save for the moonlight. Slipping back into my nest of blankets on the bed, I let my eyes adjust to the darkness. Hardly a couple minutes had passed before I let my head fall down upon the pillow and the tears continued to wet my face and tumble down my cheeks. I cried softly and mumbled things that not even I could possibly have understood. From far down the feeling started and began to rise slowly. For a moment I waited, my hands clutching the blankets. Then, the voice came, giving way to that first sharp, yapping voice which was impossible to beat or train out of my head. It was the voice of doubt. The collective voices of all my abusers. In the distance stretched before me the gray bloom between success and failure and the latter was speeding toward me like a pack of hungry wolves.

In a flash, the meaning of my life had changed and this unexpected opportunity brought with it a crushing fear. It dawned on me that I could fail and fail miserably. It was cutting me into bits and I wanted to take flight from this place. I cried more fiercely, burying my face in the pillow. Outside the summer wind continued to whine. In my room, I wept too at the empty air.

Pitching forward, I almost threw up and then settled back down onto the bed. A cry that rose shrill and scarcely human above the muffled moaning into my pillow filled the room. In my mind, I saw a single figure, small and naked, darting from my mother's room. His genitals were red and they ached. Chasing this small creature was the haunting voice of a woman laughing. It was me as a boy and I had climbed into my own bed after Mother's molestations, breathing heavily, while desperately trying to hide my sobbing as I did now.

It had been years ago and I had been only a child. Now, I was a young man by age, but still the same terrified child. The thick night soon engulfed all signs of my dorm room. Ahead of me was college and it loomed up slowly, and like now, it caused me great trepidation. I thrust my fists into the bed while weeping. The weight of what was expected of me was far too heavy.

Glancing at the mirror, I could no longer see my reflection. A sudden fear shot through me while I fought the terror. My breathing began to slow, and the panic-like knifing, which was ripping up my heart steadily subsided. I was crying still, and crying hard. My faces was hot and ached with pain. Still binding my body up in the blankets, I drew them closer to me tightly and concentrated on breathing. It was too late to quit. I had thrust myself into the opportunity of higher education and toward the possibilities of better days. *I have to ride it out*, I thought. If I didn't, I knew I'd go under, and that meant this time, for good.

Exhausted, I began to fall asleep and the room continued to whirl. Close behind me there rose that yapping and howling of Mother's voice. I groaned and rolled over to my side, curling up into a ball. I knew I had to fight. I knew I had to face the enemy: my abusers. The demons that lived and breathed inside of me. They hated this place and told me so with every panic attack, always threatening to drive me insane, once and for all.

Before falling asleep, still buried deep within the ocean of blankets, I took note of where I had ended up eighteen years later. It was the first night in my college dorm room. The first place where I had lived outside of family, friends, and foster homes. The date, which also held a measurable significance, was September 2, 1981. It was my birthday.

CHAPTER TWELVE

Finding my Way

*"Let my prayers bring back a new Spring in my aching heart.
To catch a glimpse of time when I felt glory was close at hand."*

A FTER WORKING THAT SUMMER AS a member of the maintenance and housekeeping staff scrubbing toilets, mopping floors, sweeping hallways, and painting walls, my first semester of my first year in college was about to begin. I took a full load of classes and declared a major, business administration, not having a clue what that meant, but it sounded worthy. It sounded important. The college entrance exam all incoming students had to take proved that I was lacking the fundamental skills necessary in nearly all of my required courses. Therefore, my first semester would primarily consist of prerequisite courses, which were basically a repeat of my senior year of high school.

It was a little embarrassing, but my shame was soon dashed by the fear of failing. So I studied harder than ever before and the fear tugged relentlessly at each effort. I had to make it. If I did not, I knew I would die for sure, and most likely by my own hands.

Leaving nothing unfinished, I tackled my studies with an unbroken sweep of both panic and anxiety always close and ready to burst from me. With every syllabus handed out by a professor, I felt a sudden flush in my face. The fear of failure was building with each passing day, and with it came the abrupt gust of loneliness. After a few weeks within the first semester, I fell back a little and then a little more. I was ill-prepared for this level of academics and spent all my time outside of track and work reading in order to keep up. Every spare moment was completely consumed by study and I would spend twice the amount of time on lessons than what was normally required. It was learning to read all over again, and this time, the stakes were far greater.

The heightened intensity of collegiate track was also incredibly daunting. Practices and track meets proved other teammates and competitors were better athletes. I felt as if I was no more than a practice dummy. Struggling just to keep up with the training showed there was a clear quality of athleticism I was lacking. However, the thrill of matching skill against contender brought with it the reminder whether we win or lose, it was wonderful to at least be part of a team.

Crouching low in the blocks, my spiked cleats braced against the buttress of metal blast walls for our feet, I was a different person. My emotional wounds and the uncomfortable sensation of sliding backward with regards to life in general were not present when racing. The perpetual worry of failure made me dizzy and nauseous, but on the track it was different. These feelings usually would be creeping up out of the memories of awful things done to me. Though in my lane, crouched like a cheetah ready to rifle forward from its hunkered down position, the fear and panic that consumed me was not a reality. There would be no sound before the starting gun except that of my breathing. A dark spot would grow outward within my vision, leaving only a pin-point of light, barely covering the lined and numbered lane before me. When the gun sounded, this light would then almost disappear, and grow larger the closer I got to the finish. Playing itself out in my mind was the raising and lowering of my feet, and I was convinced sometimes I could not feel the track beneath my shoes. When competing, Mother and the strangers became only shadowy figures of my imagination. And it became possible that my abusers would lose trace of me within the darkness of my lane.

I was stressed over trying to develop a business case for one of my management courses. While staring at the text, there leaped a little spurt of panic I had not felt before, and every nerve inside my body seemed to sing out at once. Pushing hard to stave off the panic that came on so quickly caused my body to buzz and hum for several minutes. Several times more during the next few months the panic sent its leaden messengers of insanity directly to the center of my brain. And, each time during these terrible moments that lasted longer as time went on, I would fight back a wild outburst of screams. Sometimes during the panic attacks, I would hear a quick metallic snap inside my head before slipping into these emotional chambers of calamity. Beyond that sound were always the low whimpers that came from straining to keep from losing my mind altogether. I would be left exhausted after the humming inside my body and head slowly died away with a grim silence, but very near was the creeping roar of another attack soon to follow without warning.

The joy of having been given the opportunity to attend college by Coach Palmer no longer seemed to matter under the weight of the trembling fear. In place of this joy was rising a thickening certainty my mind would explode one day, flying apart, leaving me absolutely mad. I wasn't giving up, but I was getting weaker by the day. Each lesson plan was a drudgery of effort and the day when the university would drop me from the roster seemed to be closing in. However, the professors were wonderful and extended themselves to each and every student, of which I took full advantage. The university also offered free tutoring services, of which again, I took full advantage.

I continued to work diligently on my studies concealing to everyone the fear in my eyes and face. My voice would be strong and cheerful, so as no one would suspect anything was wrong. It was best that no one knew of my real past. I was barely keeping up with the academics, and adding to this stress was the thought of bringing on a windfall of shame if anyone ever found out the truth. Ride it out. That's all I had to do, but I was alone.

Now and then, there'd be a girl and it offered some comfort. She would smile sweetly at my touch, but I was always unfaithful, dropping easily into the addiction of promiscuity. It helped me forget. Although it was a viciously heart-wrenching endeavor when I was caught cheating and I would say to myself I learned my lesson. But I had not learned and would repeat the behavior along with the heavy burden of infidelity. Even when staring into the face of a young girl's heart I had broken, it did not seem to move me. In high school, I had been the one faithful. Now, and without realizing it was happening, I was caught in a trap of multiple relationships, and because of me, every one of them was a lie.

The professors, along with Pat, gently worked with me on my studies. During a difficult track practice, Pat would ask how I was coming along. Sometimes, I would feel his arm around my shoulders while I stood breathing heavily with my eyes closed. Opening my eyes, he'd just be staring at me and smiling.

"You doing okay, Milligan?" Pat would ask.

"Yeah, Coach," I'd say, panting.

Pat would then slap me on the back and walk on. Every now and then, he'd stop short of asking me something else, but instead, just grin and nod his head.

"Keep up the good work," he'd say in a kind voice, still looking in another direction while walking away.

I groped for a foothold and thrust myself into both study and track, always knowing there was something of great peril waiting for me. Lurking just beyond striking distance. It was not an unusual concern because it rose from a place in which I had yet to escape. I was on the edge of something awful and could feel it. Something I had been fighting to keep back since a child rose out of the gloom growing within me.

In front of me was the incessant pounding of academic requirements; however, lifting me up as best they could were all the faculty and staff, and as always, Pat. He gave me shelter. Pure and simple, and it helped get me through the darkness, but I knew it could not keep all the demons away for long.

Education was the one thing that could save me now —the one thing left I dared attempting. I would keep my promise to Pat and do my absolute best. At least, I tried to make myself believe that I was keeping my promise. But deep in me there was an undercurrent of feelings that I could not explain. Something was keeping the secrets of what happened in Mother's house at bay. It felt a lot like shame.

It was a gathering of secrets barely kept down that swelled inside, almost to the bursting point, but the glow of a new life was so close. I was narrowly keeping ahead of the flood of emotion that teased at my brain. Racing it and losing. *When was the last time I slept without nightmares?* I wondered.

Each morning brought the imprint of wet or drying tears on my pillow. Something was closing in, other than normal academic responsibilities. There was something closing in on me, choking me, and I poured myself into the work of higher-learning to compensate as much as struggling to overcome it.

I ate and drank my studies and often needed the assistance of a tutor. Most times because of track, study and work, I couldn't see the light of day.

Little attention was given to any self-analysis or therapy, but I came close from time to time during the worst of the panic attacks. However, the panic was never as powerful and heavy as the weight of shame.

My attention was dead set on survival and education was the key. Sure, it scared the hell out of my roommates when I'd wake up with a wailing protest while smothering myself under the soaked sheets covering my bed. But they seemed not to notice or maybe just didn't know what to say. In order to dig myself out of the hole I was in, I knew I had to graduate with a college degree. What gave me this strange idea was a mystery, but I clung to it like life itself. And there was a change coming over me that seemed right. Regardless of the fear and loathing buried deep inside, the effect higher education was having on me was positive.

Turning my eyes toward a more positive path did not fully keep the figure of something menacing from slowly creeping toward me. Halfway between just barely losing and making it was the mantra of each passing moment. The choice between facing my demons or focusing on school was an easy one. The latter would win out for many obvious reasons. One of them was further setting me apart from my abusers. Knowledge was a refuge. It also unlocked more opportunities. I took up the path of higher learning and following this direction was already in play. Perhaps the university would finally end me, but at least I stood when so many others simply gave up. Those in my life that did give up were pushers of hatred and they did push as hard they could into anyone around them. And, like Pat always said, these types of people had no love. In the first eighteen years of my life already I had witnessed these same people committing heinous acts against humanity, and all with the same look on their faces, while standing idly by as of turned to stone.

The first semester was dotted with stops and starts and went by swiftly. There was a score of difficulties related to simply adjusting to college life and the complexities of balancing multiple academic subjects. After all, I had been to four different high schools and most of what I picked up with regard to study habits were things developed along the way. My last stand was to be made here and, so far, in all situations leading up to college I had not wasted precious opportunities when presented. The prearranged curriculum based on a declared major had its advantages. It was focused on a particular field of study and I liked the organization that went along with that. It was order in the chaos.

Putting action into words, I began writing down my feelings. Not a journal, but more like random and jotted notes written on scraps paper which were thrown out before the ink was dry. Too difficult to read along with the fact I did not want anyone to accidently read these inner thoughts made up of dark secrets. Awful and embarrassing things of the past. Later, I took some of these thoughts and began to incorporate them into literature assignments. Always taking great care not to give away the main character, which was me, and in them, I hinted toward the abuse. The process was instantaneous and correlative –the act did not work, but made things worse. Therefore, I stopped immediately and again focused only on the sterile confines of pure academics.

The end of the first term closing, it would appear as though not only did I find myself completing one-half year of college, but also scoring high enough to pass my prerequisites. The courses would now become exponentially more difficult. What would replace these refresher courses were the classes I now feared the most; Micro and Macro Economics, Business Law, Accounting I and II, Statistics, and the list went on.

No sooner had I successfully completed the first term, the second was already beginning. I set out at a harried pace and struggled even more, which stood to reason, due to the fact I was running wounded. The tutors knew me all too well and probably began to hide when they saw me coming. This was definitely not the case with the professors. They always welcomed me into their offices, making time to explain the lesson, and they made sure I understood it before letting me out of their sights. Having not fallen flat on my face as expected, I continued to press on with a little more vigor. It was only one semester out of the way, but no longer a black speck of despair. I had advanced and that mattered a lot. However, now that the second semester was underway, there came with it another chance at falling.

It was halfway through the second semester, I called Lauren. When she heard my voice an unpleasant laugh came through the receiver.

"So, are you still in college?" she asked in her usual condescending manner.

"Yes," I answered in my usual agreeable fashion.

It was best not to rock the boat. Lauren was still in a position of great power over me. She had Lynn, and I so dearly loved her. So much, it ached.

Ironically, the college in which I now attended was only a few miles from Lauren. Better still, it was only a few miles from Lynn. Over the phone, I pleaded with Lauren to allow me a visit. The call was strained, but that wasn't out of the ordinary. Something was different. She did not want me seeing Lynn. Not now.

As it turned out, Lauren and Tim had decided the last of us would be pushed from their home. At the end of Lynn's sophomore year of high school she was sent away and placed into the foster care system. The shining light in all this, other than being free of Lauren and Tim, was the fact the foster home was near the university. This would be the last time Lauren and Tim would have any say in my life or Lynn's, and I was going to make certain of it.

Lynn was barely on her feet for several seconds when we saw one another for the first time in far too long. She ran to me and jumped, wrapping her legs around my waist, screaming with delight.

"My brother, Gregg!" she yelled giddily.

"We're together again!"

"We're together! We're together!"

She nearly knocked me down the porch steps of the foster home as I was climbing them. Her face was so small, too thin, and childlike. Her hair was cut short, too short –Lauren had saw to that, and she wore an old sweatshirt that was much too large. Lynn was no heavier than a flea, her eyes burned wildly from out of shaggy bangs, and she was panting like a thirsty puppy. She was absolutely beautiful.

Seeing Lynn never brought back the terrible memories of what Mother wanted her to do with the strangers. Or, what I did with the strangers to protect her. Instead, seeing Lynn brought back with it the only reason I was still fighting to become something better.

I had traveled only a few miles to see Lynn, but it felt like a few hundred. She had called the university the day Lauren dropped her off at what would become Lynn's new home for the next year. The only reason it was possible to end up so close to one another was because of the State wanting to keep her in the same high school, which happened to be in the same city as the university. It had been our good fortune and something both Lynn and myself found unbelievably rare. We saw at once how lucky we were.

Seeing Lynn nearly made me cry as well. My eyes felt red and swollen as Lynn rested her head against me, sitting side by side on the porch. Every fiber in my body seemed for a moment to have lost the power of action as her head nested itself under my arm. We giggled, laughed, and stared at one another, and then Lynn finally busted through my tough exterior the minute the words left her lips.

"Gregg," she said. "I love you."

And with that, an amazing sob broke from me. I looked at Lynn, my littler pug-nosed sister and made an involuntary movement to hug her, but she was already ahead of me. I had flung my arms around her, and in an instant, was on one knee at her side, cradling her slight figure. Unashamed of who may be watching or listening, we both held one another and wept.

"I am so afraid, Gregg," Lynn said, breaking through her sobs.

"I'm here and I promise I won't leave you," I replied. This time, it was a promise I would be able to keep.

Why Lynn ended up having to leave Lauren turned out to be another mystery. The same as it was when I was evicted. Garbage talk when Lynn asked why. Smack. Nothing but. The usual bullshit that couldn't and wouldn't make sense to anyone. Especially, a scared as hell sixteen-year-old girl. I gripped Lynn's hand in mine and assured her that we'd get through this together. She was holding on tight; and Lynn looked up into my eyes, saw that she was no longer looking into the face of just anyone, but that of her big brother. I smiled and so did she.

We both drew in deep breaths, helping each other to our feet, and said our farewells for the evening. Before going inside, Lynn introduced me to her foster mother. She was a heavy-set nearly blind woman with a heart of pure gold. Lynn was still crying when I said goodnight, but they were happy tears. I could live with that. Tearing myself away from her, having squeezed Lynn one last time, I set off back to the college. She was still sobbing and talking like a crazy girl when she ran down the porch steps, into the yard and wrapped her arms around me one more time like a frightened child. It gave me new strength, and for a time longer, brought me back from the downward spiral I was heading before seeing her. As I finally got moving and had a couple blocks between us, I turned and saw her still standing in the yard. Another block later, now at least three, I could still see Lynn waving.

For the next two years, I would be faced with the daunting task of making sure Lynn graduated high school. Bearing down upon Lynn were the pressures of moving into a household of all wayward girls; albeit under the love and care of a sweet woman, it was still a transition in which she would have to adjust. In addition to my own busy schedule, I made time to help coax, sometimes pulling Lynn through her high school academics. I did not mind and leapt at the chance to be with Lynn. Falling into taking care of her was not only easy, it was fulfilling. The main reason was because she loved me so much in return.

A bit of sanity had come back into my life as I worked through helping Lynn with the normal high school homework. I was again associated with a worthwhile feeling of being appreciated. No sooner started, I successfully completed one year of college. That summer Lynn and I faced some battles together. Mostly, it was keeping her out of trouble with the boys and from partying a bit too much. But nothing serious and the close physical distance between us made it possible for us to spend a lot of time together. We supported each other and our powerful little duo kept us both balanced, or so I thought.

Summer passed and Lynn started her junior year of high school, and I, my second year of college. It was during my sophomore year, when the relentless pressing down of all that needed to come out sooner or later, finally busted through the walls of my psyche. Whatever was sloughing away at my mechanisms to avoid my past would win out in the end. It felt like the end and the most terrible death in which I feared since being a child. The death of irreversible insanity. At last, I would suffer a nervous breakdown by any definition.

As I laid in bed, for a few moments sleep seemed to begin creeping in just as difficult as usual, but something seemed strange. Sure, the anxieties were still there, but nothing I couldn't handle. Then suddenly, I was panting, clasping at my neck and trying not to choke. Slipping further into the worst of all panic attacks, none of that kind I had ever experienced.

I'm dying! I'm going crazy! I thought with certainty.

If the choking did not kill me, the insanity would be worse. It seemed liable that at any minute my mind would snap. It would not be long now. I was sure to end up crazy, just like Mother. She had come to kill me with all the terrible things and this time without laying a hand on my body. I tried, but the haunting of things was too awful and everything unchecked by way of therapy or any other sort of mental relief finally gave way to the secrets of the past to end me for sure.

At that moment, I thought of Lynn and how much she loved me and how I would no longer be able to care for her, along with Pat, and how I had let him down. I thought of these people for a long time as I struggled to hold on to reality. I thought of angels too. The sort that saved people in times of need like depicted in the Bible. The sort that were supposed to be all around when we, as humans, were at the doorsteps of our darkest hour. And God, I thought of him too and wondered if maybe He could see me. Hoped He could at least hear me, so I started to pray. I wept harder thinking that perhaps God would not hear me. That maybe, He was sleeping.

There was a giant marble statue of Jesus that stood upon a pedestal outside the college library. His hands were outstretched and He had a solemn look of mercy chiseled across His face. Many times, when certain no one was looking, I would kiss His feet. No prayer was said, only a quick kiss atop His toes. I thought the gesture was enough, and that to Jesus, no prayer was necessary.

Inside my ears was a loud buzzing that turned into what sounded like ringing within a closed metal box. A box in which I was trapped. Like the metal child's rocket ship where I hid and cried in the pouring rain after one of many terrible fights with Father. I was so cold then, but now I burned with a fever. My bed was soaked with sweat and piss. I don't remember urinating. Even though I was on the edge of death, insanity or both, I did not dare want to die or go crazy. It could not end like this, so I made a concerted effort to pull it together. First, concentrating on breathing, and after that, I pushed the covers from me and began to pull myself out of my bed that felt like a coffin.

I fell out of bed and half-crawled, half-walked out of my dorm room, and began working my way toward the hallway phone. There was only one person to call. Only one person I felt could help me, other than Pat. His name was Dr. Ed Skinner, a professor of psychology at the university. His contact number was on an old syllabus I still had after taking his course as an elective. The hallway, like my room was empty. It was a break during the semester and most of the other students were home, along with my roommates. Breaks were usually more enjoyable for me. Having no home to go to, I stayed at the university and used the alone time to collect myself. I stood using the wall where the phone hung to pull myself up. The fear was so overwhelming, I was no longer too embarrassed to seek help. I was dying, goddamnit.

"Dr. Skinner?" I said, my voicing shaking and cracking. "It's Gregg Milligan and I really need your help."

Once the words were out, I realized that it could have been anyone on the other end of the phone. I dialed a number from the syllabus, but had no idea if I had written it down correctly when Dr. Skinner gave it out in class. Or if the number had been changed, disconnected, or belonged to someone else. But thankfully it was Dr. Skinner and he didn't sound surprised, upset, rattled or even slightly confused. As a matter of fact, he sounded as if he were expecting my call. He wasn't, of course, but he was a well-trained psychologist and worked for the local Sherriff's Department as a suicide prevention counselor in addition to teaching at the university. I wasn't his first basket case.

"Listen to me, Gregg," Dr. Skinner, who insisted I call him Ed, said sternly.

"Meet me at the Sherriff's Department in twenty minutes."

It had to be 1:00am, but Ed also sounded like he wasn't sleeping. This did not occur to me until I was well on my way, driving like a bat out of hell, in a borrowed car of a schoolmate while he was home with his parents during the short semester break. I got there in ten minutes but Ed was already there waiting.

For the next several weeks, at no charge, Ed met with me in his office twice a week. I told him everything. The past poured from me in a torrent. Ed would often need to tell me to slow down, while gently smiling, slightly raising his hand in an up and down motion. I was finally exposed. The ruse was up and I didn't care. The breakdown left me terrified of going crazy and if telling all would stop my mind from flying apart, so be it. In that first meeting with Ed, the night the panic attack was worse, while he calmly spoke to me from his office, all I could do was smile wanly into Ed's eyes and weep.

"You came to the right place," he said coaxing me to speak.

"And, from what I see – just in time."

This was supposed to be humorous, I'm sure. But it wasn't as funny as Ed had hoped. During all of our sessions, Ed spoke as if he had known me a lifetime. He covered each emotion I was suffering gently, and in spite of himself, his eyes always showed brightly the love he had for me. There was something incredibly special about Ed.

A few weeks into our sessions, I broke into a racking sob that made my nose bleed. Ed saw the look of desperation on my face.

"What haven't you told me?" was all he asked. It was all he needed to.

My voice barely a whisper with the crimson stain of blood still around the small circles of my nostrils, I felt the choked grief rise up inside as I began to tell of the first molestations by Mother, the prostitution, the strangers.

I took Ed through the first of the incest and over the secrets I was afraid to admit –even to myself. I should have told him the first night he saw me in desperation, but I did not know that until afterward. After I trusted him. While I spoke it was as if he stopped breathing.

"Keep talking," Ed said in his usual gentle way, but this time it had a bit of an edge to it. A firmness. As if he were telling me not to stop now.

Ed reached across his desk and took one of my hands. I went to pull it away, but he detained it within his. He was crushing both his thin, warm hands in my own, but said nothing else. He just waited, fighting to stifle the sobbing grief that hitched in his breath.

When Ed spoke again, it pulled years of remorse from my heart.

"You were good to her –good –good to her," he repeated weakly.

"You loved her –and it was right, because you were innocent and only a child."

"I'm glad you loved her. You've been good and honest and I want someone like you in this world." Ed then watched my face in earnest and then spoke some more.

"I'll let your hands go, but not until I've told you something, Gregg."

"This isn't your fault." I read the same words in books secretly scanned in the university library about sexual abuse, but they meant nothing to me. They never struck any real chord. However, this time, while Ed held my hands from across his desk and looked at me with those bright shiny and kind eyes, the words finally made sense. All of his words made sense.

"You're not going crazy," Ed continued.

"And, you're not going to die … not today anyway." He smiled and I even managed one too.

Ed gently let my hands go free and his face was tense, staring straight into my eyes.

"I'm not going to give up on you, Gregg," he said.

"You need someone and you are so goddamn alone."

I started to cry softly, but when Ed rounded his desk, bent on one knee and laid my head on his shoulder, I wept until it echoed off the walls of his office. Still on his knee, he swore to me that together we would make it through. My rigid body relaxed, and I sank into Ed's arm with a sign of relief. I always believed in God –regardless of all the terrible things done to me, He sent me Pat, and now Ed. A sudden light of hope came into my heart.

I rose from the edge of death while Ed held me and my sobs turned to stuttered hitched breathing. In a few minutes, we both were giggling which turned to a thrilled, half-silly laugh. My eyes were still closed when Ed tenderly pushed me from his shoulder. Ed spoke and his voice was as though the words he were uttering came from out of a dream. I saw the end was not near, but it was only the beginning. Ed bent down one last time to catch the look on my face. His hands were again holding mine. His eyes were red and shiny and then Ed whispered:

"You did not lose your innocence –it was stolen," he said.

"Gregg, you're not a bad person –you are good."

Ed smiled and bent lower so that now our mouths were almost touching.

"I'm going to help you."

I made no answer. I did not really hear what he was saying until later when I was playing the words over and over in my head and even wrote them down. The smile never faded from Ed's lips and I knew we had made a great deal of effort together over the past several weeks. With a glimpse anticipation of better days, I gripped Ed's hands in return. He let go of one hand and patted my back. We laughed, and suddenly Ed caught me in his arms one more time, just before I crumpled forward from exhaustion and relief –sobbing severely. There he stayed, kneeling on the floor of his office before me. And now, Ed sobbed just as hard as well.

CHAPTER THIRTEEN

The Promise Fulfilled

"To know all I had to do in return for Grace –
was simply live and breathe."

IT WAS WAY PAST AMAZING that I completed my sophomore year of college having taken the more difficult courses so far and that I had also helped Lynn get one more year closer to graduating high school, all while suffering a massive nervous breakdown. Managing to keep this from Coach Palmer proved easier due to the fact I took a year off track. What made up for lacking the monies I would have received for the partial athletic scholarship were student loans and working for a plastics molding factory near campus. It was all I could do to pull myself together while trying to focus on my studies.

Pat was worried and I'm sure a bit disappointed, but what helped the both of us was the occasional greeting as we passed one another, generally on my way to class with a ton of books under my arm. I'm sure Pat just figured I was swamped with academics. He knew of my lack of educational training and I'm sure when making a choice between track or study, Pat would have had me choose the latter. I wasn't going to set the world on fire running collegiate track or make the U.S. Olympic Track Team anyway.

During the healing process, post the breakdown while Ed and I worked diligently on getting me better, it was difficult to stop crying at the drop of a hat. Going to class had its challenges already, but now I wept like a baby when watching a goddamn soap commercial. What was also difficult was watching any kind of horror movie, especially the Twilight Zone. Two things that I once enjoyed immensely now became far too strange to stand. The genre was mentally just too close for comfort. Another after-effect of the nervous breakdown was my inability to have any intimate contact with another human being. Therefore, I took an apartment off-campus, so I could go to bed and wake up alone. Outside of class and work at the factory I was alone most of the time.

Before the breakdown however, I had been dating another student. There was even talk of marriage after college. She was simply, Lana. Beautiful, with long wavy brown hair and eyes to match. Bright red full lips and the disposition of a saint and the patience of one as well. I should know, because of my frequent infidelity. Lana always took me back. She was sweet and I was a fool with more baggage than an airline.

She too lived off campus and was in an apartment only a block away from mine. I broke off the relationship soon after my breakdown. Lana was both hurt and angry, telling me we could work it out. It was Lana who had enough strength for the two of us and what plans were made regarding our relationship, it was she who made them. The only plan I participated in was when it came time to part ways. When I told her, there was a fresh redness in her eyes, and she puffed in and out trying to breathe. I thought of that parting often in the days that followed. How Lana stood in the door of her apartment, and in her face was a look I wished never to have seen. In my own heart was the dread and the fear of caring for another, the thing until my nervous breakdown, I would not name.

For years I could not shake off the gloom that oppressed me. It was buried deep in the recesses of my mind and asleep. I did not want to wake it, because that meant not only was I damaged —that Mother did leave with me something ugly, but that I may never be able to have a normal relationship. It wasn't until the shelter of therapy with Ed that it was awakened, laughing at me while I dug it out of its nest.

I set about the work of accepting the fact monogamous intimacy, normal relationships in general, were far from my capabilities mentally and emotionally. I just did not want to take care of anyone else. The history of having done so and failed miserably with Mother haunted me.

For the first time in my life I was admitting to this and doing something about it. However, it meant getting free of any and all relationships; short and long-term. By the time I came to realize the work ahead of me and the damage left behind, Lana had become no more than fodder. It wasn't her fault which made it even worse and made it all the more terrible telling her goodbye. I dragged her through hell because of my infidelity, mood swings, violent temper tantrums, and now, after she had invested so much, I was saying goodbye.

The day I told her, of course, she looked more beautiful than ever. It was nearing September and the start of my junior year of college. She had been wearing a hooded sweatshirt, and her pretty doll-like face seemed to glow. The light danced auburn and gold in the tangled curls that jutted from under the hood. As I spoke to her of the break-up, I saw more and more of what I knew I would find in the woman who was no longer a viable option for me.

When finished, Lana produced a small box from her pocket wrapped in tissue paper. Fold by fold she smoothed back the paper revealing what was inside. My heart was beating fast knowing what was in the box. It was an engagement ring and I remember slipping it on Lana's finger. It had been a spur of the moment thing, not really wanting to marry, but I had treasured the memory regardless.

After returning to my apartment, I could still picture Lana. How her face was framed by the cinch of the hood covering her head, allowing just enough light to enhance her beauty. As I lay in bed that evening I thought of our first meeting and was once more in the presence of her beauty floating in front of me in the darkness of my room.

And then troubling visions came to me and I was filled with the shuddered dread of remembering what she had done when catching me cheating for the first time. She had broken a light bulb and with the glass cut her wrist. It had happened only a few feet from my dorm room door and another student found her unconscious. The cut was not deep enough to cause any damage nor deep enough to leave a scar. Not like the one down the belly of my right forearm. But the first glimpse of blood caused Lana to pass out.

The student who found her quickly summoned me and I ran to where Lana now lay. Her face gleamed a ghostly white against the thick blackness of the old tile. I had to turn my own face away before the panic stole my senses. The sight of her attempted suicide reminded me of Mother and filled me with the oppression of a leaden hand. The hand that pressed down hard on my heart when it came to accepting responsibility for another's actions. A thing that was both dread and fear. I could feel the presence of Mother while trying to rouse Lana. A presence like a warning, stirring familiar thoughts within me and for a long time I could not forgive Lana for what she had done. Mostly for what she had stirred inside of me.

Right before finally drifting to sleep, there was a knock on my apartment door. I rose out of bed, dressed and walked down a short flight of stairs. Through the glass of the door there stood Lana. A warmth that was not joy leapt into my face, and I gathered up my patience and opened the door. Lana pushed me aside and ran up the stairs. I followed her and when reaching the top, she began screaming at me in anger. When Lana finally stopped, there were tears in her eyes and a filmy mist of the same in mine. She was an image of lost hopes and I was flooded with emotion. My heart ached for her, but it was over. Here was again a bitter reminder. She was all heart and soul, but not for me. Not the way I was. Not for a broken man. Someone like Lana became menacing without meaning it and that made her dangerous. She had to go, so I pleaded with her but she would not. Therefore, I physically carried her down the stairs and gently put her out, shutting the door and locking it behind me.

As I began to ascend the stairs there was a horrible crash of glass. When I turned toward the sound, Lana was walking down the porch and away from my apartment. The upper-window portion of my front and only door was shattered. Shards of glass, some large and small, were scattered all over the floor of the foyer.

Continuing up the stairs, I went to retrieve a broom and dustpan, taking one more look where Lana was heading. She was already across the street and walking toward her apartment, but something was wrong. In an instant I was out the door and running after her. I watched as she swayed, stopped, and then fell in place, all while her back was still to me. The distance between my foyer and where Lana was before dropping like a stone was a good twenty feet. Something caught my eye though. It was her right arm, which was a deep crimson red against her lily white skin. Before hitting the sidewalk with a thump, I heard Lana faintly call out my name.

I ran to her side and gently rolled Lana's body over. Looking first into her pale face, I then checked for a pulse. For some kind of bodily movement, but there was none. Checking her pulse, I found a heartbeat and with every lub-dub, the blood oozed from her arm. She must have punched the window after I had locked the door. The glass ripped through every layer of skin, deep into her flesh, past veins and into an artery. Lana was dying on the sidewalk and it had been all my fault.

I did not wait for help, but lifted Lana up, cradling her in my arms, and ran to her apartment. It wasn't closer, but I did not have a phone. I did not have a key to her apartment either, so I kicked in the door still holding her bleeding body.

"Hang in there!" I said.

Once in Lana's apartment, I laid her on the couch and applied a thick, tight tourniquet above the wound. I knew basic triage since only a child. It was necessary for survival. The place she sliced open her arm was almost exactly where my scar still remained and I knew it was a killer cut. One that was easy to bring death.

Lana was in and out of consciousness, whispering incoherently, while I phoned the police. One after another, I had to keep replacing towels quickly soaked with blood and soon I was on to clothing. Anything to stop the bleeding. Anything to save her life.

There were still love notes and pictures of me strewn about her apartment and I thought for second I should try and hide them. They were evidence and somehow I feared a link that would implicate me when the authorities arrived. Soon, I was back to redressing Lana's gaping wound and forgotten about the memorabilia. She'd want to save the love notes for sure because they came from me.

On her counter there was a worn and faded envelope and inside of it was the wedding date written on a scrap of paper. It was my writing. This, I shoved inside my pocket after peering at it for awhile. The guilt was terrible. There were other things in plain view from our relationship. Lana must have taken a walk down memory lane before coming to see me. No wonder she wanted to put her fist through glass.

My heart gave a sudden throb when I saw the blue flower petals I had given her pressed inside wax paper laying on the counter. Back to the issue at hand, I laid my ear against her breast and listened. There was barely a beat and I nearly wept when my cheek touched her skin. I was trying to revive Lana when I heard movement within the hallway of the apartment. Then radio static. I thought it had to be either the police or paramedics, so I walked to the open door of Lana's apartment to beckon them to hurry. An officer saw me, drew his weapon, and suddenly dove behind a staircase. I dove myself back into Lana's apartment.

What in the fuck did the dispatcher radio!? I thought to myself.

"I'm unarmed!" I yelled.

A perfect day: broke up with girlfriend, she committed suicide, accidentally of course, which was not how it looked right now to the cops, and then got shot trying to save her life. If it weren't so tragic, it'd been funny.

"I'm unarmed!" I yelled, again.

Keep it simple when telling the cops what the hell is going on. I learned that too from my childhood. Reverently, the cops began the task ahead of them and slowly crept into the apartment. What assured them that I was not a threat was the fact I was kneeling with my hands above my head in the middle of Lana's living room.

The first cop entered, then the second, followed by a couple paramedics. To my relief, they finally holstered their weapons. They were still breathing rapidly and one of them actually scolded me for jumping out in the open. Normally, I would have told him to go fuck a duck, but saving Lana was more important. The two paramedics worked on Lana and spoke quickly to one another. I was questioned by the police and asked the same questions over and over.

"If you need proof she slammed her goddamn fist through a window then go look for yourselves!" I said, raising my voice to one of the cops.

"Calm down," he responded in that tone that always meant they were in control and you were guilty.

Apparently, the cops believed my story because I was allowed to ride up front in the ambulance. Not a sign of emotion came into my expression, not even with a flicker of an eyelash did the immobility of my face change as we drove to the hospital, sirens blazing. Nearly there, I turned and looked at Lana laying prone strapped to a gurney. Fully conscious once the intravenous solution began kicking in, she tilted her head up and backward looking directly at me. In a low, clacking monotone sound she began to speak, and there was an expression of grief in her voice. Before Lana's mouth formed the words, I knew what she was trying to say.

"I'm sorry," she uttered weakly.

The look of guilt on her face was heart-wrenching and I understood now that in my heart it was best to stay clear of all relationships, friend or otherwise. Realizing how ill-prepared I was at caring for another person was obvious. After Lana mouthed her sincere apology, I stared at her for a few seconds, then turned and without a word in reply, went back to looking out the windshield of the ambulance.

For the next several weeks, Lana healed and kept to herself. We barely spoke, and before long, I was out of her life completely. Because of the incident, the landlord of my apartment saw fit to evict me and so I moved back on campus. I continued my therapy sessions with Ed, registered for courses, and again earned a place on the track team. The therapy helped considerably and I began to see life as not so much a burden, but a real opportunity. Putting these new feelings into action, my grades began to improve dramatically and the academic struggles subsided. I was catching on. Finally.

I quit my job at the factory and began working for the university as part of the housekeeping crew. Mostly I scrubbed toilets and mopped floors, but it was income to help pay for school. My dear friend Pat Palmer took another position and the track coach position was handed over to a capable young man who had proven himself worthy. Not only as a supreme athlete, but a wonderful coach as well. Pat's shoes were tough to fill, but he did so splendidly. Things were falling into place for me academically, athletically, and emotionally. I was delighted to earn another varsity letter and also received the college's third-year award in athletics. Due to my efforts academically, I was also asked to be treasurer on the university newspaper, which I accepted cheerfully. In all, it appeared that I finally found my groove.

Pat stayed very close to me even though he was no longer my coach. He watched me like a doting father. There wasn't a week that went by my junior year that Pat wasn't shaking my hand gladly while passing in the hallways and cheering me on during track competitions. It wasn't that he wanted to keep an eye on someone in which his reputation hinged, although that was true. I knew it was because he loved me. Pat also didn't like the idea of losing at anything. Especially those things most important in life and that was remembering we are here to save one another.

Half the semester over, I wasn't convinced a degree was a sure thing; however, for the first time in my life, I was confident there was nothing that would cause me to fail. In the words of one of many wonderful professors at the university, "Only a bullet could stop me now."

Lana had graduated at least three years before me, but still lived in the local area. I stayed away not wanting to give her any further trouble. Like a possession you have to give up, but still to know it was tucked away somewhere safely. It was selfish of me to feel this way and I did not deserve the right to do so. Every now and then I would have to fight the urge to find her and confess to all of the things I had done in which she did not know, but the result would yield no grand benefits and would only break her heart all over again in the end.

Lynn was still very much a part of my life. I'm sure Lynn kept some secrets from me even though we were close. Just as I had kept so many things from her, including the nervous breakdown. We loved each other dearly, but sometimes even we were unable to tell all of our secrets. To fully report to one another the sins others had forced upon us would have been more than difficult. It was perhaps the love we had for one another was so strong –to the death, that in admitting to these things we might let out the truth and it would ruin us for sure.

Other than Lynn, all contact had diminished with every other member in my family. My mother and father were dead to me and the healthier I became while working through the problems brought on by abuse, and just being raised poor in general, the more I felt sorry for them. From where I started a lot of ground had been covered. I had come a long way since the mother who I had fallen in love with, of the kiss I had longed to give her without retribution, and of the abuse, the pursuit of happiness, the recapturing of my life, and that final moment when the chains of ugly secrets were beginning to loosen from my wrists.

Once I began the journey of healing with Ed, I left nothing untold, even the molestations, rapes, incest, and forced sex for money with strangers. And, about Lynn too who was paraded in front of the men in nothing but a pair of dirty and urine-stained panties. How Mother showed the men what they could have at a price, but instead I would tell Lynn to run and hide. In her place I gave myself freely to the men, and with a tremble in a child's voice, there came a persuasive agreement in order to throw them off her trail. Make them forget Lynn was even in the house somewhere. Hiding, weeping, alone and sucking her thumb while scared to death, and so sad –so goddamn sad.

When I spoke of the sexual abuse, there was always a mistiness in Ed's eyes. And, each time I finished, he'd reach across gripping my hand or come round and hold me. Sometimes, I wept when he held my hand, but mostly it was when I could bury my face in the crook of his neck, hiding my own face, the deep sobs came like torrential rain.

"All your dreams are coming true," Ed would tell me.

During the more difficult conversations, I thought he was lying.

"No, they're not," I would say holding my head down.

"They are, and the happiness is bringing about a change in you," Ed would interrupt firmly.

"Jesus, Gregg. Just because your heart is breaking doesn't mean you won't find happiness," Ed would say and this rang true.

It lifted a weight from my heart and it struck down Mother's voice a little more each time he said it. I made plans to graduate college and set out to do so. I went to the door of possibilities, opened it, and looked out. The future was getting brighter. No further were the panic attacks as prevalent or strong. There were still the chronic nightmares. They stayed and were just as awful as before. So awful that I still woke hearing myself wailing like the steady sobbing of a surf on a seashore. But there were forming small circles of light of a better day, growing larger and brighter. I was master of my destiny, exhausted and footsore from the journey, but there was a present and strange hope broken only by the low moaning coming from me during the nightmares. However, I kept getting up and out of bed each morning. *Fuck it.*

I was seated on Billy's bed, also a junior, and we were studying for finals, when Julie came running into the room screaming frantically. She was a sophomore and what happened next would end her college career. Julie stared into my face trying to mouth some words. She looked like a fish and Billy laughed; however, the look on her face made Billy stop, and when his laugh ended, Julie screamed even louder. She grabbed my shoulder and squeezed and I found that her fingers tightened so hard that it hurt. Julie's red long hair was tousled and windblown. Her top was torn, leaving two buttons popped, exposing her breasts. She wasn't wearing a bra and I noticed her nipples were as red as her hair. Julie pulled me to the partly opened door still trying to speak. All of Billy's good humor was now completely gone and he looked worried. I hadn't noticed Julie wasn't screaming any longer until the room got deathly quiet. In place of Julie's screams, I could hear her sobbing, then she abruptly stopped, and now I heard neither.

Julie then spoke and the words didn't make any sense.

"Gregg! Come with me!" Julie panted while laboring for breath.

"It's Sandy and she's hanging from the window!"

Normally this would not have been a problem, but we were on the third-floor of the university and the drop was a long way down. No time for discussion, Billy and I took off running with Julie leading the way.

We had run to the other end of the hallway when suddenly Julie bolted inside an open doorway of a dorm room. It was Sandy's room, a freshman who was about to finish her first year. Billy and I quickly followed Julie inside. I noticed it was quiet. Too quiet.

"Where's Sandy?" I asked Julie with a puzzled look on my face.

I had not quite understood what she meant. Julie pointed to an open window missing a screen. As a matter of fact, the screen laid inside the room against the wall near the window. I listened for a shout, breath or a sob, and heard nothing. A curtain was sucked outside the window and was blowing eerily in the wind. The three of us just stood unable to move and stared at the open window. It was light inside the room and dark outside, making it difficult to see anything past the blowing curtain. I instinctively made out something strange on the window ledge and when realizing what it was, my heart beat faster, and I called to Sandy. It was her fingers. There was no answer. I looked at Julie and Billy and began to slowly walk toward the window, calling out to Sandy. Halfway between the door of the room and the window, I suddenly broke into a dead sprint. I was filled with a sort of horror and my hand was extended as if to reach through the window before my body had arrived.

I kept assuring myself Sandy was okay, but then one set of fingers disappeared, then the other. Julie grabbed my shoulder again and this time thrust me backward.

"Don't look!" she yelled.

"She's fallen!"

Her voice pierced my ears like a knife, and there came again that scream Billy and I heard in his room only moments before. Moments that now felt like hours. Then Julie's voice became this low-moaning and the three of us reached the window and looked down at the same time. Julie fell back and stopped, then screamed again.

"Call 911!" I shouted and ran out of Sandy's room and down the hall to find the nearest exit outside. It was dark and all I saw was a twisted lump of something in the cement drainage basin directly underneath the window in which Sandy was hanging. When I arrived, it was evident what used to be Sandy now lay perfectly still and not breathing. I put two fingers against her neck and felt a weak pulse. I felt her hand, which was damp, clammy with a cold perspiration and wondered how long had she been holding on before finally becoming too weak and letting go. Julie was by my side, knelt next to Sandy, and began weeping. *Billy must be calling for help from the hall phone*, I thought. A momentary dizziness nearly made me throw up, but I pulled myself together for Sandy. For Julie and her words came in a fresh feverish childlike whimper.

"She's dead, Gregg," Julie wept.

"She's dead. She's dead. She's dead!"

The cool air did me some good by keeping the dizziness from coming back a little, but not much. I covered Sandy with a jacket Julie was wearing. In the distance, I heard the wailing of sirens.

By the time the police and ambulance arrived, a crowd of students had formed a semi-circle around Sandy's limp body. Some jeered. Some cried. Most just gawked and did not know what to do or say. The paramedics worked on Sandy, getting her on the gurney and into the ambulance. Julie, Billy, and I hurriedly sped to the hospital where they would be taking Sandy. Among the other emergency room's unfortunate victims, we waited. The hopelessness of our position impressed itself swiftly upon us. It felt as though Sandy, if she survived, would never be the same again. I knew better than most no one was immune to danger and I shuddered at the thought of Sandy living paralyzed for the rest of her life. Stricken down in her prime and something like this being the furthest from her parents' mind when they sent her off to college.

Julie sat next to me trembling with fear as she looked into my eyes. I tenderly caressed her long soft beautiful red hair and brushed it from her face. We had dated, but it was more than that. I was Julie's first. When we first discussed making love, she sat quiet and wondering. Then, smiling she looked up and nodded. Loneliness was not new to either of us. Along with the solitude and frightening uncertainty that came with an alcoholic parent. We had that in common. Me much worse, but still Julie had suffered and pain was pain.

Right before the act itself, she hesitated, wondering if I was to whom she would give her most prized possession. Her love. The excitement was too much for both of us and we eagerly went through with it. Afterwards, Julie turned her head away from me on the pillow and wept. After telling me to leave, I did. Twenty minutes later, she was in my room weeping and asking for assurance I would not leave her. I made every effort not to, but in the end it was the fear of responsibility for another's heart that caused me to first drift slowly and then speed away. Julie chased me for months, but my rejection was as strong as she was relentless in her pursuit. She could see that I was exerting every effort to place distance between us. And, adding to the speed of my heels was how Julie meant how much she loved me.

The doctor walked up to the three of us and a sudden, sickening pain shot through me. It was over in an instant, but when he explained Sandy would live but need the assistance of a wheelchair for perhaps the rest of her life, this seemed to repeat itself over and over in my head.

I had flung out my arms to keep Julie from falling to the emergency room tile when she fainted. When the nurse passed the smelling salts under her nose, Julie's eyes flashed open and then seem to take their time focusing on the room. Panting as if she had run a race, Julie slowly recovered. Billy and I helped her up and to the car. Sandy's walking life was cut short.

The doctor explained how the fall was as if a knife-blade had cut into her neck. The doctor seemed to go on forever explaining in medical terms what exactly had happened. It was driving all three of us crazy and reminded me of old medical text books for children I once found in the public library when first learning how to read. They were all in the third-person, but I didn't know what that meant back then. The books would explain the heart by describing in detail the inner-workings as, *"This is George's heart. It is has four valves. Two on the top of the heart. Two on the bottom. This is George's heart."* They were creepy and because of this, I didn't want to read them. *"This is Sandy's neck. It is fucking broken. She will never walk again. This is Sandy's neck."*

Billy drove Julie's car back to the university. We all sat in the front seat, Julie in the middle, but she laid her head on my shoulder and cried. Every now and then Billy would whisper to himself, "What the fuck," while staring at the road.

Sandy returned weeks later to campus, but true to the good doctor's word, she was wheelchair bound. Sandy also never came back the next year. It was selfish, but I was relieved. It was hard to look at her and I wondered often had I not hesitated those few seconds in her room, if she'd be okay. I would have gotten to her in time, grabbing her hands, and pulling Sandy back to safety. A second glance around the goddamn room, that's what cost me those precious seconds.

Part of me said that I was wrong, but the other part, the well-beaten part, told me I cost Sandy her legs. I went over that evening many times and always came to the same conclusion. It was my fault. Making it worse was the fact when Sandy fell she made no sound whatsoever. No scream for help. Julie's shouts carried a mile, but Sandy said absolutely nothing. It was as if she made peace with death. Then, letting go of the ledge she fell back into the darkness. Well put, Billy. *What the fuck. What the fuck, for sure.*

My junior and senior year of college proved to be my finest both academically and athletically. I received the Most Improved Runner my senior year, and was NAIA-ranked as third-man on the university 1600m indoor relay team. Finishing my junior year strong, I began diligently working that summer on my undergraduate thesis, titled, *"The Personnel Manager's Role as Agent of Change."*

There was a restlessness in the air as to what would happen after college, but first things first and that was to graduate. With eyes wide open to the dream of graduating college, once not even a figment of my imagination, I hunkered down for the final stretch. My family, except letters I would share with Ashley every now and then during my junior and senior year, were motionless as if they were actually dead. They did not matter to me. Some distance away, like a star, there gleamed the small and steady light of my future made possible by one man's belief in me –Pat. Thank God, I would not let him down.

For the next summer and full two semesters of what would become my last year of undergraduate college, I worked harder than ever. At intervals there were, among the stony ground of ups and downs, sharp pebbles, but I managed to traverse them with great deft and skill compared to before. And also for a few moments there would be the threat of panic-like the wailing of the wind, the swish of a low-hanging sky, and the crackling of Mother's laughter inside my head. But there was another sound too. The sound of something chanting for me to keep moving. Keep fighting. Something bigger and better than me. Than all of us. I could no longer hear the low lament of my abusers while awake. So they came to me in dreams, but that was to be expected. Those in the nightmares had already dug their own graves early in their lives and lay inside them waiting to be covered by dirt and forgotten. I would lean over their shallow holes in the earth and know, to me, they were already gone.

I graduated. Not with honors or any special academic chords, ribbons, medallions or recognition. No matter. Because what I did graduate with was the one thing I wanted and nearly died, nearly lost my mind in which to obtain. A college degree. From this piece of invaluable parchment came the knowledge that has propelled my life forward. It pulled me from the edge and toward a light. A light that for years to come would swallow the darkness.

Years of loneliness plagued me on this pilgrimage and I had known loneliness, the heartbreak and the longing of it, in the black and silent chaos of physical and sexual abuse. I had almost gone insane because of it, and I had nearly died for a glimpse of Mother's love. But things were getting better now. The panic was still there, but it didn't eat at my soul each day and each night; except for the nightmares. I had once believed that my caring for Mother would make me happier, but I was just a child, and that was many years ago. I thought the next time I would see Mother again would be on her deathbed, but in this I was mistaken.

It wasn't until years later a picture was shown to me of my graduation day.

Mother was standing among the people posing along with me. I don't even remember her being there. Though there would be days before and after her death that would not lend themselves to forgetfulness, and on these days Mother's voice seemed nearer and more real to me. And, she became more and more insistently a part of my thoughts, but this too would fall away in time. She stayed with me in the nightmares each night and the dread would be upon me soon after waking up that she would be there again the next time I sleep.

There was an overwhelming desire to return to Mother that possessed me from time to time, but I fought against this desire as one would fight against death. Because it was death. I knew, once surrendering to the temptation, I would lose what I had already won in my struggle in the years since leaving her. So all my efforts carried me steadily onward, while Mother's invisible hands tugged at me from behind.

It was not an easy road with all those others doing their best to take from me what did not belong to them. Sell me on their lies and peddle their hatred. Ugly, mean-spirited people who called me many names, including son and brother. Then there was the nearly three months I spent in constant therapy after having my nervous breakdown. If it weren't for the love and compassion of a learned man, who just so happened to live the mission of my undergraduate university, I would have gone insane or committed suicide. I had more than once also half-expected Pat to pass on his belief in me, but he never wavered. Never faltered. Urging me on and begging me to join the living. I jumped at the opportunity, and remained under the guidance of Pat for four years and still to this day. However, the years of abuse have had their effect on me and I do suffer occasionally through the storms of anxiety, but the medication helps. My history is tragic, but my present is not.

These are the worst of my days I wrote about, and the best —so far. During the worst of times, something dragged me into the light. There was suffering, terrible dreams, and agony. But there was triumph too. Even when I was thinned by starvation, somehow I found bread or it was given to me. The belief in something came from somewhere and this faith decided me when only a child. I was torn and ragged at the edges, and soiled from abuse in its most decadent form; incest. Some left me for dead emotionally and I am not ashamed to say I wept.

Here and there while searching for a better day, not believing for a second it'd be there, I was obliterating all the statistics. Of course, my heart nearly dead did not see the triumph. Instead, only the stony faces of all my oppressors, leaving me dry inside as though I had passed through a fever. Therefore, to them I say they are nothing more than a water-stain and unintelligible blur. I crushed their hatred and laughed in spite of the terrible deeds done unto me as I walked out into the blinding chaos of a storm.

In August of 1985, before a distinguished panel of faculty, I made my thesis argument. A week later, moving along a procession of caps and gowns, I was one of the chosen few donned in the colors of the university. As the recent graduates made their way into the building where the ceremony was held, the wind was blowing more strongly and I had to quickly secure my cap before it blew off my head. There is a picture of this Lynn had taken while trying to snap the shutter and wave to me at the same time. A few minutes later, we were all inside what was referred to the Field House, and coincidently, the place where I had competed in many track events. Moments later I stood only a few paces away from the stage, where I would be handed a bachelor's degree. Fighting back the tears, I could hear Lynn's voice above the din of the crowd while joyfully shouting my name.

Epilogue

SOMETHING UNHEALTHY KEPT ME FROM telling my secrets, but not any longer. There is a spirit with me at times, walking at my side, and hovering about my life. It called to me and I responded with a promise. A promise I would give back and help as many people as possible. With this effort, there is an undercurrent of a feeling I cannot explain. I never thought that unconditional love could exist, except perhaps between a father and a son. However, I know now that it can exist between anyone. With it, in all the castles we build are the dreams we dream, the alpha and omega of love that remain with all people willing to remember the difference between right and wrong.

Therefore, keep searching for the answers. You will find them in the most obscure places and generally quite by accident. How they reveal themselves will be subtle and I found the answers to exist either in one's actions or within the words they put down to paper –not speak. There is oppression everywhere and broken hopes brought on by the cruel and stupid. When they do speak, clench your fists and do not listen. Keep moving and you will leave these people far behind. There is something there in the silence and the gathering light that calls the good souls away from the darkness. Do not keep back the secrets and take them to your grave. It is a dead waste of time to allow the sins of others time to linger, fester, and break you. Instead, put those terrible things out there for those compassionate who are willing to help you. They are there, like me –waiting.

Behind [we] who suffer is an owl hooting its lonely mating song.

Years later, I would go on to receive a masters degree, graduating *Magna Cum Laude*. And, also serve honorably in the United States Air Force. In addition, I have held several engineering and executive positions. I was also recognized by my undergraduate university for work within the area of child abuse prevention. An incredible honor, and made even more so, coming from the university that saved me. However, my greatest accomplishment is having raised a child to know only love and compassion. Because of my son, for the first time in my life, I would know what it felt like to be loved by someone. To be loved by him and so many others. I owe these people my life. They have given more than I will ever be able to repay. They helped me. They saved me. And, together, not alone, [we] have broken the cycle of abuse. We fighters: known to each other, and to the world, as Survivors.

God, you might be sleeping but I am wide awake. Best of all, I am still here and as long as I am, I will be doing my best to make this a Beautiful World.

They had dug their graves early in lives meant for so much more. Where fires they could have built would have lighted up the darkness. Instead, they chose to stay hidden in a deep shadow. One would be cremated and the other buried in a grave his children would never visit. Not even the one that was by his side only hours before his death: me. After their deaths, not the sound of mourning fell upon their bodies, but that of regret. Leaning over their coffins, their children looked upon these savage people. Their work was crude and done before it even began, and like a thin black shadow before it is blotted out by the sun, all that remained was nothing to guard them from the devils to come and steal their souls within the first hours of death. They were cut down by their own hands. A cross was carried over a beaten shoulder for them for nothing. Stripped of what remained, dulled by hatred, and returning to the grave was the path they chose. The darkness was allowed inside and it swallowed them whole; nearly taking me with them as they fell into the gloom. They were done and it was too late to pray. I am sorry. God knows I am sorry. I wish it would have been different.

Regarding Mother and Father.
October 2010

CPSIA information can be obtained at www.ICGtesting.com
Printed in the USA
BVOW08s2153070616

451145BV00001B/10/P